The Center for South and Southeast Asia Studies of the University of California is the coordinating center for research, teaching programs, and special projects relating to the South and Southeast Asia areas on the nine campuses of the University. The Center is the largest such research and teaching organization in the United States, with more than 150 related faculty representing all disciplines within the social sciences, languages, and humanities.

The Center publishes a Monograph series, an Occasional Papers series, and sponsors a series of books published by the University of California Press. Manuscripts for these publications have been selected with the highest standards of academic excellence, with emphasis on those studies and literary works that are pioneers in their fields, and that provide fresh insights into the life and culture of the great civilizations of South and Southeast Asia.

RECENT PUBLICATIONS OF THE CENTER FOR SOUTH AND SOUTHEAST ASIA STUDIES:

Richard I. Cashman
The Myth of the LOKAMANYA:
Tilak and Mass Politics in Maharashtra

Edward Conze
The Large Sutra on Perfect Wisdom

George L. Hart, III
The Poems of Ancient Tamil:
Their Milieu and Their Sanskrit Counterparts

Tom G. Kessinger
Vilayatpur, 1848–1968:
Social and Economic Change in a North Indian Village

Robert Lingat
The Classical Law of India (translated by J. Duncan M. Derrett)

MARRIAGE AND RANK IN BENGALI CULTURE

This volume is sponsored by the
Center for South and Southeast Asia Studies,
University of California, Berkeley

RONALD B. INDEN

MARRIAGE AND RANK IN BENGALI CULTURE

A HISTORY OF CASTE AND CLAN IN MIDDLE PERIOD BENGAL

UNIVERSITY OF CALIFORNIA PRESS
BERKELEY · LOS ANGELES · LONDON

UNIVERSITY OF CALIFORNIA PRESS
Berkeley and Los Angeles, California

University of California Press, Ltd.
London, England

ISBN 0–520–02569–5
Library of Congress Catalog Card Number: 73–85789

Printed in the United States of America

To

Gilda, John,

and

Margaret

CONTENTS

TABLES

ACKNOWLEDGMENTS

This account, a revision of my Ph.D. dissertation (University of Chicago, 1972), rests heavily on my knowledge of Bengali language and culture. Were it not for the training received from Edward C. Dimock, Jr., it would not have been possible; for his guidance and warm encouragement I am deeply obligated.

To J. A. B. VanBuitenen I owe my knowledge of the Sanskrit language and classical Indian culture, the knowledge of which were indispensable to this study.

Bernard S. Cohn has been my guide to the study of Indian history with a social science perspective. For his reading and criticism of the many drafts of this study, I extend my heartfelt thanks.

McKim Marriott urged me to focus on the problem of marriage and rank in my study of the indigenous genealogies on which the dissertation is based. His patient and detailed reading of earlier drafts are responsible for much that is of value in this finished version.

Ralph W. Nicholas has provided me with helpful guidance and critical comments generated from his extensive field work in West Bengal.

David M. Schneider, whose ideas on culture and kinship play a central role in this account, was kind enough to read an earlier draft and suggest improvements.

Many of my other colleagues at the University of Chicago and elsewhere have also contributed to this study. Some of these, in alphabetical order are, Philip B. Calkins, Leonard A. Gordon, Barrie M. Morrison, Maureen L. P. Patterson, and A. K. Ramanujan. I must also thank the Committee on Southern Asian Studies whose good works have long sustained the interdisciplinary study of South Asia.

I am also grateful to the Foreign Area Fellowship Program for its generous support, which made possible the doctoral research done in India and East Pakistan in 1964 and 1965.

Many persons provided indispensable help while I was doing

this research abroad. Nirmal Kumar Bose, Director of the Anthropological Survey of India, and Gaurinath Sastri, Principal of Sanskrit College, supplied me with introductions to people who inevitably proved very helpful.

Siddiq Khan, Director of the Dacca University Library, extended all courtesies and full use of the library facilities while I was in Dacca. Without his assistance, I would not have found and copied the manuscripts of the genealogies from which this study has emerged.

Srikumar Mitra and his father, Saratkumar, offered invaluable guidance to me on Kayastha society in Calcutta. Their hospitality and kindness cannot be repaid.

Tarasish Mukhopadhyay, Manik Sinha, and Pradip Sinha made possible my productive research in rural West Bengal.

Finally, I am also deeply grateful to Ashin and Uma Dasgupta and Arun and Manashi Dasgupta. They fed my body and nourished my mind on innumerable occasions during my Calcutta stay.

INTRODUCTION

Purpose

This study gives an account of marriage and clan rank among the highest castes of Bengal. I use the cultural categories contained in their genealogical records as the categories of social and historical analysis. Many of the higher castes of India have historically been organized into ranked clans or lineages. The highest Hindu castes of Bengal, the Brāhmaṇ or "priest" caste and the Kāyastha or "writer" caste, are no exception to this widespread pattern. Like the higher castes elsewhere, the internal organization of these castes was complex. The Brāhmaṇ and Kāyastha castes of Bengal were organized into smaller territorial units which I shall refer to as "subcastes." Though this study encompasses all of these subcastes, it will focus on two of them, the Rāḍhī Brāhmaṇ, found in western and southeastern Bengal, and the Dakṣiṇa-rāḍhī Kāyastha, found in southwestern Bengal.

The Rāḍhī Brāhmaṇs were, according to their genealogies, organized into fifty-nine clans arranged into five ranked grades. The Dakṣiṇa-rāḍhī Kāyasthas were organized into eighty-three clans arranged into three ranked grades. The higher grades of eight clans in the Rāḍhī Brāhmaṇ and three in the Dakṣiṇa-rāḍhī Kāyastha subcastes were referred to as Kulīna, "of high clan rank". The lower grades of clans in the Rāḍhī Brāhmaṇ subcaste were referred to as Śrotriyas, those in the Dakṣiṇa-rāḍhī Kāyastha subcaste, as Maulika. These are the two subcastes among whom I was able to do field work while I was in India as a Foreign Area Fellow in 1964–1965. The information I was graciously given by the modern representatives of these subcastes and the observations I was able to make while among them have provided me with invaluable insights into the historical organization of their ancestors.

The period of time covered by this account begins with the formal organization of the larger Brāhmaṇ and Kāyastha castes into smaller subcastes and still smaller ranked grades of clans around 1500 A.D. and ends with the first attempts to reorganize into larger more homogeneous units around 1850. This period, which I shall refer to as the "middle period," begins with the success of the Muslim rulers of Bengal, who had conquered that region around 1200 A.D., in consolidating their political hold over Bengal. This was achieved in part by reaching an accommodation with the local Hindu *zamindārs* or landholders of Bengal, many of whom were Brāhmaṇs and Kāyasthas, and by opening up administrative posts in the regional government to persons of these "elite" or "dominant" castes. The succeeding, relatively stable centuries saw the expansion of the area under rice cultivation and with it the spread of the Brāhmaṇs and Kāyasthas into the new "frontier" areas. This expansion of a largely rural society both by migration and by incorporating local populations seems to correlate well with the tendency on the part of the Brāhmaṇs and Kāyasthas of Bengal to organize themselves along increasingly localized and particularistic lines during this period. The middle period ends with the centralization of British administrative and economic control over Bengal. The centralization of power and the transformation of Bengal's economy, both of which continue today in independent India and Bangladesh, have been accompanied by an increasing tendency to unite formerly distinct caste units or even to do away with them as the primary units of social organization.

Sources

The genealogical records of the Brāhmaṇs and Kāyasthas, the major sources for this study, are referred to in Bengali as *kulajī*, *kula-kārikā*, or *kula-pañjikā*, all of which terms mean "book of clan rank." These texts, written either in Bengali or Sanskrit, were not the property of individual families but the corporate property of the subcastes and were recited, usually from memory, on the occasions of weddings and kept up to date by professional genealogists (*ghaṭakas*). Their contents were judged for accuracy at the time of recitation by the persons of the subcaste assembled for the wedding, and their contents had to be approved before the genealogists received remuneration. These texts were, thus, the corporately approved "charters" of the subcastes.

The complete books of clan rank are divided into three "sections" (*prakaraṇa*). The first relates the "creation of the clans" (*kula-sṛṣṭi*), beginning with the creation of the world and ending with the division of the Brāhmaṇ and Kāyastha castes of Bengal into their territorial subcastes and the arrangement of the clans into high and low grades within the subcastes at the outset of the middle period.

The second section details the "codes of the clans" (*kula-kārya, kula-karma, kula-kriyā, kula-dharma, ḍhākuri*), the actions (*karma*) to be performed by their members during the "present" (*adhunā, varttamāna*) of the middle period in order to preserve their clan ranks (*kula*). Most of the actions prescribed here have to do with the "rules" (*vidhāna*) governing the "gift" (*dāna*) and "acceptance" (*grahaṇa*) of "daughters" (*kanyā*) in "marriage" (*vivāha*), including the honorific gifts of wealth (*paṇa*) to be made on the occasion of a marriage. In addition, this section gives the arrangements to be made for the convening of subcaste wedding "councils" (*samāja, sabhā*), including the criteria to be used for selecting a person to act as "master of the council" (*samāja-pati*) or genealogist. Often particular parts of the code are illustrated with tales of particular persons and events in the subcaste. These codes all presupposed knowledge of earlier Sanskrit texts on codes for conduct, such as the *dharma-śāstras* and *purāṇas*, and the *kulajīs* occasionally cite passages from them.

The third section contains the "truth" (*tattva*) concerning the "births" (*vaṃśa, janma*) and "marriages" (*aṃśa, karma*) of the clans. As the strict "genealogy" (*vaṃśāvalī*) portion of a book of clan rank, it is by far the largest, containing fifty to hundred manuscript folios and uninterrupted records of births and marriages over ten to twenty generations during the middle period. Though these records always include judgments on the results of the marriages made by the male members of each clan and often include the names of the villages where persons were settled, they very seldom refer to a person's occupation or "livelihood" (*vṛtti*) or to the land or other property he might own. The moral evaluations of marriages that were made tell whether particular persons obtained "respect" (*sanmāna*) or "disrespect" (*apamāna*), "praise" (*praśaṃsā*) or "blame" (nindā), "fame" (*yaśa*) or "infamy" (*apayaśa*) as the "fruits" or "results" (*phala*) of their marriages. These records, therefore, constitute an invaluable source for the cultural and historical study of marriage and clan rank in Bengal.

A number of the texts used in this study exist either partly or wholly only in unpublished, undated manuscripts. The texts contained in these manuscripts often date back to the fifteenth century, but the physical manuscripts themselves must all, on paleographic grounds, be assigned to the late eighteenth or early nineenth centuries.

I was very fortunate while in India and East Pakistan in 1964 to find these manuscripts in the University of Dacca library. A great interest in caste affairs arose among English-educated Brāhmaṇs and Kāyasthas around 1850 and lasted until about 1935. During this period numerous caste associations were founded, and many Bengalis, scholars and otherwise, spent their time collecting *kulajis* and publishing histories of their caste, often claiming ranks higher than those traditionally accorded them. Much of this activity was at least in part a response to the attempts of the British Census Commissioner, Herbert H. Risley, to produce ranked lists of castes in the Census of India. While some of these accounts are unreliable and propagandistic, many of them contain useful ethnographic data relating to the nineteenth century end of the middle period. I have used them to supplement the often sketchy evidence on marriage gifts and feasts found in the books of clan rank.

Nagendranāth Vasu was probably the most important of the Bengalis who did research on caste history. Although many of his own arguments about the origin of the Kāyasthas of Bengal cannot be taken too seriously, I have relied heavily on the hundreds of texts which he collected and published in his extensive history of the castes of Bengal, *Vaṅger Jātīya Itihāsa*. After his death, the historian R. C. Majumdār, who was the vice-chancellor of the University of Dacca and wished to reexamine the evidence on which Vasu's arguments were based, bought for the university most of the manuscripts which Vasu had collected. It is these manuscripts which form the foundation of this study.

Methods

I shall argue that in the middle period, marriage exchanges, as understood in terms of Bengali cultural concepts, were the defining actions by which high and low clan ranks among the Brāhmans and Kāyasthas were maintained or altered. When I began this research, however, I thought that an "aristocratic" or "class" model (based, of course, on European cultural concepts) would explain the system of clan ranking in the Brāhmaṇ and Kāyastha subcastes. I knew before I began that the patterns of marriage exchanges made among the clans were somehow closely connected with the ranking of the clans. One of the early British ethnographers, Denzil Ibbetson, observed in 1881 that the "tribes" (clans) inside the higher castes of Punjāb—Brāhmaṇ, Rājput, and Khatri—were ranked high and low and that the pattern of marriages between clans or lineages of equal rank differed from that obtaining between clans of unequal rank. In fact, Ibbetson was the first one to use the terms "isogamy" and "hypergamy" to refer to these two patterns:

> They also may be referred to two laws, which I shall call the laws of isogamy and hypergamy. By isogamy or the law of equal marriage, I mean the rule which arranges the local tribes in a scale of social standing and forbids the parent to give his daughter to a man of any tribe which stands lower than his own. By hypergamy or the law of superior marriage, I mean the rule which compels him to wed his daughter with a member of a tribe which shall be actually superior in rank to his own. In both cases a man usually does not scruple to take his wife or at any rate his second wife from a tribe of inferior standing.[1]

Wise and Risley were the first Western ethnographers of Bengal to adopt Ibbetson's terms in describing the correlation between marriage patterns and clan rank in the Brāhmaṇ and Kāyastha clans there.[2] The marriages of the Rāḍhī Brāhmaṇs are, in fact, used in Indian anthropological literature as a "classic" example of how hypergamy works.[3]

Despite these strong hints about the importance of marriage, I continued to pursue the problem of rank in terms of an aristocracy model, for that model, adjusted to take into account Hindu cultural concerns, has been the prevailing explanatory one since the turn of the century. For example, Baines, writing of the north India Rājput warrior caste in 1912, asserts that the title of Rājput denotes "an order of hereditary nobility, access to which is still obtainable, and whose circle, accordingly, is being constantly enlarged upon.... The essentials of the position are the chieftainship of a tribe or clan and the command of an armed force, with the possession of a substantial landed estate and a scrupulous regard for the strict regulations

[1] Denzil Ibbetson, *Panjab Castes* (Lahore: Superintendent of Government Printing, 1916), pp. 23–24.

[2] Herbert H. Risley, *Tribes and Castes of Bengal. Ethnographic Glossary* (Calcutta: Bengal Secretariat Press, 1891), I, 144–48, 440–42.

[3] J. H. Hutton, *Caste in India: Its Nature, Function, and Origins* (Oxford: University Press, 1961), pp. 53–54. Third edition.

as to marriage, domestic customs and intercourse with other classes."[4] While the pattern of ranks and hypergamous marriages were seen to correlate with each other, something appeared to be wrong with his aristocratic interpretation, for he concedes that hypergamous marriage patterns did not always coincide with chieftainship.[5]

W. H. R. Rivers argued in 1921 that clan ranking in such castes as the Rājput or Rāḍhī Brāhmaṇ was based, essentially, on political power. In his view, higher ranked clans were clans of invaders which imposed themselves on indigenous clans. A hypergamous pattern of marriages arose between invading and indigenous clans because the invaders did not object to forming unions with the daughters of the indigenous men but refused to give their own daughters to them and had the military strength to prevent it.[6] The refusal to give daughters to lower indigenous clans was based, in turn, on the Hindu invaders' cultural conception of blood purity and its preservation through women: "Especially important in this interaction was the belief of the invaders in the essential need for purity of blood as a necessary condition for the performance of religious ceremonial. . . ."[7] Thus, while clan rank was based on political power, it was also thought by Rivers to be connected with Hindu ideas about purity and religious or ritual status.

The more recent views of Yalman in his studies of the Goyigāma caste of Ceylon do not depart radically from these earlier views. According to him, this caste is divided into three grades—the highest, consisting of "a few aristocratic families" which are considered "pure" and "good," the ordinary "good" people (cultivators), and the lowest (serfs) which are considered "impure" and "bad." Marriages between those of different economic or ritual status are seen to validate or express these ranks and are almost always hypergamous because of the Goyigāma concern for female purity.[8] Dumont's account of hypergamy and rank among the Sarjupari Brāhmaṇs of Uttar Pradesh comes closer to the mark in asserting that

[4]Athelstaine Baines, *Ethnography* (*Castes and Tribes*) (Strassburg: Trübner, 1912), pp. 29–30.

[5]*Ibid.*, p. 32.

[6]W. H. R. Rivers, "The Origin of Hypergamy," *Journal of the Bihar and Orissa Research Society*, 7 (1921): 9–24.

[7]W. H. R. Rivers, *Social Organization*, ed. W. J. Perry (New York: Knopf, 1924), p. 155.

[8]Nur Yalman, *Under the Bo Tree* (Berkeley: University of California Press, 1967), pp. 177–79.

ranks are given by birth on the one hand and created by marriage on the other.[9] Instead of developing this idea, however, Dumont reverts to the aristocratic model. He refers to the higher "houses" as a "small aristocracy" and conjectures that the ranks of the lineages "might be the result of a codification by some sovereign or court intending to establish a clear order of precedence."[10]

A number of particular difficulties arose in trying to explain clan rank in Bengal with this modified aristocratic model. Clan rank did not correlate with the political offices held by the Brāhmaṇs and Kāyasthas in the Muslim regional administration or under the local Hindu *rājās* or landholders. Nor did it correlate with landholding sizes. In fact, some of the largest, most powerful landholders of the middle period were not Kulīnas but Srotriyas or Maulikas. Conversely, passages in many of the genealogies suggested that poor Kulīnas depended on these lower ranked but wealthier persons.

The hypothesis that clan ranks were based on conquest and its connection with the cultural notions about the purity of blood and ritual status seemed to be echoed in the Brāhmaṇ and Kāyastha accounts of the creation of rank. Brāhmaṇ and Kāyastha Kulīnas are there portrayed as outsiders who were considered to be more pure and higher in "ritual status" in relation to the indigenous castes and clans. They are not, however, portrayed as conquerors able to refuse gifts of their daughters to inferiors because of their superior military strength.

There were also difficulties with the hypergamy hypothesis. I had expected that marriages among the ranked clans in all of the subcastes would be regulated by rules allowing or enjoining hypergamy, but prohibiting hypogamy (marrying daughters to inferiors). To my surprise, I discovered that two of the subcastes, Uttara-rāḍhī and Dakṣiṇa-rāḍhī Kāyastha, actually enjoined clans to make hypogamous marriages. Thus, the notion that high caste Hindus refused to make hypogamous marriages out of concern for the ritual purity of their women seemed not to apply here.

Finally, there was the problem of social mobility. This not only raised doubts about the validity of the aristocratic models but also about the conventional definition of a caste or subcaste as a hereditary social unit. This conception of a caste generally precludes the

[9]Louis Dumont, "Marriage in India: The Present State of the Question," *Contributions to Indian Sociology*, 9 (December 1966): 107.

[10]*Ibid.*, 108.

possibility of an individual changing his caste. Yet the genealogies not only contained many illustrations of precisely such events; they even appeared to structure the Brāhmaṇ and Kāyastha subcastes around such possibilities. Thus, as these particular difficulties accumulated, I began to feel that the problem of understanding rank among the Brāhmans and Kāyasthas was a deeper and more general one than I had anticipated.

The attribution of high and low rank to persons or groups is necessarily a "subjective" concern, based on the cultural premises held by persons inside a given social system. The more I worked with books of clan rank, the more it became clear that the cultural premises of the Bengali Brāhmaṇs and Kāyasthas were quite different from those of the European and American scholars who were trying to understand these and other Hindu systems of ranks. The attempts to understand clan rank in terms of an aristocratic model rooted in European cultural concepts, but "modified" to take into account Hindu concerns for purity and ritual status, looked more and more like Ptolemy's attempt to account for the movements of the heavenly bodies by adding epicycles. The fundamental distinctions that were being made between "ritual," "religious," or "ceremonial" ranks on the one hand, and "secular," "political," and "economic" power on the other appeared to be the root of the problem, for these are distinctions that the Brāhmaṇs and Kāyasthas appeared not to make, at least not in the same ways that European and Americans do.

The need for a deeper understanding of Hindu concepts of society has received recognition in recent studies of castes and caste rank. Dumont has moved the Hindu concept of the "pure" and the "impure" from the periphery to the center of the stage, arguing that it is the "fundamental opposition" underlying hierarchy or rank in Hindu society.[11] Marriott, concerned with the "interactions" among castes rather than their "attributes" as "indicators" of rank, has demonstrated that a high correlation exists between opinions on caste rank and the pattern of food transactions among them.[12] Both of these scholars have noted the centrality which the Hindu

[11]Louis Dumont, *Homo Hierarchicus* (Chicago: University of Chicago Press, 1970), pp. 42–49.

[12]McKim Marriott, "Caste Ranking and Food Transactions: A Matrix Analysis," in *Structure and Change in Indian Society*, ed. Milton Singer and Bernard S. Cohn (Chicago: Aldine, 1968), pp. 133–72.

concern for the body occupies in Hindu society and culture.[13]

While the work of Dumont and Marriott has greatly influenced the approach taken in this account, the most direct inspiration for the method I have used comes not from a study of Indian society but from David M. Schneider's cultural account of kinship in American society. Fundamental to Schneider's approach is his relative emphasis on the cultural system of a society. A cultural system, according to Schneider, is "a system of units (or parts) which are defined in certain ways and which are differentiated according to certain criteria. These units define the world or the universe, the way things in it relate to each other, and what these things should be and do."[14]

This account of clan rank in Bengal is a cultural account. It will concern itself totally with the categories used by the Bengali Brāhmaṇs and Kāyasthas, their cultural premises, definitions, views, and normative rules. Thus, this study is not a "behavioral" or "quantitative" study. I shall not be concerned with the distribution of population, birth rates, migration rates, household composition, or the amounts of land controlled, the incidence of adherence to traditional caste occupations, or rates of upward and downward social mobility. As a history, this account will be less concerned with the "objective" explanation of "actual" social changes that took place over time than with the Bengalis' views of change and their explanations of these changes.

Of the many analytic tools used by Schneider, one of the most useful for this study has been that of the "distinctive" or "defining" feature, borrowed by him from linguistics.[15] Schneider found that two features, operating either singly or in combination, defined the domain of kinship in American culture—shared or inherited natural substance (blood) and a particular code for conduct (one enjoining love).[16] Interestingly, shared or inherited substance and code for conduct prove also to be the two features by which castes and clans are defined in Bengali culture. However, there is a fundamental difference between the way the Americans and Bengalis conceive of and connect these two features.

[13]Dumont, *Homo Hierarchicus*, pp. 49–52; Marriott, "Caste Ranking," pp. 142–46.

[14]David M. Schneider, *American Kinship: A Cultural Account* (Englewood Cliffs, N. J.: Prentice-Hall, 1968), p. 1.

[15]*Ibid.*, p. 32.

[16]*Ibid.*, pp. 49–53.

The organization of people into castes and clans is premised on the Bengali Hindu cultural assumption that all living beings are organized into *jātis* ("castes") or *kulas* ("clans"), each of which is defined by its particular bodily substance and "moral" code. This classification of all living beings into castes or clans is further premised on the assumption that natural substance and moral code are and should be inseparable. The moral code for conduct of a particular caste or clan is thought to be imbedded in the bodily substance shared by the members of a caste or clan and is inherited by birth. Thus, no distinction is made, as it is in American culture, between an order of "nature," defined by shared biogenetic substance, and an order of "law," defined by code for conduct. Similarly, no distinction is made between a "natural" or "secular" order and a "supernatural" or "sacred" order in Bengali Hindu culture. Thus, the orders of nature, morality, and divinity are conceived of as a unity. The natural substance by which a caste or clan is defined is also its divinely endowed and embodied moral rank. And the particular divinely generated moral code for conduct of a caste or clan is also its inborn, natural code, imbedded in its inherited bodily substance.

Thus, the cultural connotations of this fundamental unit which the Bengalis refer to as *jāti* or *kula* are much broader than and also different from the conventional concepts of "caste" and "clan." In fact, the criteria used to define these natural units are much closer to those used by biologists to classify plants and animals than to those used by social scientists in constructing social typologies. So, I have adopted the notion of "genus" to designate in its broadest sense the natural, divine, and moral units defined in Bengali culture by the words *jāti* and *kula*. I have also used such expressions as "coded substance" and "coded bodily substance" to refer to the nondualistic features that define them.

The culturally assumed unity of substance and code and the unity of the natural, divine, and moral which derive from this assumption have important implications for the study of Hindu society. It is my hope that some of these implications will emerge in the study of rank and marriage offered in the following pages.

Chapter I

CASTE, CLAN, AND COMMUNITY

Jāti (Caste) and *Kula* (Clan) Defined

Jāti *as Genus and* Kula *as Generic Collectivity*

Castes are conventionally defined by social scientists as hereditary, endogamous, and ranked occupational groups, while clans are defined in the Indian context as the exogamous lineal descent groups into which the members of castes are organized. The social systems of South Asia, which are constructed out of these units, have often been characterized as closed, rigid, unchanging, and lacking a sense of "history." Recent studies, which have shown that social mobility does take place within such systems, tend to assume that mobility occurs "despite 'cultural' (values and ideologies) disapproval or opposition."[1]

These characterizations of South Asian, especially Hindu, society rest on the dualistic opposition drawn between "natural substance" and "code for conduct" implicit in our definitions of caste and clan as social units. Hindu society is closed, rigid, and unchanging because Hindus have constructed their society out of units defined primarily by "blood," an entity "out there" in the natural order and essentially beyond the control of man. Euro-American societies, by contrast, are open, flexible, and changing because we have constructed our societies primarily out of "law," a thing that is made by man and can be changed by him.

Bengali Hindus did conceive of castes and clans as defined by "bodily substance" and "code for conduct." However, these two elements were not conceived of dualistically in Hindu culture. They were not considered to be irreducibly different and opposed elements drawn from contrasting "natural" and "moral" orders

[1]Bernard Barber, "Social Mobility in Hindu India," *Social Mobility in the Caste System in India*, ed. James Silverberg (The Hague: Mouton, 1968), p. 29.

having their own distinct rules. Instead, they were conceived of as mutually interdependent elements each of which may be shaped by or even reduced to the other because they were in fact drawn from the same single "bio-moral" order.

Cultural definitions are made out of words, so let us begin by looking at the words which Bengali Hindus have used to define "castes" and "clans." A variety of Sanskrit and Bengali words—*jāti*, *varṇa*, *jana*, *śreṇī*, *kula*, *vaṃśa*, and *gotra*—were used to designate these social units. Of all these words, however, the words *jāti* and *kula* were the most important, for they were the most general and varied in their usage and application.[2]

The word *Jāti* is derived from the Sanskrit root *jan* meaning to generate, produce, or be born and was used to designate classes or collectivities of living beings which generate or reproduce their own kind. Because *jātis* were conceived of as generative or reproductive groups, I shall use the term "genus" (from the same Indo-European root as the word *jāti*) to translate the word *jāti* in its most general sense. There is good justification for introducing a term other than "caste" to translate the word *jāti* in English. The word *jāti* is no stranger in anthropological and historical accounts of Hindu society. It is often cited as the "native" word for caste in the sense of an endogamous, hereditary, occupational group. The difficulty here is that occupational castes are not the only sets of people or other beings referred to as *jātis* in Sanskrit, Bengali, and other Indian languages. It is used in combination with modifiers to designate a wide variety of units ranging from those which we would classify

[2]The material used in reconstructing the Bengali Hindus' conception of caste and clan in this chapter is drawn not from one but from a variety of middle period sources. Though much is taken from the genealogical accounts, not all of it is. Some is also drawn from texts of *purāṇas* and *tantras* and commentaries (*nibandha*) on the *dharma-śāstra* having middle period Bengal as their provenance. These will be referred to in place. A large part of the data, especially that dealing with the clan organization of the Brāhmaṇs and Kāyasthas does, of course, come from the *kulajīs* themselves. One of the most important "secondary" accounts used here is *Sambandhanirṇaya*. Written by a learned Bengali *paṇḍita*, Lālmohan Vidyānidhi, and published in 1875 just as important changes were beginning to occur in Bengali society, this treatise presents a retrospective picture of medieval Hindu society in Bengal based on references to and often long passages quoted from medieval texts. Other published works that have proven invaluable in providing definitions of words and concepts include the two-volume dictionary of Jñānendramohan Dās, *Bāṇgālā Bhāṣār Abhidhāna*, and the multivolumed encyclopedia, *Śabdakalpadruma*, compiled from ancient and medieval sources under the guidance of one of the most influential Hindus of early nineteenth-century Bengal, Rāja Rādhākānta Deva.

as "species" and "sexes" to those we would classify as "religions" or "nations." Since the cultural definition of all of these units is, as we shall see, the same, it is important to view all of these units as forming a single cultural class.

Distinctive modifiers of the word *jāti* were used to designate *jātis* of six different classes in Bengali. Three of these were classes of genera both human and nonhuman. The first of these included genera defined by their mode of reproduction and designated by modifiers such as *jarāyuja-*, "womb-generated," *aṇḍaja-*, "egg-generated," etc. The second class contained genera defined by their bodily morphology and designated by such modifiers as *manuṣya-*, "human," *paśu-*, "domesticated mammal," *vṛkṣa-*, "tree," etc. A third class included genera defined by their sex or gender and designated by the modifiers *strī-*, "female," and *puruṣa-*, "male."[3]

Three other classes of *jātis* were confined to humans alone. The first of these included *jātis* defined by their modes of worship (*yajña*, *pūjā*, etc.).

The earlier modifier *ārya-*, "respectable" and a later one, Hindu-, were used to designate the *jāti* or *jātis* which possessed combinations of powerful words such as the Veda, Puranas, Tantras, *śāstras*, etc., and were used to worship the Vedic and Hindu gods. Other negative modifiers such as *anārya-*, "nonrespectable," *dasyu*, "thief," and *mleccha*, "barbarian," were used to describe those *jātis* who did not worship the Vedic and Hindu gods.[4] Positive modifiers, such as Musulmān (Muslim) could be substituted for the more negative ones. *Jātis* of this class often appear as "religions" in English. I shall refer to them as worship *jātis*.

The second of these classes included genera defined by their places of residence or "countries" (*deśa*). The whole of the Indian subcontinent, referred to as Bhāratavarṣa, was seen to contain five countries—Madhya-deśa, the middle country, Udīcya-deśa, the northern country, Paścād-deśa, the western country, Dakṣiṇa-deśa, the southern country, and Prācya-deśa, the eastern country. Two of these, Madhya-deśa (roughly the equivalent of modern Uttar Pradesh) and Prācya-deśa (roughly the equivalent of modern Bihar

[3] *Sāradātilakatantram*, ed. Arthur Avalon (Calcutta: Sanskrit Press Depository, 1933), pp. 28–30. See also G. Bühler's translation of Manu's *Dharmaśāstra*, entitled *The Laws of Manu* (Delhi: M. Banarsidass, 1964), pp. 13–16.

[4] *Brahma-vaivartta Purāṇa*, trans. into Bengali by Pañchānana Tarkaratna (Calcutta: Natavara Chakravartti, 1925), p. 34.

and Bengal) figure prominently in our story: the former because it was considered to be the original home of the highest Brāhmaṇs and Kāyasthas of Bengal; the latter because it included the Bengal region itself.[5]

Prācya-deśa itself contained a number of smaller countries. From at least the tenth century A.D. the city of Gauḍa (in modern Malda District) was held to be the premier city of the eastern country and the major capital of its ruling dynasties. As a result, the entire eastern country came to be called by that name. Subsequently, during the middle period, the term "Gauḍa" was also applied to a smaller area roughly coterminous with modern Bengal, an area containing a set of three countries—Vārendra (northern Bengal), Vaṅga (southern Bengal), and Rāḍha (western Bengal). The last was again subdivided into Uttara (northern) and Dakṣiṇa (southern).[6]

All of these terms, or adjectival terms formed from them, such as Rāḍhī- or Vaṅgaja-, were used as modifiers to designate the *jātis* of those particular places. Another word, *jana* (derived from the same root as *jāti*), has also been used to distinguish this kind of *jāti* from others and since very early times. When it is used, a *deśa* or country is referred to as a *jana-pada*, the "place" (*pada*) of a "people" (*jana*). In more recent times, terms such as Bharatiya, "Indian," or Bengali, Panjabi, etc., are used as direct modifiers of the word *jāti*. The *jātis* of this class are often dubbed "nations," "linguistic groups," or "regional populations" in English. I shall refer to them as territorial *jātis*.

The third and last class of purely human *jātis* included genera defined by the same means of "livelihood" *jīvikā*) or "occupation" (*vṛtti*, *vyavasā*). Such *jātis* were designated by a wide variety of modifiers. Some Bengali examples, with rough English translations, are Brāhmaṇ-, "priest-preceptor," Kāyastha, "writer," Gopa-, "cowherd," Kumbhakāra-, "potter," Nāpita-, "barber," and Gandhavaṇik-, "spice merchant."[7] When the word *jāti* was used in middle period Bengal without any modifier, it usually referred to a

[5] D. C. Sircar, *Studies in the Geography of Ancient and Medieval India* (Delhi: M. Banarsidass, 1960), pp. 172–73.

[6] *Ibid.*, pp. 110–22; *History of Bengal*, ed. R. C. Majumdār (Dacca: University of Dacca, 1943), I, 10–22.

[7] History of Bengal, I, 565–79; Lālmohan Vidyānidhi, *Sambandhanirṇaya* (Calcutta: M. C. Bhaṭṭāchārya, 1949), I, 1–274; and *Śabdakalpadruma*, comp. by Rājā Rādhākānta Deva (Calcutta: New Bengal Press, 1874–75), 2nd ed., III, 1305–6.

jāti of this class, indicating that the occupational *jāti* was the most important, par excellence *jāti* of Hindu society. Occupational *jātis* are, of course, the "castes" we read so much about in studies of Hindu society.

The Bengali and Sanskrit word *kula* means a "generic collectivity" (*eka-jātīya-samūha*). One could speak, for example, of a *go-kula*, a generic collectivity of cows, or of a *mānava-kula*, a generic collectivity of humans. The term *kula* was used more specifically in combination with the names of specific men to refer to units which are designated as "clans," "lineages," or "families" in English. As the above definition suggests, *kulas*, clans or families were generic collectivities contained within the larger *jātis* or "castes." Thus, within the Kāyastha-*jāti*, the Ghosh-*kula* was the generic collectivity or clan of persons who had a particular person named Ghosh as their "first ancestral male" (*ādi-puruṣa*). In conjunction with a variety of places, names, personal names, and other modifiers, the word *kula* was used to refer to smaller portions of a larger *kula*. Two other words, *gotra* and *vaṃśa*, which were sometimes used as synonyms for the word *kula*, were usually more restricted in their application and will be explained later.

Dhātu (*Substance*) *as Defining Feature*

The different classes of *jātis* were all conceived of as belonging to a single category, the set of "living beings" (*jīva*), beings defined as "possessing bodies" (*śarīrī, dehī*). Hindus have made many important cultural distinctions with respect to the human body. Since some of these are of crucial importance to this study of caste and clan, I shall give a brief account of them. A whole body in the Hindu view consisted of two complementary parts, a "subtle body" (*sūkṣma-śarīra*), consisting of "mind" (*manas*) and the various "senses" (*indriya*); and a "gross body" (*sthūla-śarīra*) consisting of seven "sustaining substances" (*dhātu*): "digested food" (*rasa*), "blood" (*rakta*), "flesh" (*māṃsa*), "fat" (*meda*), "bone" (*asthi*), "marrow" (*majjā*), and "reproductive substances" (*śukra*). Of these, blood and reproductive substances are of greatest concern to us, for these were considered the essential bodily substances of a genus, whether a caste or a clan. Blood was the general bodily source of a genus' nourishment and, hence, of its well-being. In particular, it was the source of its reproductive substances, the source of a female's "uterine blood" (*śoṇita*) and of a male's "semen" (*śukra*),[8] and these in turn were the substantial source of a genus' offspring and continued existence.[9]

Thus, one of the defining features of a human *jāti* or *kula* was is particular shared "bodily substance" (*dhātu*). Human bodily substance was, however, not the only substance feature which defined a human *jāti* or *kula*. Nonhuman *jātis* and *kulas* may have been defined by bodily substance alone, but human *jātis* and *kulas* were defined by the combination of human bodily substance with three other life-giving substances as well—"worship," "territorial," and "occupational"—to yield the three classes of *jātis* described above.

Worship substances consisted of the various implements or items, such as food, used in the worship of the gods. The par excellence "substances" of worship, however, consisted of the uttered sounds (*śabda*), the powerful words (*mantra*) of texts such as the Vedas and the Tantras. Now, the Westerner, dualistically habituated to thinking of the "Word" in religion as a transcendent spiritual entity independent of material substances, will undoubtedly find it difficult to think of the words of a "sacred" text as substances. But that is exactly how the Bengali Hindu treated them. For him, the words of the Veda consisted of the uttered sounds themselves and were considered to be immanent, not transcendent with respect to human flesh, as combinable with other substances, such as those of the human body, as food. In fact, it was precisely the combination of these sounds with human bodily substance that defined a *jāti* as *ārya* or Hindu. Territorial substances consisted of the land, rivers, animals, crops and so on of a particular country. When blended with human bodily substance, they defined a *jāti* as Rāḍhī, Vaṅgaja, etc. Occupational substances consisted of the wide variety of tools, products, and other items used by persons to gain their livelihoods and operated when combined with human bodily substance to define *jāti* as occupational. For example, the combination of ink, pen, and paper with human bodily substance defined a *jāti* as Kāyastha or writer (*lekhaka*) by occupation.

This classification of substances in a tripartite scheme was not, however, a mutually exclusive one. Substances that were used to define a *jāti* as a worship, territorial, or occupational *jāti* in one

[8]The term *śukra* applies in its more general sense to "reproductive substance"; in its more restricted sense, to "male substance" or "semen" alone.

[9]*Śabdakalpadruma*, 2nd ed., III, 1318–19, 1778–79.

context could operate to define it differently in another, depending on the purpose for which it was used. For example, the use of worship substances to gain a livelihood defined a *jāti* as Brāhmaṇ or priest by occupation.

Kulas or clans as subdivisions of *jātis* were defined not only by bodily substances, the semen of particular ancestral males, but also by their combination with the worship, territorial, and occupational substances as well. Since clans were considered to be the human units most intimately involved with generic reproduction, the distinction between these other substances and bodily substance alone was most explicitly made here. It can be seen in the contrast between the usages of the two words *vaṃśa* and *kula*. While both of these terms could be used as synonyms to refer to a clan, they were also used differently. The term *kula* was used to refer to all of the shared substances of a clan blended together. By contrast, the term *vaṃśa* was used to refer to shared bodily substance alone, namely, the semen of its males, and was often used as a synonym for male children (*santāna-santati*). The term *gotra*, used as a synonym for *kula* to refer to a clan, was used in yet another sense to refer to persons of a clan who shared not the same bodily substance but the same Vedic personal name, a worship substance.

To sum up, one of the defining features of a *jāti* or *kula* was shared substance. As a genus of living beings, each and every worship, territorial, or occupational *jāti* was defined by its own particular shared and inherited bodily substance. But human bodily substance was not the substance feature that distinguished the worship, territorial, and occupational *jātis* from each other. The substance feature that distinguished each of these types of *jātis* from each other was, appropriately, the possession of worship, territorial, and occupational substance. However, the sharing of these substances alone did make a social unit a *jāti*. There were also units in Hindu society defined by the possession of each of these substances. For example, a collectivity consisting of a preceptor (*guru*) and his disciples (*celā*, *śiṣya*) drawn from different occupational *jātis* was defined by shared worship substances; a village (*grāma*) consisting of persons of different occupational *jātis* and even from different worship *jātis* was defined by shared territorial substance. But these units were not classed as *jātis* because their defining substances were not combined with shared bodily substance. Thus, the substance feature that defined a worship, territorial, or occupational *jāti* was a "composite" substance feature consisting of human bodily substance combined with worship, territorial, or occupational substance. Clans, conceived of as subdivisions of the worship, territorial, and occupational *jātis*, were defined not only by shared bodily substance but by shared substances of the other three types as well. Yet, because clans more than *jātis* were concerned with generic reproduction, the distinction between shared bodily substance (*vaṃśa*) and shared composite substance (*kula*) was sharpest here.

The Hindu use of these different substances to define *jātis* and *kulas* was explicitly monistic, for it did not involve any of the dualistic contrasts postulated to exist between opposed moral and natural or ritual and material orders. To the contrary, all of these substances were seen as homologous in their uses and characteristics. Each of them was shared and inherited in a homologous manner and each shaped and was shaped by the other in defining a genus. Finally, all alike were endowed with powerful life-giving qualities, for all possessed the same "natural" and "moral" or "ritual" and "material" capacity, handled in the right and proper manner, to bring about the well-being and prosperity of the genera which they made up and defined.

Dharma (*Code for Conduct*) *as Defining Feature*

The other defining feature of a *jāti* or *kula* was designated by the Sanskrit and Bengali word *dharma*, a word that receives much discussion in accounts of Hindu society. This word has been one of the most difficult to gloss in English. It has variously been translated as "law," "civil law," "sacred law," "ceremonial law," "duty," "right conduct," "nature," "morality," and even as "spiritual merit."[10] The problem with these glosses is that they attempt to classify *dharma* as an element in one or the other of the dual orders postulated in Euro-American culture. This is incorrect, for in the single, monistically conceived order of Hinduism, the word *dharma* was applied not only to divine or human *jātis* and *kulas* but to virtually every differentiated set of substances and beings. Everything ranging from a metal or rock to a human *jāti* or king was said to have its own particular *dharma*.

[10]Bühler's *The Laws of Manu* contains nearly all of these glosses; an interesting essay on *dharma* as conceived by Manu is V. Raghavan's "The Manu Saṃhitā," *The Cultural Heritage of India* (Calcutta: The Rāmakrishna Mission Institute of Culture, 1962), II, 335–63.

Hindu *dharma* was, thus, not only, in Euro-American terms, a sacred, spiritual, and moral element; it was also a secular, material, and natural one. To avoid any of these dualistic connotations, I usually prefer to translate the word simply as "code for conduct." This is virtually identical with the gloss preferred by the eminent scholar of *dharma-śāstra*, P. V. Kane.[11]

While this simple and neutral gloss of *dharma* as code for conduct is helpful in avoiding unnecessary dualistic connotations, it only begins to bring about an understanding of what *dharma* is in its Hindu cultural setting. The word *dharma* is derived from the Sanskrit root *dhṛ* meaning to "sustain" (*dhāraṇa*) or "nourish" (*poṣaṇa*).[12] This rightly suggests that the code for conduct of a *jāti* or *kula* was that particular code which sustained and nourished it as a distinct genus of living beings. Commonly, this code for conduct was conceived of as a bundle of interconnected "attributes" (*guṇa*), "powers" (*śakti*), and "potential actions" (*kartavya-karma*). These are thought of as inherent in the *jātis* or *kulas* to which they belong. When realized through actual conduct (*ācāra*), a code for conduct is believed to bring about the "well-being" (*maṅgala, kalyāna*) and good fortune or prosperity (*śrī, lakṣmī*, etc.) of its genus. Taken in this sense, *dharma* is not simply a code for conduct; it is the highest of the three goals of man as an embodied being, taking proper precedence over the "enjoyment of desires" (*kāma*) and the "acquisition of wealth" (*artha*). As a goal, *dharma* is the "proper order" of things that brings about the good of the whole world, a goal that is achieved only by the constant striving of people. Thus, *dharma* is not only a synchronic state of beings but also a diachronic process of becoming, inherent in the units that make up the world.

The concept of *dharma* as a particular bundle of inherent attributes, powers, and potential acts raises the question: inherent in what? The answer is that a particular code for conduct was considered to be inherent in its own particular, homologous substance. Since

[11]According to him, "The writers on *dharma-śāstra* meant by *dharma* not a creed or religion but a mode of life or a code of conduct, which regulated a man's work and activities as a member of society and as an individual and was intended to bring about the gradual development of a man and to enable him to reach what was deemed to be the goal of human existence." See P. V. Kane, *History of Dharmaśāstra* (Poona: Bhandarkar Oriental Research Institute, 1930–62), II, 2.

[12]For definitions and usages, see *Śabdakalpadruma*, 2d ed., III, 1764–67; and Jñānendramohan Dās, *Bāṅgālā Bhāṣār Abhidhāna* (Calcutta: The Indian Publishing House, 1937), I, 1128–32.

jātis were defined by shared bodily substance, the code for conduct of a *jāti* was appropriately seen to inhere in its distinctive bodily substance. For example, the code for conduct of the human *jāti*, *manuṣya-dharma*, inhered in its distinctive bodily part, its mind (*manas*) while the code for conduct of the female *jāti* inhered in its distinctly female bodily substances. Among the three classes of purely human *jātis*, generic code for conduct was thought to inhere not only in shared bodily substance but also in the other defining substances with which it was combined. Thus, the code for conduct of the *ārya* or Hindu *jāti*, *ārya-dharma* or Hindu-*dharma*, inhered not only in its shared bodily substance but also in the Vedas, Tantras, and other words which made up the shared worship substance by which it was defined. Similarly, the code for conduct of a territorial *jāti* or *jana* was contained not only in its shared bodily substance but also in its shared territorial substance (*deśa*) and was often referred to as its *deśa-dharma*.

The code for conduct of an occupational *jāti* was referred to as its *jāti-dharma*. As the term *jāti* referred in a par excellence sense to an occupational *jāti* or caste, so the compound term *jāti-dharma* had as its par excellence meaning the occupational code for conduct which inhered in the bodies of persons of the same caste as a result of the combination of their occupational substances with their shared bodily substance. Since an occupational *jāti* was also combined with a worship *jāti* and a territorial *jāti*, its defining substance was a composite, and so, too, was its code. The term *jāti-dharma* was thus also used to refer to a caste's code in its composite aspect.

The code for conduct of a clan, *kula-dharma*, was conceptualized in much the same way as *jāti-dharma*. Just as the defining substance of a clan was its ancestral male's reproductive substance, so its defining code for conduct was a code enjoining proper marriage and reproduction. Yet a clan's code was also a composite code, for it also included the occupational, worship, and territorial codes of the *jāti* to which it belonged. Hence, the term *kula-dharma* could be used either in a general sense to refer to this composite code or in a more restricted sense to refer to its marriage and reproductive code alone.

Jāti *and* Kula *as Coded Bodily Substance and Rank*

That a particular code for conduct was always conceived to be inherent in a particular, homologous substance is an important point, for it is precisely here that the difference between substance and code as the two defining features of a caste or clan collapses. Code for conduct was not a spiritual or moral-legal entity which transcended matter and nature in the Hindu social order of *jāti* and *kulas*. Rather, it was an element immanent in the *jāti* or *kula* to which it belonged. Conversely, the defining substances of *jātis* and *kulas* were themselves inherently coded. Whether liquid or solid, substances ranging from blood through the words of the Veda—the implements of worship, ink, pens, or land, water, and crops—were conceived of not as unstructured, inert matter but as structured, living things having their particular purposes and uses in sustaining life. In other words, there were no castes or clans defined either by substance or code for conduct alone, for substance and code were in the Hindu view really two aspects of the same thing. As inseparable elements of the same order, both operated in the same way according to the same rules. The derivation of the words for both substance, *dhātu*, and code for conduct, *dharma*, from the same root, *dhṛ*, meaning to sustain (*dhāraṇa*), belies their non-duality as that is precisely what both do; the defining substances of a genus sustain it as a living thing and so, too, does its defining code for conduct.

Thus, *jātis* and *kulas* were not really defined by two opposed and contrasting features—natural substance and moral code for conduct. To the contrary, they were defined by a single feature, one which might best be termed "coded substance." The words *jāti* and *kula* were often used in contexts where they may, in fact, be glossed as "coded bodily substance." For example, when a person said that his *jāti* was "ruined" (*naṣṭa*) or that his *kula* had been "realized" (*siddha*), he was not using the words *jāti* and *kula* to refer to his caste or clan but to the composite coded substance of his caste or clan which he himself possessed. Finally, the terms *jāti* and *kula* could be used in conjunction with modifiers such as *ucca*, "high," *nimna*, "low," *śreṣṭha*, "superior," etc., to compare the relative qualities or conditions of the coded bodily substances of different *jātis* or *kulas* or to refer to the "prestige" (*maryādā*) or "honor" (*sanmāna*) held by them. In such contexts, the words *jāti* and *kula* can best be translated as "rank," for the rank of a caste or clan was in fact the relative quality or condition of its coded bodily substance.

So far our concern has been to abstract at a very general level the irreducible, culturally defined elements by which Bengali Hindus defined castes and clans. We have seen that substance and code were conceived of as inseparable elements drawn from a single order. Hence, the features that defined social units were really single features which we can best refer to as "coded substance." The single feature that defined a human social unit as a *jāti* or *kula* was the sharing of the same "coded bodily substance." The combination of coded bodily substance with three different kinds of coded substances, those of worship, occupation, and territory, yielded three different classes of *jātis*. *Kulas* were defined by a combination of all of these features. What distinguished one *kula* from the other was the sharing of the coded bodily substance of a particular ancestral male. We turn now from these more abstract definitions to the more concrete problem of how coded substances were used to define the particular sets of castes and clans that made up the total community of Bengal as conceived by medieval Bengali Hindus.

Two Caste and Clan Systems in One

Community (Samāja) *as Four* Varṇas *and Many* Jātis

The population of Gauḍa or Bengal was conceived of as organized into a single, distinct community by Bengali Hindus of the middle period. The word which was used to refer to community in the most general sense was the word *samāja*, a word having as its etymological meaning, "going together." As its etymology implies, it was used to refer to aggregates of persons or to sets of *jātis* and *kulas*, or villages, kingdoms, councils, etc., that were conceived of as belonging together and forming a whole—a totality endowed with "proper order" (*dharma*) among its parts and possessed of the power to bring about the well-being of the persons it contained. The word *samāja* was a good word for community in the Bengali setting. Since it was "neutral" with respect to caste and clan, it could be used to refer either to *jātis* and *kulas*, aggregates of persons who shared the same coded bodily substance, or to other units such as villages, aggregates of persons who did not share that but rather some other coded substance as defining features. Most importantly, it could be used to designate the larger community of Bengal as a whole, the total community conceived of as embracing sets of smaller communities defined in both ways. Our concern here will be to explicate the "sets" or "systems" of *jātis* and *kulas* that made up this community.

The task of reconstructing the caste and clan system of middle period Bengal is a complex one, for imbedded in the particular regional system of Bengal was a more universal, all-India caste and clan system, that of the four *varṇas*, a system familiar to most students of Indian society and elaborately described in ancient Indian texts.

The persistent appearance of this ancient system in the medieval Bengali texts puzzled me for a long time. It is well known that Bengal lies outside the "middle country" or Madhyadeśa, the area where the four-*varṇa* system arose, and that there were many glaring discrepancies between this system and the caste and clan system of Bengal as defined by the Bengalis. As I became more sensitive to the meanings of the statements made in Bengali accounts of their caste and clan system, I began to realize that the four-*varṇa* system was not an empty set of ideal social categories and norms.

This system was, it is true, considered to be one of Hindu society as it had existed in the past. Yet this past society was not held to be a dead thing from which people of the "present" (the middle period) were separated. Nor was it considered to be an imposed, exogenous ideal which Bengalis could only poorly approximate. To the contrary, it was conceived of as a living thing coming down continuously into the present, and the substances and codes that defined *jātis* and *kulas* in it were held to exist concretely in the caste and clan system of middle period Bengal. As a system of combined elements, however, they had not come down through time unchanged. The middle period system was thought to have developed as a result of a series of "key events" which occurred over time. The *jātis* and *kulas* of the past thus existed in the present but in a transformed state. In other words, the caste and clan system of middle period Bengal is better understood as a later, regional variant of the earlier, all-India system, and any correct analysis of it must also be an historical one.

The remainder of this chapter is devoted to a "synchronic" description of this system, comparing and contrasting the particular Bengal variant with the universal, all-India matrix out of which it arose. The succeeding chapter will then turn to a "diachronic" account of the key events by which the society of Bengal was transformed into its middle period state.

Jātis ("*Castes*") *Defined by Occupation* (Jīvika)

Bengali Hindus conceived of the total Hindu community as originating from a single source, the living body of a gigantic (*virāṭ*), primordial (*ādi*) Code-Man, entitled Puruṣa or Prajāpati, who was possessed of the most powerful and subtle of coded substances, the words of the Veda, and was a form of *brahman*, the all-powerful neuter entity out of which the entire universe was generated. After he had produced a set of male and female genera for the purpose of generating mankind by dividing himself into halves, this Code-Man proceeded to generate a set of four named and ranked occupational *jātis* in the Madhyadeśa or middle country of India. Each of these had its own "livelihood" or "occupation" (*jīvikā*). Frequently, the word *varṇa* was used in place of the word *jāti* to describe these four genera. Derived from the root *varṇ*, meaning to describe, it was employed to describe definite sets of things such as syllables (*akṣara*) and colors (*raṅ*) and was used here to distinguish these four occupational *jātis* as a "primary" set from other "secondary" occupational *jātis* thought to be derived from the "mixing" (*saṅkara*) of these four. These four *varṅas* are, of course, the four "classes," "estates," or "castes" so widely discussed in accounts of "classical" Hindu society. The first to be born, the Brāhmaṇ, was generated from his mouth, the second, the Kṣatriya, from his arms, the third, the Vaiśya, from his loins, and the fourth, the Śūdra, from his feet. Here is an excerpt from a Bengali text purporting to convey the views of the ancient *dharma-śāstra* of Manu. It should be noted that the four-*varṇa* system, as presented here by equating the "twice-born" with the Brāhmaṇ alone, has already partially transformed it into its middle period state:

> When Prajāpati (the Lord of People) generated (*sṛṣṭi*) people (*prajā*), the Veda Brāhmaṇs were generated (*udbhava*) first from his mouth. The Kṣatriya, endowed with a bow (*dhanu*) was generated from his arms, and the Vaisya, attached to agriculture (*kṛṣi-karma*), was generated from his loins. In order to serve (*sevā*) the Brāhmaṇ, the Śūdra was generated from his feet. And so, from the body (*aṅga*) of Brahma, the four *varṇas* were born. The proper place for the four Vedas—the injunctions (*vidhāna*) of the Sāma, Ṛk, Yajuḥ, and Atharva—is in the mouth of the Brāhmaṇ. Continually worshiping for himself (*yajana*), worshiping for others (*yājana*), learning the Veda (*adhyayana*), teaching it (*adhyāpana*), and accepting gifts (*dāna-grahaṇa*) are the

> marks (*lakṣaṇa*) of the Brāhmaṇ. Because he recites the *sandhyā* and *gāyatrī* and knows the injunctions of the Veda, interprets the code-books (*śāstra*), engages in *yoga*, and possesses knowledge (*jñāna*), he is perpetually endowed with powerful heat (*tapānvita*). The code for conduct (*dharma*) of the Kṣatriya enjoins good conduct (*sadācāra*) involving knowledge of the bow. He takes care of people (*prajā-pālana*), is distinctively adept at giving (*dāna-śīla*), and expert in warfare (*yuddha*). The code for conduct (*dharma*) of the Vaiśya enjoins him to engage in agriculture (*kṛṣi-karma*), take care of domesticated mammals (*paśu-pālana*) and trade (*vāṇijya*), this is the order. The code for conduct (*dharma*) of the Śūdra enjoins him to do the service of the twice-born (*dvija-sevā*) and be subordinate to the twice-born. These are the codes for conduct of the four *varṇas* according to the injunctions (*vidhi*) of the Veda. He who preserves his own code for conduct (*svadharma-pālana*) in accord with the views of the code-books (*śāstra*) is superior (*śreṣṭha*) in *varṇa* and becomes renowned.[13]

As this account implies, each of these four occupational *jātis* or *varṇas* was generated by combining occupational codes and substances with homologically coded bodily substances or parts. Also implied here is the notion that the four make up a complete set, a totality having as its symbol and source the single Code-Man. The units of this set are conceived of as interdependent; the well-being of the whole and of the persons making it up rested on the occupational exchanges made among the *varṇas*.[14] Thus, the code for conduct of the Brāhmaṇ, inherent in his mouth and in the Vedas or *śāstras* and the worship implements which he possessed, enjoined him to gain his livelihood by teaching the Veda (*adhyāpana*), performing Vedic worship for the Kṣatriya and Vaiśya (*yājana*), and accepting gifts (*pratigraha*) in return. The Kṣatriya's code for conduct, inherent in his strong arms as well as in the weapons he possessed, enjoined him to bear weapons (*śastrāstrabhṛt*) and "protect" or "take care of" (*pālana, rakṣā*) people in general and the Vaiśya in particular. The Vaiśya's code, inherent in his generative loins and in the wealth, animals, and grain he accumulated, enjoined him to trade (*vāṇijya*), take interest (*kusida*), care for domestic mammals or engage in culivation (*kṛṣi*), and give taxes (*kara*) to

[13]Nibandha, Dacca University Library MSS (uncataloged), n.d., fol. 1.

[14]For accounts of the four *varṇas*, see *Śabdakalpadruma*, 2d ed., VI, 4096–4104. 4115–19; Kane, *History of Dharmaśāstra*, II, 19–45; and Manu, *Manu-smṛti* [*Dharmaśāstra*], ed. Ganganātha Jhā (Calcutta: Asiatic Society of Bengal, 1932–39), I. 87–91 and X. 74–131.

the Kṣatriya in return for the protection he received. Unlike the three higher *varṇas*, the Śūdra was not originally combined with distinct occupational substances. His code for conduct, inherent in his body and especially his lowly feet, enjoined him to engage in the bodily service (*sevā*, *śuśruṣā*) of the three higher *varṇas* in return for which he was to receive maintenance (*bharaṇa*).

The set of occupational *jātis* which existed in combination with the territorial substance of Bengal in the middle period differed from that combined with the territorial substance of Madhyadeśa in the earlier period. The population of middle period Bengal was seen to be organized not into a set of four great universal occupational *varṇas*, but into a set of smaller, more particular occupational *jātis*. Furthermore, these *jatis* were seen to be particular variants of only two of the four *varṇas*, the Brāhmaṇ and Śūdra.

The particular ranked Brāhmaṇ castes of Bengal were considered to belong to the Brāhmaṇ *varṇa*. Of these, the highest was the Brāhmaṇ caste marked by its possession of the Veda. The particular non-Brāhmaṇ castes of Bengal, stereotypically seen to form a set of thirty-six, belonged to the Śūdra *varṇa*.[15] These Śūdra castes were not all equal. Instead they were ranked high and low in two major subsets, *sat* ("good"), and *asat* ("not good"). Among the *sat* Śūdras, the Kāyastha was considered the highest. The highest of the Brāhmaṇ castes, the Vedic, and the highest of the Śūdra castes, the Kāyastha, are, of course, the major subjects of this study.

Occupational exchanges among these Brāhmaṇ and Śūdra castes also varied from those in the earlier system. Unlike its predecessor, the Vedic Brāhmaṇ castes of Bengal performed acts of worship (*yajña*) with Vedic utterances (*mantras*) for the Śūdra castes, but only for the higher ones.[16] This distinguished it from the lower or Varṇa-yājī Brāhmaṇ caste which performed non-Vedic worship for the lower Śūdra castes.

The Bengali Śūdra, too, was different. Unlike his forebears, he was combined with occupational substances and codes apart from his own body. The *sat* Śūdra castes such as the Kāyastha or writer, the Vaidya, or physician, and the castes of the *nava-śākha* ("nine branches") set—Mālākāra, garland-maker, Kumbhakāra, potter, Kāmār, blacksmith, Nāpita, barber, etc.—were each combined with their

[15] Rāmānanda Śarmā, "Kula-dīpikā," Dacca University Library MSS (uncataloged), n.d., fol. 3b; and Vidyānidhi, *Sambandhanirṇaya*, I, 91–92.

[16] Vidyānidhi, *Sambandhanirṇaya*, I, 133, 145; and *Brahma-vaivartta Purāṇa*, p. 28.

own occupational substances and codes.[17] So too were the *asat* Śūdra castes such as the Hele, cultivator, Suvarṇavaṇik, gold-merchant, Dhopā, washerman, Hāṛī, scavenger, Ḍom, basket-maker, etc.

This did not, however, excuse them from serving. The many Śūdra castes of Bengal, like their single predecessor, all shared a code for conduct enjoining them to serve the twice-born, though in Bengal, of course, this meant the Brāhmaṇ alone. On the other hand, services were distinguished in accord with the two types of Brāhmaṇs and Śūdras present in the Bengali variant. The higher Śūdras served only the Vedic Brāhmaṇs; the lower Śūdras not only served the Vedic Brāhmaṇs, they also served the higher Śūdras, even though the latter were not twice-born. Thus, one can see that in the Bengali variant, the *sat* Śūdras, as patrons of Vedic worship and receivers of service became partial replacements of the absent Kṣatriya and Vaiśya.

Another characteristic which distinguished this prolific Bengali variant from its matrix was the perceived lack of simplicity and clarity with respect to the generic attributes and codes of its constituent parts. This confusion was said to be the result of *varṇa-saṅkara*, the "mixing of castes." According to both ancient and medieval texts, the four *varṇas* formed a complete set of occupational *jātis*, capable of filling all of the occupational needs of the community: "Three *varṇas* are twice-born, Brāhmaṇ, Kṣatriya and Vaiśya. The fourth, the Śūdra, is only once-born; there is no fifth."[18] Other occupational *jātis* were considered to have as their source the improper "mixing" or "confusion" (*saṅkara*) of these four original *varṇas* and were referred to as *varṇas-saṅkara* or *saṅkara jātis*: "those born as a result of the mixing (*saṅkarya*) of those four castes (*jāti*), that is, from females (*strī*) and males (*puruṣa*) of two different castes, became known as *varṇa-saṅkara*."[19]

The generation of new occupations could have occurred through the mixing of different occupational substances, but the generation of new occupational *jātis* logically required not only the mixing of occupational substances but of bodily substances as well. Hence, the generation of new occupational *jātis* was held to be caused by

[17] Vidyānidhi, *Sambandhanirṇaya*, I, 145–77.

[18] Manu, X.4.

[19] *Brahma-vaivartta Purāṇa*, p. 28; see also Vidyānidhi, *Sambandhanirṇaya*, I, 222–37; *Śabdakalpadruma*, 2d ed., VI 4121–25; and Kane, *History of Dharmaśāstra*, II, 59–61.

improper marriage and reproduction on the part of men and women of different *varṇas*. Semen and uterine blood were the bodily substance by which persons of a *jāti* transmitted their compositely coded bodily substances intact to their offspring. The improper mixing of differently coded bodily substances resulted in offspring which possessed coded bodily substances that were, therefore, mixed or confused. Since the generation of new occupational *jātis* occurred as a result of improper mixtures, they were invariably considered inferior in coded substance or rank and classed as Śūdra. All thirty-six of the Śūdra *jātis* of Bengal were considered to be such *varṇa-sankara jātis*.

The result of these improper mixings was a certain perceived confusion of coded occupational substances. The ancestors of the highest ranking Vedic Brāhmaṇs of Bengal were, as we shall see, made to look like warrior Kṣatriyas when they arrived in Bengal to settle. Moreover, as we have already seen, not all of the Brāhmaṇs in the Bengal variant possessed livelihood codes marked by their combination with the Veda; only the highest did. Some of the lower Brāhmaṇs had livelihood codes which enjoined the performance of worship for others, but they did it without the Vedic *mantras*. Still others, the Graha-vipra, or astrologer, and the Agradāni, or performer of funerals (*antyeṣṭi*), had even lower, more restricted occupations. Conversely, one of the highest of the Śūdra castes, the Vaidya,[20] did possess one of the Vedas, albeit an inferior one, the Āyur-veda.[21]

These were not the only explicitly confusing occupational features of the Bengali variant. The occupations of *vaṇik* (merchant), cultivator (*hālika*, *cāṣi*), and cowherd (*gopa*), all of which formed the livelihood codes of the single Vaiśya *varṇa* in the earlier model, appeared as the codes for conduct of particular, discrepantly ranked Śūdra *jātis* in the Bengal variant (for example, the Sadgopa was included among the *sat* Śūdras while the Suvarṇavaṇik and Hele were included among the *asat*). Finally, kings, who were appropriately drawn from the Kṣatriya *varṇa* in the all-India system were drawn from a variety of non-Kṣatriya castes including the Vedic Brāhmaṇ and Kāyastha Śūdra castes. Even the two powerful kings

[20]The name of this caste appears to be derived from the word Veda itself. Another, and perhaps older, name for this caste is Ambaṣṭha. See Nripendra Kumar Dutt, *Origin and Growth of Caste in India* (Calcutta: Firma K. L. Mukhopadhyay, 1965), II, 65–81; and D. C. Sircar, *Studies in the Society and Administration of Ancient and Medieval India* (Calcutta: Firma K. L. Mukhopadhyay, 1967), I, 113–18.

[21]The Veda of "long life" (*āyuḥ*).

said to have rule in Bengal before the Muslim conquest, Ādiśūra and Vallāla Sena, were, as we shall see, considered to be Vaidya Śūdras and not Kṣatriyas. Thus, there was no sure correlation in the Bengali system of castes between observable occupational attributes and inherently possessed occupational codes; nor was there any neat correspondence of *varṇa* occupational code and caste rank.

Jātis ("*Subcastes*") *Defined by Territory* (Deśa)

The particularity characteristic of these occupational castes of the Gauḍa or Bengal country did not end at the regional level, for these regional occupational castes were themselves seen as divided into sets of smaller, territorially differentiated *jātis* that were not ranked high and low. These are *jātis* which are often referred to in the literature as "subcastes." Here, too, there was some confusion as well as complexity; not all were divided into the identical territorial *jātis*. For example, the Kāyastha *jāti* of Bengal was divided into four territorial *jātis* named after the four "subregions" or countries of Gauḍa in which they were settled—Dakṣiṇa Rāḍhī, Uttara Rāḍhī, Vārendra, and Vaṅgaja. The Brāhmaṇ *jāti*, on the other hand, was divided into only two territorial *jātis*—Rāḍhī and Vārendra. There was no separate Vaṅgaja Brāhmaṇ *jāti*; Rāḍhī and Vārendra Brāhmaṇ were seen to share this country between them.[22]

Worship (Yajña, Pūjā) *as the Primary Definer of* Jāti *Unity and Rank*

So far we have seen that territorial substance was held to embrace complete sets of occupational *jātis*. Madhyadeśa in the past contained within it the complete set of four *varṇas* whereas the country of Bengal in the "present" contained its full complement of occupational *jātis*. However, neither territorial nor occupational substances were accorded primary stress in defining the total community. The feature that was accorded this distinction was the coded substance of worship. The correct possession and use of the words and implements of worship were thought to be more powerful than the other two in

[22]Many other "confusions" of the territorial variety could be enumerated. The reader who wishes to acquaint himself with these may consult the ethographic glossary in Herbert H. Risley's *Tribes and Caste of Bengal* (Calcutta: Bengal Secretariat Press, 1891).

bringing about well-being because it was the source not only of well-being on earth but also of a higher state after death. The coded substance of worship was also the par excellence source of *dharma* as "proper order" among the castes and clans of the community. Since the differential possession of worship substances acted to define castes as divine and higher in rank in relation to others, it is of particular importance in this study.

The words or "coded substance" of two sets of texts, the Veda or *nigama* and the Tantra or *āgama*, operated to define the occupational *jātis* of all of the countries of Bhāratavarṣa as a single *ārya* or Hindu genus in the earlier system. Since the possession of these words defined beings or genera as divine and were considered to be properly combined with all persons who belonged to the *ārya* or Hindu community, it is proper to speak of the entire community as divinely endowed. The catch in this, of course, was that not all beings and genera were equally endowed with divinely coded substances. A number of important distinctions operated to define some as divine in relation to others. The most important distinction was that made between those who possessed only the *āgama* words and those who possessed both the *āgama* and *nigama* words. The possession of the *āgama* words, and especially of the powerful Tantric *mantras* or utterances contained therein, was seen by Bengalis to have incorporated virtually the entire past population of Bhāratavarṣa into a single *ārya* or Hindu genus. The coded substance of the *āgama* contained a code for conduct enjoining persons of the two sexes and four *varṇas* to be combined through "initiation" (*dīkṣā*) with the powerful Tantric utterances and to perform the worship, here called *pūjā*, of the all-powerful Hindu deities such as Viṣṇu, Kṛṣṇa, Śiva, Durgā, or Kālī in the form of an embodied, enlivened image with offerings of flowers, fruits, and other foods.

This combination with the coded substance of the *āgama* defined the men and women of all four *varṇas* in a general sense as a single divinely endowed *ārya* (or Hindu) genus and opposed it to other *anārya* genera such as those mentioned earlier.

The additional possession of the *nigama* or Veda operated not to unify the total Hindu community but to draw and maintain major distinctions of rank within it. In the caste system of the past it acted to make a clear distinction between men of the three higher *varṇas* on the one hand and their women and the Śūdras on the other. These men were seen to be combined directly with additional *mantras* or utterances of the Veda itself in the course of a *saṃskāra* or "life-cycle act of worship" referred to as the *upanayana*, "initiation," or *dvijāti*, "second generation." Appropriately, the men of the three *varṇas* who underwent this combining, generative act were referred to as the "twice-generated" or "twice-born" (*dvija*).

The sustaining code for conduct contained not only in the Veda but in the bodies of the twice-born themselves enjoined them to learn the Veda (*adhyayana*) and to perform the Vedic type of worship, called *yajña*, or more narrowly, *homa*, in which food was offered to a multitude of Vedic gods. This form of worship contrasted with *pūjā* in that it was performed "with fire" (*sāgni*) which was held to convey cooked food upward to invisible rather than concretely embodied deities and required the use of Vedic *mantras*. In addition, this code also enjoined the giving of gifts (*dāna*), especially to Brāhmaṇs.

Śūdras and women, who were thought unworthy to possess the Vedas, were enjoined not to learn the Veda or perform the Vedic type of worship. They combined themselves with the Veda only indirectly as servants and wives of the twice-born. In keeping with this distinction, the twice-born were considered to be the *āryas* par excellence within the larger *ārya* community whereas the Śūdras (and women) were considered in relation to them to be *anārya*. Appropriately, twice-born men were considered to be divine and themselves worthy of worship in relation to their once-born wives and Śūdra servants. Service of their twice-born masters was, in fact, their form of worship. The divine benefits that were received from the gods by the twice-born as a result of Vedic worship were, according to the texts, received from the twice-born by their wives and Śūdra servants as a result of service. Thus, the three twice-born *varṇas* taken together and the single Śūdra *varṇa* were not only defined as occupational *jātis*; they were also defined as worship *jātis*. And it was primarily as worship *jātis* that they were ranked high and low.

There were two major contrasts between the earlier matrix and the middle period variant. One had to do with the presence of Muslims in Bengal, the other with the diffusion of the Veda among the Hindus themselves. First, the entire population of Bhāratavarṣa, of which Bengal was a part, was no longer combined with the coded substances of the Hindu texts. Part of it was now combined with the texts of Islam. As a result, the contrast between *ārya* and *anārya* became a contrast between Hindu and Musulmān in the Bengal variant.

Consistent with this shift, terms such as *dasyu*, "thief," *mleccha*, "barbarian," and Yavana, Greek, which had been applied in the past model to *anāryas*, were sometimes applied to Muslims in the Bengal variant. Yet these Muslims were not excluded, as were the earlier *anāryas*, from the larger community to which Bengali Hindus belonged. Mukundarāma, a sixteenth-century Hindu writer who described the establishment of a local Bengali community having a full complement of genera, unquestioningly includes within it a large set of Muslim genera (*jātis*).[23]

The second contrast involved a different alignment between the coded substances of the Veda and the bodily substance of the occupational *varṇas* and *jātis* as a result of their mixing. Here, too, as with the occupational substances themselves, the combination in the Bengal variant was marked by differences, but not by the systemic confusion characteristic of occupational and territorial substances. Since the Kṣatriya and Vaiśya were missing in the Bengal variant, the terms twice-born and Brāhmaṇ became synonymous. Not all the Brāhmaṇ *jātis* in Bengal, however, were considered worthy to possess the Veda. Some of the lower *jātis*, especially those performing worship for the lower Śūdra, were held to have lost possession of the Veda. Hence, in relation to the higher Brāhmaṇ, he did not possess the Veda. The Śūdra, who was not to combine himself with the Veda in the past model, was enabled to do so in the Bengal variant. Even so, the Śūdra was still not to learn the Veda. He could engage Vedic Brāhmaṇs for the performance of Vedic worship and give them gifts in return, but he himself was not to recite the Vedic *mantras*. Therefore, in relation to the Brāhmaṇ, the Śūdra of the middle period was only partially combined with the coded substance of the Veda. Yet, just as the possession of the Veda operated to distinguish high and low Brāhmaṇs, so, too, did it operate to distinguish high and low Śūdras. Only the *sat* Śūdra who had worship performed for him by the Vedic Brāhmaṇ was considered partially combinable with the Veda. The lower or *asat* Śūdra whose worship was performed by a "fallen" Brāhmaṇ was considered unworthy. The *asat* Śūdra in relation to the *sat* Śūdra was, thus, not even partially combined with the Veda. Thus, as a result of the mixing of the *varṇas*, the coded substance of Vedic worship was more confusingly and widely diffused in the Hindu community of the present than it had been in the past.

[23]Mukundarāma Chakravarti, *Kavikaṅkaṇa-Caṇḍī*, ed. Srikumar Bandyopadhyay and Visvapati Chaudhuri (Calcutta: University of Calcutta, 1958), I, 343–46.

The point of major significance, however, is that the differential possession of the coded substance of Vedic worship defined high and low rank relationships. Sets of occupational *jātis*—Brāhmaṇ, *sat* Śūdra, *asat* Śūdra—were ranked not by their occupations or by the wealth or land that they possessed, but by the degree of Vedic power they embodied. It was the Veda and Vedic worship, however diffuse they might be, which were seen as the ultimate source of well-being and prosperity for each *jāti*, and so it was the Veda which produced an ordered community of ranked *jātis*.

Gotra *as Worship Clan and* Kula

Each of the *varṇas* in the community of the past was divided into an indefinite number of equal clans defined by the possession of the compositely coded bodily substances of their particular ancestral males and an inherent code for conduct enjoining the persons of the same clan not to marry with person of their own clan, but with those of other clans of the same *varṇa*. Of particular importance in this model was the *gotra* aspect of clan organization. In fact, the *gotra* is so important that in the *śāstras*, the clan marriage codes are usually associated with the *gotra* rather than the *kula*. *Gotras* were the personal names of the original Brāhmaṇ priest-preceptors (*ṛṣis*), and all persons who shared the same *gotra* name were said to be of the same *gotra*. These names, like other words of the Veda, were considered to be subtle and powerful substances necessary to the correct performance of Vedic worship.

The *gotra* names of the Brāhmaṇs were acquired in the same way as their bodily substances, for their clan and *gotra* ancestors were considered to be one and the same. This was not so, however, for Kṣatriyas and Vaiśyas. Like the Brāhmaṇ, they were twice-born and were enjoined to perform Vedic worship using *gotra* names. Yet the Kṣatriya and Vaiśya did not acquire their *gotras* from their ancestral males. Rather, they acquired them from their ancestral Brāhmaṇ priests (*purohitas*). The Śūdras, who in the community of the past did not have Vedic worship performed for them, did not possess *gotra* names.

Kulas or clans, whether combined with *gotras* or not, were divided in the all-India system into smaller *kulas* or "joint families." While the larger clans were units whose persons all shared the bodily substance of a dead ancestral male, these smaller families were units who all shared the bodily substance of a living male who acted as their "master" (*kartā*).

Worship Jātis (*"Grades"*) *Within Territorial and Occupational* Jātis

The clan organization of the Brāhmaṇs and Śūdras in the middle period variant of this community was much more complex, exhibiting a "baroque" degree of elaboration, and it was also, of course, more garbled. The population of each of the territorially distinguished Brāhmaṇ and Kāyastha subcastes was organized into a definite number of named *kulas* or clans, though the numbers and names of these clans of course varied from subcaste to subcaste. Most importantly, the clans in each of these subcastes were organized into smaller named sets of two or more clans that were ranked high and low with respect to each other. These sets, referred to variously as *jāti*, "genus," *bhāva*, "mode," or *śreṇī*, "section," are conventionally dubbed "grades," a term implying rank. As I have, for convenience, retained the terms "caste" and "subcaste" in this study, so I shall, for the same reason, use the term "grade" to refer to these ranked sets of clans.

There was, inevitably, some variation by subcaste in the names and numbers of these grades. The major variation in nomenclature occurred between four of the subcastes—Rāḍhī and Vārendra Brāhmaṇ, Dakṣina-rāḍhī and Vaṅgaja Kāyastha—and the other two—Uttara-rāḍhī and Vārendra Kāyastha. The highest grade in each of the first four subcastes was named Kulīna. The lower ranked grades in the two Brāhmaṇ subcastes were named Śrotriya, and the lower grades in the two Kāyastha subcastes were named Maulika. The Rāḍhī and Vārendra Brāhmaṇ subcastes contained four and two Srotriya grades, respectively, while the Dakṣiṇa-rāḍhī and Vaṅgaja Kāyastha subcastes contained two and three grades, respectively. Terms such as Siddha and Sādhya were used to name these lower grades. The Uttara-rāḍhī and Vārendra Kāyasthas did not use the terms "Kulīna" and "Maulika," relying more simply on the terms "Siddha," "Sādhya," "Kaṣṭa," and "Amūlaja" to name the ranked grades in their subcastes. The meanings of these terms will be examined shortly. A list of the grades contained in the Brāhmaṇ and Kāyastha subcastes is given in Table 1.

Table 1

Brāhmaṇ and Kāyastha Clan Grades

Subcaste	Clan grade	Number of clans
Rāḍhī Brāhmaṇ	Kulīna	8
	Śrotriya	
	Susiddha	34
	Siddha	3
	Sādhya	4
	Ari, Kaṣṭa	7
Vārendra Brāhmaṇ	Kulīna	7
	Śrotriya	
	Siddha	9
	Kaṣṭa	84
Dakṣiṇa-rāḍhī Kāyastha	Kulīna	3
	Maulika	
	Siḍdha	8
	Sādhya	72
Vaṅgaja Kāyastha	Kulīna	4
	Maulika	
	Madhyalya	4
	Mahāpātra	4
	Acala,Sādhāraṇa	87
Uttara-rāḍhī Kāyastha	Siddha	2
	Sādhya	3
	Kaṣṭa	4
Vārendra Kāyastha	Siddha	3
	Sādhya	4
	Amūlaja	40

Each of these ranked sets of clans was defined by its own *kula* or coded bodily substance. Earlier it was stated that *kula* as a coded substance was a composite of occupational, territorial, and worship substances which were combined with the bodily substances of a clan's persons. Hence, the coded substances by which a clan was defined was thought to consist of "attributes" (*guṇas*) or "characteristics" (*lakṣaṇa*) of all of these substances. As we shall see later in more detail, what distinguished one ranked grade of clans from another was the presence or absence of one or more of these attributes in its coded substance and the overall quality of its coded substance—its relative capacity to bring about well-being and prosperity. Given the centrality of the coded substances of Vedic worship as differentiators of rank in this concept of community, those differentiating attributes upon which primary stress was placed were, of course, those emanating from the Veda.

In accord with the differences in their embodied attributes, the clans of each ranked grade also possessed their own codes for conduct. These codes for conduct all centered on the complex act of marriage, which was itself—consistent with the emphasis on worship as the ordering act—considered to be a form of worship and enjoined the lower clan grades to worship the higher clan grades with offerings of daughters and, above all, wealth and food.[24]

Thus, the *jātis* or sets of clans ranked high and low within the territorial *jātis* of Brāhmaṇs and Kāyasthas were defined primarily as worship *jātis* or grades. They were not ranked by their occupations or by the wealth, land, or political offices they might have held. Instead, each was defined and ranked in relation to the other by the degree to which its embodied rank was marked by the power of the Veda, and each lower grade was enjoined to state its inferior rank by worshipping grades higher in rank.

Just as the ranked castes were seen to be characterized by confusing and diffuse combinations of occupational, territorial, and worship substances with bodily substance in the middle period variant, so, too, were the ranked grades of clans. Take, for example, the combination of the *gotra* name, a worship substance, which marked high and low ranks, with the Śūdra clans. The Śūdra of the past was enjoined from performing Vedic worship and had no need, therefore, to be combined with the *gotra* names used in that kind of worship. In the middle period Bengal variant of this matrix, the higher *sat* Śūdra was enjoined to perform Vedic worship, for which purpose he had to combine with a *gotra* name. After listing the major *gotra* names, the Bengali text which elaborates on Manu's *dharma-śāstra* describes how Śūdras acquired *gotra* names:

> Thus the *gotras*. . .are declared in accord with the Veda. They shall be pronounced in conjunction with the utterance of its injunctions

[24]The problem of how persons of one grade could accept wives from other grades without mixing and inferiorizing the coded bodily substance of their offspring centered on the complicated question of what constituted "proper" and "improper" marriages and is dealt with in Chapter III.

> (*vidhi*) and for the purpose of performing its enjoined actions. The *gotra* of the Brāhmaṇ derives from the name of his ancestral man (*pūrva-puruṣa*), but the other castes (*jātis*) obtain the *gotra* and so forth of their priests (*purohita*). And so the Kṣatriya, Vaiśya, Śūdra and all the mixed castes (*varṇa-saṅkara*) obtain the *gotra* and so forth of their *purohita* in accord with the code-book (*Śāstra*). Those twice-born Brāhmaṇs were the priests of all those Śūdras who were their dependents, and the Śūdras obtained their *gotras* from those twice-born. Thus the *gotras* of the Śūdra were set in order in the code-book of Manu.[25]

The clarity with which ranked grades combined with *gotras*, however, varied. Generally, the higher the rank and the more a grade was marked by the presence of the other coded substances of Vedic worship, the clearer was the combination of its clans with *gotras*. Thus, each Kulīna clan in a Kāyastha subcaste was held to be combined with one *gotra* name different from those of the other Kulīna clans of its subcaste. This was not so for the Maulikas. Clans of the higher Maulika grades were invariabley found to be combined with two or more *gotra* names whereas clans of the inferior Maulika grades were often found to have no *gotra* names at all, suggesting that they perhaps did not perform Vedic worship.

Still more significant in this connection was another aspect of grade organization. The texts of the Brāhmaṇs and Kāyasthas persistently tended to identify persons of the lowest grades in their subcastes as persons belonging to or descended from the lower Brāhmaṇ and Śūdra occupational *jātis*. They did not, in other words, see their own *jātis* as neatly bounded units distinctly separated from lower ones. Past mixtures of coded substances made it difficult, in their view, to identify and classify persons. The organization of their own *jātis* into ranked grades of clans was a middle period attempt to solve this problem of confusion by providing Bengali Hindus with a kind of "dual organization" scheme. According to this scheme, Brāhmaṇs and Śūdras could be classified under some circumstances as persons belonging to distinct, ranked occupational *jātis*. Under other circumstances, however, the same persons could be classified as persons belonging to ranked grades of the highest Brāhmaṇ and Śūdra subcastes.

A brief review of the modifiers used to designate ranked grades in one of these subcastes, the Dakṣiṇa-rāḍhī Kāyastha, will provide

[25] Nibandha, fol. 2.

a preliminary view of how this dual organization scheme operated. The term "Kulīna," an adjective formed from the word *kula* meaning of "high" (*ucca*) or "superior" (*śreṣṭha*) clan, that is, possessed of the highest coded clan bodily substance or rank, was used to refer to the highest grade of clans in the Dakṣiṇa-rāḍhī Kāyastha subcaste, the one possessing the coded substance of the Kāyastha *jāti* in its highest and fullest form. The term "Maulika," derived from the were *mūla*, "root," was used to refer to the two lower grades of clans in the Dakṣiṇa-rāḍhī Kāyastha *jāti* and tagged their coded bodily substance or rank (*kula*) as "having roots" or "possessing a foundation" yet not, relative to the Kulīna, superior. These two were, in other words, grades that possessed the coded bodily substance of the Kāyastha *jāti* but not in its highest or fullest form.

Two additional modifiers, Siddha and Sādhya, were employed by contrast to distinguish the two Maulika grades themselves. The word "Siddha" was used to mark the coded bodily substance of the higher Maulika grade as "realized" or "actualized" while the word "Sādhya" was used to mark that of the lower Maulika grade as "latent" or "potential." In other words, the Siddha Maulika grade possessed the coded bodily substance or rank of the Kāyastha *jāti* in an "actualized" or "realized" form. The Sādhya Maulika grade, on the other hand, possessed it only in a "potential" or "latent" form. Persons classified here were those who appeared to belong to the lower Śūdra occupational *jātis* but themselves claimed to be Kāyasthas.

Past mixtures of coded substance meant that almost any Śūdra could possess the coded bodily substance of a Kāyastha in a latent or potential form. Those apparently inferior Śūdras who claimed so could be classed as Sādhya Maulikas; should they actualize the coded substance of a Kāyastha, they could then be classed as Siddha Maulikas. Clearly, then, the organization of the highest occupational *jātis* of Bengal into ranked grades of clans was important, for as we shall see in subsequent, fuller discussions, it was closely connected with the process of social mobility in middle period Bengal.

Kulas or clans of the same worship *jāti* or grade did not have bodily substances endowed with different attributes, nor did they have different marriage codes, and they were not ranked high and low with respect to each other. Neither did they possess their own discrete countries, nor did they share any wealth or property in common. What distinguished one of these clans from the other, like the clans in the all-India matrix, was their possession of the semen (*śukra*) or "seed" (*bīja*) and surname (*paddhati*, *gāñi*) of one particular common ancestral "seed-male" (*bīja-puruṣa*) as opposed to another.[26] The names of the clans and the grades to which they belonged are given for the two major subcastes of the study, the Rāḍhī Brāhmaṇ and Dakṣiṇa-rāḍhī Kāyastha, in Tables 2 and 3. Even with regard to

Table 2

Rāḍhī Brāhmaṇ Clans

Clan grade	Clan name		
Kulina and *Vaṃśaja*	Bandya	Caṭṭa	
	Mukhaiṭi	Pūtituṇḍa	
	Kāñjilāl	Gāṅgulı	
	Ghoṣāl	Kundalāl	
Śrotriya Susiddha	Māscaṭak	Kaḍiyāl	Śāṭeśvarı
	Kuśāri	Ambuli	Bhaṭṭa
	Pākḍāśī	Bhūri	Kulkuli
	Baṭbyāl	Bāpuli	Dāyāri
	Śimlāyī	Siyāri	Puṃsi
	Simlā	Sahuri	Siddhal
	Poṣalī	Basuyāri	Nāyāri
	Pāladhi	Dagdhabāṭi	Ākāś
	Kāñjāḍī	Tailabāṭi	Ghosalī
	Palsāyī	Dīghal	Seuk
	Pūrbba	Koyāri	Mūlī
	Nandī	Pāri	
	Kusumkuli	Bāli	
Siddha	Pippalī	Diṇḍī	
	Dirghāṅgī		
Sādhya	Mahintyā	Guḍ	
	Had	Parihāl	
Ari	Keśarkonī	Ghaṇṭā	
	Rāyī	Kulabhı	
	Pitamuṇḍī	Cautkhaṇḍı	
	Gaḍgaḍī		

[26]It would be premature to infer from this sharing of the same semen that the Bengali *kula* was a "patrilineal descent group" as defined by anthropologists. The difficulty with this is that an out-marrying daughter did not belong to her father's *kula*, while an in-marrying wife, on the other hand, did. The Bengali Hindu concept of marriage, to be explicated in Chapter III, held that the coded bodily substance (*kula*) of a properly married woman was transformed into that of her husband and resolves this difficulty.

Table 3

Dakṣiṇa-Rāḍhī Kāyastha Clans

Clan grade	Clan name			
Kulina and *Vaṃśaja*	Ghosh			
	Basu			
	Mitra			
Maulika				
Siddha	Datta	Pālit		
	Guha	Sen		
	Deb	Sinha		
	Kar	Dās		
Sādhya	Hoḍa	Bhui	Nāth	Arṇab
	Svar	Chandra	Śāmi	Āś
	Dhar	Rudra	Heś	Śakti
	Dharaṇi	Rakṣit	Man	Bhūt
	Bān	Rāj	Gaṇḍa	Brahma
	Āic	Āditya	Rāhā	Śān
	Som	Bisṇu	Rāṇā	Kṣem
	Pai	Nāga	Rāhut	Hem
	Sur	Khil	Sānā	Barddhan
	Sām	Pil	Dāhā	Raṅga
	Bhañja	Gūt	Dānā	Gui
	Binda	Indra	Gaṇ	Kirtti
	Guha	Gupta	Khām	Nandi
	Bal	Pāl	Kṣom	Śil
	Lodh	Bhadra	Ghar	Dhanu
	Śarmā	Oṃ	Baios	Guṇ
	Barmmā	Ankur	Bīd	Yaś
	Hui	Bandhu	Tej	Kuṇḍu

surnames there was confusion, especially among the Kāyasthas. For example, the names of the Kulīna and Siddha Maulika clans in the Dakṣiṇa-rāḍhī Kāyastha subcaste did not vary from one account to the other; the names of the Sādhya Maulika clans, however, did vary. The names listed in Table 3 are those most frequent.

Kulas *Within* Kulas

While clans of the past were held to be divided simply into smaller family units, the clans of the middle period Brāhmaṇ and Kāyastha subcastes, and especially their Kulīna clans, were held to be divided into many, more complex units. The Kulīna clans in these subcastes were divided like the subcastes themselves into ranked genera also referred to as *kulas*. The Kulīna clans in the Rāḍhī and Vārendra Brāhmaṇ and Dakṣiṇa-rāḍhī and Vaṅgaja Kāyastha subcastes were divided at the highest level into two major genera. These ranked genera were distinguished by the quality of their clan blood and their codes for conduct. The higher genus or grade contained the proper or par excellence Kulīnas, those who had followed the particular marriage codes of their clan since its founding. The lower genus, named Vaṃśaja, contained the Kulīnas and their descendants who had departed from the Kulīna code for conduct: "He who, though born in a clan of high rank, does not follow the rules, becomes a Vaṃśaja."[27]

The differentiation into particular ranked genera did not stop here. The higher or par excellence Kulīna genera in each of these subcastes were themselves divided into a varying number of ranked genera. The smallest number, three, was found in the Vaṅgaja Kāyastha subcastes; the largest, thirty-six, in the Rāḍhī Brāhmaṇ. Though each of these genera was distinguished from the other by the possession of its own bodily substance and marriage code, the principle by which they were differentiated varied from subcaste to subcaste. Among the proper Kulīnas of the Vaṅgaja Kāyastha subcaste, the bodily substances and marriage codes of three ranked grades were distinguished in accord with the degree of interruption their substances and marriages had suffered over time. Their subcaste genealogist describes these metaphorically by referring to rivers and trees. The shift from the one to the other symbolizes the sharp distinction made between continuity on the one hand and varying forms of interruptedness on the other:

> In the view of some, Kulīnas are of three types—Ḍambura, Dhustūra, and Gaṅgāśrotā. That family whose marriages are in the proper order is proclaimed a Gaṅgāśrotā (stream of the Gaṅgā, continuous and pure in its flow); that whose marriages are with superiors (Kulīnas) afterwards rather than first are Dhustūra in form (a thorn-apple, beautiful to look at, but poisonous); and those whose marriages are occasionally with inferiors (non-Kulīnas) is declared Ḍambura in form (a fig tree), which rarely blossoms.[28]

[27] Śarmā, "Kula-dīpikā," fol. 16b.
[28] *Ibid.*, fol. 10a.

The bodily substances and marriage codes of the nine ranked grades among the proper Kulīnas of the Dakṣiṇa-rāḍhī Kāyasthas were differentiated according to the seniority of their birth:

> Listen, everyone, to this treatise on the seniority grades (*kula*). Mukhya (elder), Kaniṣṭha (younger), Chabhāyā (six-brother), Madhyāṃśa (intermediate), and Teoja (fourth-born) are the main ones. Listen to a narration of the designations and qualities of the remaining seniority grades, namely, Kaniṣṭha Dvitīya-putra (younger's second son) and Chabhāyā Dvitīya-putra (six-brother's second son); I also recognize Madhyāṃśa Dvitīya-putra (intermediate's second son) and Teoja Dvitīya-putra (fourth-born's second son). I speak now of high rank (*kula*) in nine forms in Rāḍha.[29]

And still there were boxes inside of boxes, for the highest of these ranked *kulas* was differentiated into still three more: "The form of Mukhya is three-fold, hear about it—Prakṛta (original), Sahaj (easy), and, last of all, Komala (soft)."[30]

The bodily substances and marriage codes of the thirty-six ranked genera of the Rāḍhī Brāhmaṇ Kulīnas were differentiated according to their distinct "defects" (*doṣa*). Since their codes enjoined the exchange of daughters between reciprocally linked clan segments, their grades were referred to as "unions" (*mela*):

> Thirty-six unions were proclaimed previously by the *paṇḍitas* of the past. The rules by which the birth of these took place are now clearly related. A union evolves from the mixture (*melana*) of defects (*doṣa*). And a mixture is declared to be the mutual interaction of faults. For that reason they come in pairs, the original source (*prakṛti*) of the fault and reciprocator (*pālṭī*) of it. Thus, the designations original source and reciprocator mean "primary" and "secondary." The one who is distinguished and active is the original source, endowed with the primary defect. The reciprocator, the one whose gain is minor, would then be the one who gains it in person and by intent. And so, he who is endowed with secondary faults is entitled the reciprocator.[31]

The larger *kulas* of all grades (including the ranked grades of the Kulīna clans) were also divided into smaller *kulas* ("localized clan segments"), which were combined with the particular named villages

[29] Vācaspati, "Kula-sarvvasva," in Nagendranāth Vasu, *Vaṅger Jātīya Itihāsa* (Calcutta: Viśvakoṣa Press, 1911–33), VI, Pt. I, 112.

[30] *Ibid.*

[31] Vācaspati, "Kularamā," in Chandrakānta Ghaṭaka-vidyānidhi, *Kulakalpadruma* (Calcutta: Bhavanipur Press, 1912), p. 22.

in which their less remote ancestors had settled. Often the persons of such a clan segment added the title its founder had received from the regional Muslim government to its clan name. Examples of localized clan segments were the Mitra-Mustauphīs (Dakṣiṇa-rāḍhī Kāyastha) of Ulā or Bīrnagar in Nadia District and the Basu-Rāychaudhuris (Vaṅgaja Kāyastha) of Ulpur in Faridpur District.[32]

Localized clan segments that were more than three or four generations in depth seldom continued to exercise joint control over land. The inheritance rules, which Bengali Brāhmaṇs and Kāyasthas adhered to, commonly enjoined uterine brothers to partition their paternal property in equal shares after both parents had died.[33] Thus, the joint control of property by a corporate localized clan of a great population or generational depth was thought to be improper.[34] Nonetheless, the members of a localized clan often continued to exercise joint control over such items as temples and tanks (which were difficult to divide). They might continue to worship the same clan deity (*kula-devatā*) and act jointly as sacrificer (*yajamāna*) for their worships (*pūjās*). In such circumstances, one male clansman (not necessarily the most senior) was often recognized as the ad hoc leader of the localized clan.[35]

The genus conceived of as a fully corporate economic and political unit among the Brāhmaṇs and Kāyasthas of Bengal, as in the all-

[32]Reasonably good accounts of both of these localized clans were written in Bengali by their members early in the century. The one written by Srijanāth Mitra Mustauphī (*Ulār Mustauphī Vaṃśa* [Ula: By the Author, 1930]) is well-documented but rather contentious. The other, written by Dīnabandhu Ray Choudhury (*Paricaya: Vaṅgaja Kāyastha-gaṇer Sāmājika Itihāsa saha Dakṣiṇa Farīdpurer Bil-pradeśer Vivaraṇa* [Calcutta: Amūlya Chandra De, 1937]) is less well-documented, but more honest and insightful.

[33]The Hindus of Bengal were supposed to follow inheritance rules which differed in several respects from those in the rest of northern India. These rules are known as the Dāyabhāga rules after a text of that name written by Jīmūtavāhana in the thirteenth or fourteenth century. For explication of these rules, see Pandurang Vaman Kane, *History of Dharmaśāstra* (Poona: Bhandarkar Oriental Research Institute, 1946), III, 543–661; for an English translation of Jīmūtavāhana's text, see *Mitacsharā and Dāyabhāga: Two Treatises on the Hindu Law of Inheritance*, trans. by H. T. Colebrooke (Calcutta: B. Banerjee, 1883), Pt. II, pp. 1–205, i–xii. For discussions of inheritance rules in modern Bengali villages, see Tārā Krishna Basu, *The Bengal Peasant from Time to Time* (Calcutta: Asia Publishing House, 1962), pp. 89–95; and Ralph W. Nicholas, "Economics of Family Types in Two West Bengal Villages," *Economic Weekly*, Spec. N. (July 1961), pp. 1057–60.

[34]Basu, *Bengal Peasant*, p. 90.

[35]Ray Choudhury, *Paricaya*, p. 119.

India paradigm, was the smallest segment of a clan, the family (*parivāra*), often referred to in legal and sociological literature as the "joint" or "extended" family. It was thought normally to contain a man who acted as *kartā* or manager, his wife, and their sons and sons' wives together with their children. What distinguished one family in a clan from others was the possession of a house (*ghar*, *bāḍī*), in which its members lived, and wealth or property (*viṣaya-sampatti*), such as land over which it exercised defined rights. Often Bengalis used the words for house as rough synonyms for family (or even clan). The two, however, were conceptually distinguished, for the house or household possessed by a family might also contain persons such as servants not considered to be members of the family defined as a genus. The *ghar-jāmāi*, the husband (*jāmāi*) who lived in the house (*ghar*) of his wife's father, is a good "institutionalized" example. Though clearly considered a relative, neither the *ghar-jāmāi* nor his wife and children were considered to belong to his wife's father's family or clan.

The *kartā*, a married male who had "mastery" (*adhikāra*) over a family, was the person defined as the primary actor in the community. His code for conduct enjoined him to perform all those actions by which the family and its rank were upheld. Hence, it was the *kartā* who made the marriages of his children. Since the persons of his family were conceived of as depending on him for their bodily substance and its nourishment, they were thought to obtain the fruits or results of the actions he performed. If their *kartā* made good marriages, they obtained the good results (as did their descendants, those who inherited their bodily substance). This made the family the primary unit of social mobility. If the *kartā* settled in a new village, so did his family, and if he obtained higher embodied rank as a result of his acts of worship, so did his family.

The smallest unit distinguished in the community was not a genus but the person (*mānuṣa*, *loka*) himself. So far we have been looking at the person defined as a casteman or clansman. The casteman or clansman defined as a person, however, is a different kind of unit. Each person had his own discrete code for conduct (*svadharma*), which was a composite of the generic codes which he possessed. The code for conduct of a person might, for example, consist of his codes for conduct as a Bengali, a Hindu, a Śūdra, a Kāyastha, a Dakṣiṇa-rāḍhī Kāyastha, a Kulīna, a person of Ghosh clan, a person of a particular village, and of a particular family. Thus, while each person defined as a casteman, clansman, etc., was seen to be a representative or embodied microcosm of the genus to which he belonged, the person as a total composite being was seen to be the unique product of past births and actions, uniquely embodied and encoded.

Kings (Rājā) *and Community Councils* (Samāja)

The job of maintaining *dharma* in the sense of "proper order" among the castes and clans of the Hindu community belonged in the past society to a single "great king" (*mahārāja*); in middle period society it belonged to a plurality of lesser kings (*rājā*) and councils (*sabhā*). The king of the past was conceived as an incarnation (*avatāra*) of the supreme god Viṣṇu or Kṛṣṇa. Characterized as a deity who ruled the entire earth, his royal code for conduct (*rāja-dharma*) enjoined him to maintain the well-being of the world by causing people to adhere to the codes for conduct of their *jātis* and *kulas*. As we shall see, he was to maintain proper order by examining the conduct (*ācāra*) of others and appropriately rewarding or punishing it, by resolving disputes (*vivāda*, *vyavahāra*) through the use of his high power of "judgment" or "discrimination" (*vicāra*), and by relating the constituent parts of the community to each other through his own correct exchanges with them.

Since the "proper order" was seen to emanate more from the coded substance of worship than from any other, the king, himself a divine being in relation to his people (*prajā*), was held to be concerned with the proper execution of these exchanges as enjoined in the *śāstra* and especially with those considered to be acts of worship. The well-being and prosperity of society depended on the maintenance of proper order, and that, in turn, rested on the correct performance of acts of worship. No wonder then that the king was styled the foremost patron of worship (*yajamāna*) in his kingdom and that he was held responsible for retaining and supporting Brāhmaṇs learned in the Veda and capable of performing Vedic worship, for the Veda was seen as a symbol and source of everything good in the world.

The primacy of the coded substances of worship and the concept of the royal code for conduct were no different in the middle period. What did vary was the concentration of royal power. The single Hindu king of the earth was replaced in the middle period by a

Muslim king at the level of the total community including both Hindu and Muslims; and, at the level of the Hindu community of Bengal itself, he was replaced by a plurality of Hindu kings. These kings, less powerful than their single predecessor, were thought unable to inspect conduct and maintain proper order within the Brāhmaṇ and Kāyastha subcastes. The power to do this was held by subcaste councils which consisted of the masters (*kartā*) of subcaste families and professional genealogists (*ghaṭaka*) retained by the council as a whole. The word most often used to designate these councils was the word *samāja*,[36] a usage suggesting that these councils, rather than local kings, were the regulators of their subcaste communities. Local kings of the Brāhmaṇ and Kāyastha subcastes did play a role in maintaining order in their respective subcastes, but it was a secondary one. Such a king could make a decision only after he had convened the council, been given the honorific post of *samāja-pati*, "council-master," taken the advice of the genealogists, and obtained consent from the council as a whole.

To summarize, the two features that defined castes and clans, shared substance (*dhātu*) and code for conduct (*dharma*), were conceived of nondualistically. The words *jāti* and *kula* which were used to refer to castes and clans as social units were also used, again nondualistically, to refer to the features that defined them. In this context, the words *jāti* and *kula* did not refer either to shared substance or to code for conduct but to both as aspects of a single feature, one which can best be characterized as "coded substance." Since the terms *jāti* and *kula* were also employed to refer to the "prestige" or "respect" (*maryādā*, *sanmāna*) of a caste or clan, it is clear that the coded substance which defined a caste or clan was also, in relation to other castes or clans, its "rank."

Jātis and *kulas* were all conceived of as particular aggregates or genera of living beings (*jīva*), beings that possessed bodies (*śarīrī*). Hence, the coded substance feature that defined a *jāti* or *kula* and distinguished it from other kinds of social units was coded bodily substance. However, coded bodily substance alone was not the feature that distinguished human *jātis* and *kulas* from each other. Other coded substances, those of livelihood (*jīvikā*), country (*deśa*), and worship (*yajña*, *pūjā*), all of which were considered vital to the

[36]Another term, *goṣṭhī*, a synonym of the word *samāja* current in the Dakṣiṇa-rāḍha country, was used to refer to the community councils of the Dakṣiṇa-rāḍhī Kāyasthas.

life and well-being of humans, operated in combination with bodily substance to yield *jātis* of three classes—occupational (for example, Brāhmaṇ, Śūdra), territorial (for example, Rāḍhī, Vaṅgaja), and worship (for example, Hindu, Musulmān). Since the persons of a particular clan were considered to belong to *jātis* of all three classes, these were not, strictly speaking, the features that distinguished one clan from another. What did was the sharing of the compositely coded bodily substance (*vaṃśa*) of a particular ancestral seed male (*bīja-puruṣa*).

The concept of "community" (*samāja*) postulated by medieval Bengali Hindus was a complex one, for imbedded in their concept of a "present" community was the concept of a "past" community. Of central significance in both concepts was the stress placed on the coded substances of occupations, countries, or the human body were by it. In both alike the coded substances of worship, more than the coded substances of occupations, countries, or the human body were considered to be the symbol and source of order and of the power to do good and bring about the prosperity of the community. Persons of the Hindu community were related by the sharing of worship substances of two kinds, each of which acted in a different way. One was the sounds of the Tantra enjoining the performance of a particular kind of worship called *pūjā*. All persons of the Hindu community were thought to be equally related by the sharing of these sounds and the performance of *pūjā*. The sounds of the Veda comprised the other coded substance of worship and enjoined the performance of a particular kind of worship called *yajña*. The sounds of the Tantra and Tantric worship operated as a unifier of the Hindu community as a whole, endowing each of its parts with the power to sustain life and bring about prosperity irrespective of *jāti* or *kula*. The Veda and Vedic worship operated as a differentiator. The Veda was not combined in the same way with all *jātis* and *kulas*. To the contrary, it was combined differentially with the *jātis* and *kulas* making up the Hindu community. The higher ranked *jātis* and *kulas* were considered to be those more fully endowed with the Veda and were, consequently, thought of as more fully endowed with the power to do good and cause prosperity not only for themselves but also for lower, less divinely endowed *jātis* and *kulas* when these worshipped the former. Thus, the whole issue of caste and grade rank revolved around what we might call the symbols and ideology of Vedic worship.

Finally, let us review the characteristics that distinguished the past community from its middle period variant. The combinations of coded substances which defined units in the past were held to be relatively clear and simple and easy to perceive. Quite the opposite was true of the present community. It was characterized by a great degree of particularity and a prolific quality not found in the past. More important was the perceived confusion and diffuseness of the coded substances that defined *jātis* and *kulas* in the present, a state of affairs that had come about as a result of the improper mixing of castes (*varṇa-saṅkara*). This made it difficult to ascertain just what coded substance or rank a person or family possessed. On a canvas painted in many hues it was difficult to identify the primary colors. The organization of the Brāhmaṇ and Kāyastha subcastes into ranked grades of clans was a response to this situation, for it amounted to a "dual organization" scheme according to which the same persons could be classified as Brāhmaṇs or Śūdras of lower caste or as Vedic Brāhmaṇs and Kāyasthas of lower grades.

Chapter II

HISTORICAL TRANSFORMATIONS OF THE HINDU COMMUNITY

Myths, Cycles, and Stages

While the older view of Hindu society as a static, changeless society having no history and, in particular, no written history is no longer tenable, the view of what constitutes proper historical sources is still a rather narrow one.[1] Most historians still reject the vast bulk of myths and legends generated by ancient and medieval Hindus as unhistorical in scope. The "historical" portions of the *kulajīs* have been placed in this category. They have been roundly criticized by historians as "unreliable" and "fanciful," but that is because historians were attempting to reconstruct an accurate, blow by blow, chronological account of Benga's history.[2] I would be the last to assert that the *kulajīs* have much value in this respect, but that is not the point. The point I wish to make here is that locked up in these "mythic" or "legendary" accounts are descriptions and explanations not of day-to-day events but of the major structural transformations that occurred over time in Bengali Hindu society. Even more important, these views of how and why changes took place in the past informed the actions of those who knew them. Thus, even if the events described bore no relation to "what actually happened" (and I do not believe this), they are worthy of study on that score alone.

Bengali Hindu views of their own past were influenced by a widespread cyclical concept of time. According to this concept, Puruṣa generates the universe out of his cosmic body, sustains it for a time, and then causes it to degenerate and become reabsorbed

[1] U. N. Ghoshal, *Studies in Indian History and Culture* (Bombay: Orient Longmans, 1965), pp. 1–167,

[2] *History of Bengal*, ed. R. C. Majumdār (Dacca: University of Dacca, 1943), I, 625–33.

in him, only to begin the cycle anew.[3] The three great gods of Hinduism, each embodying a complementary aspect of Puruṣa—Brahmā, the god of generation (*sṛṣṭi*), Viṣṇu, the god of sustenance or protection (*pālana*), and Śiva, the god of degeneration or destruction (*nāśa*)—symbolized the three kinds of actions by which this cylical process occurred.[4]

As far as human society was concerned, this cylical view was found in the concept of the four ages (*yugas*), the Kṛta or Satya, Tretā, Dvāpara, and Kali.[5] Each succeeding age after the Kṛta was characterized by a progressive decline in the quality of human life and was seen to be marked by its own less rigorous code for conduct (*dharma*) until, at the end of the Kali age, the universe degenerated and the cycle began again. Thus, at the cosmic level, there was no notion of a unique series of events in human history having a single beginning and a single serious and purposeful end. In fact, the whole process was often looked upon as *līlā*, the "play" of the gods.

This macrocosmic theory of time and society informed Bengali Hindu views of their own past as well, but not in an absolute way. Generally, they saw their "past" community as that which existed in the previous three ages while viewing their own "present" community, replete with its mixtures and confusions, as belonging to the fourth and final or Kali age. Even within this framework, however, a given period of time, for example, that ushered in by the Muslim conquest of Bengal, could be characterized as a Kali age in relation to its predecessor. The tone of skepticism or even pessimism which pervades some of the texts is probably traceable to this self-characterization. On the other hand, there is often also a humorous side to the stories, an element which undoubtedly was due to the idea of world process as divine play.

The transformation of the Hindu community of the "past" into that of the middle period (c. 1450–1800) takes place in four stages. It begins during the reign of an evil king Veṇa who forces men and women of the four *varṇas* to intermarry; the occupational *jātis* generated as a result are classified by his virtuous son Pṛthu and

[3]Mukundarāma Chakravarti, *Kavikaṅkaṇa-Caṇḍī*, ed. Srikumar Bandyopadhyay and Visvapati Chaudhuri (Calcutta: University of Calcutta, 1958), I, 35–38.

[4]*Ibid.*, I, 39.

[5]For a vivid comparison of the four, see the *Mahānirvāṇa-tantra*, ed. Jībānanda Vidyāsāgara (Calcutta: New Valmiki Press, 1884), pp. 5–11.

Brāhmaṇs as Brāhmaṇs and Śūdras. Subsequently, king Ādiśūra of Bengal recognizes the immigrant ancestors of the Brāhmaṇ and Kāyastha Kulīnas to be superior in rank to the indigenous Brāhmaṇs and Śūdras by virtue of their superior life-giving power and good conduct. During the reigns of the succeeding twelfth-century kings, Vallāla Sena and Lakṣmaṇa Sena, the ancestors of the Brāhmaṇs and Kāyasthas are divided into territorial *jātis* or subcastes and these in turn are organized into ranked grades of clans, thereby initiating the dual organization scheme of medieval Bengali society. The descendants of the immigrant Brāhmaṇs and Śūdras who have conducted themselves properly are honored as Kulīnas while the indigenous Brāhmaṇs and Śūdras, depending in their conduct, are accorded the ranks either of "realized" or "latent" Vedic Brāhmaṇs and Kāyasthas. The reign of the Senas is followed by the thirteenth- and fourteenth-century Muslim conquests of Bengal. As a result of these conquests, new and improper mixtures of coded substances occur; newly formed subcaste councils meet this challenge by reorganizing the Brāhmaṇ and Kāyastha subcastes at the outset of the middle period.

KINGS VEṆA AND PṚTHU: THE MIXING OF THE *Varṇas* AND THE GENERATION OF THE BENGALI *Jātis*

Of these four stages, only the last three can be found in the genealogical literature of the Brāhmaṇs and Kāyasthas. The code-books of the Brāhmaṇs and Kāyasthas already assume that the Hindus of Bengal are organized into only two *varṇas*, Brāhmaṇ and Śūdra, the latter of which consisted of thirty-six *varṇa-saṅkara jātis*. Fortunately, the transformation of the universal four-*varṇa* community of India into the particular two-*varṇa* community of Bengal is related in a thirteenth- or fourteenth-century *purāṇa* originating in Bengal. Though this text, the *Bṛhad-dharma-purāṇa*, is late in relation to other *purāṇas*, it does predate the earliest of the genealogical texts, which do not appear before the fifteenth century.[6] Since the account given in this *purāṇa* falls outside the purview of the genealogies, I shall provide only a brief summary of it here. By royal proclamation, an evil king, Veṇa, forbids persons from acting in accord with their generic codes for conduct and forces men and women of the

[6]A summary and critical discussion of this important text are found in R. C. Hazra, *Studies in the Upapurāṇas* (Calcutta: Sanskrit College, 1963), II, 396–465.

four *varṇas* to make improper inter-*varṇa* marriages and beget offspring. After some time, the Brāhmaṇs, who had warned Veṇa against this, kill him by shouting *mantras* at him, rub both his hands together, and cause a son, Pṛthu, and his wife to be born. Pṛthu, a good king, sees that previous misconduct has caused a lack of food for his people, stops the improper marriages, punishes those who made them, and asks the Brāhmaṇs to determine the *varṇas* and occupations of the mixed castes. The Brāhmaṇs then proceed to examine their qualities and conduct. They classify all thirty-six of the "mixed castes" (*saṅkara-jāti*) as Śūdras, leaving no Kṣatriyas and Vaiśyas. Twenty of the Śūdra *jātis* they class as *uttama* ("best") or *sat* ("good"), the remaining as *madhyama* ("medial") and *adhama* ("inferior") or *asat* ("not good"). The Brāhmaṇs then declare that they, as Śrotriya Brāhmaṇs, will perform Vedic and Tantric worship for the twenty *sat* Śūdras, while "fallen" (*patita*) Brāhmaṇs will perform inferior worship for the remaining sixteen. Once the king and the remaining Vedic Brāhmaṇs had thus reestablished "proper order" (*dharma*) among these newly generated castes, prosperity returned.

What do we learn from this story? First, one must note the central part played by the king in maintaining proper order. The king was the symbol of the entire Hindu community. Hence an evil king was seen to be the source of disorder and lack of prosperity throughout the entire community whereas a good king was seen as the source of its order and prosperity. Second, proper marriage and reproduction were considered to be crucial to the maintenance of proper order among the *jātis*. Since the coded substances of worship and occupation were seen to be combined with homologous bodily substances, improper marriages had the capacity to ruin the entire order of *jātis* in the community, for the improper combination of coded bodily substances necessarily entailed the improper combination of worship and occupational substances and codes as well.

Next, there is the question of power. The king possessed coercive power (*daṇḍa*). Yet his power was considered to be subordinate to and derived from an even higher power, that of the Veda possessed by the Brāhmaṇ. The coded substance of Vedic worship was the ultimate source of the power to bring about order and well-being. Hence, when the Vedic Brāhmaṇs saw that the king had gone astray, they were able to kill him with Vedic *mantras*. Even more, they were able to intervene in the reproductive process of the king and cause a good king and his wife to be born through the mere but extraordinary act of rubbing Veṅa's hands together.

Finally, and most important, change takes place. The old order of *jātis* was not restored. The new *jātis* that had been generated by the improper mixing of bodily substances did not, however, constitute a new order in and of themselves. Rather they constituted a disorderly state of affairs. It was only after the king had assembled these new castes, examined them in conjunction with the Brāhmaṇs, and honored them with new ranks and relationships that a new and transformed order appeared in the Hindu community.

King Ādiśūra: The Coming of the Kulīna Brāhmaṇs and Kāyasthas and Vedic Regeneration

The second stage in the transformation of the Hindu community of Bengal begins when five Brāhmaṇs, fully endowed with the highest, most powerful of coded substances, the Veda, come, accompanied by five devoted Śūdras, to Bengal. This was thought to have happened in 954 of the Śaka era (1032 A.D.) during the reign of the paramount ruler of Bengal (Gauḍa), the "great king" (*mahārāja*) Ādiśūra (literal meaning, "first hero").[7] Here is the Ādiśūra story of the Dakṣiṇa-rāḍhī Kāyasthas as related by their foremost genealogist, Nandarāma Mitra, toward the end of the middle period. Addressed to a Śūdra audience and set in the fourth and lowest age, the Kali, it begins with a prelude in which Viṣṇu, the kingly god who upholds *dharma*, playfully agrees to give birth to five superior Śūdras who possess the worship code for conduct of the higher twice-born as well as the service code of the Śūdra. They are born not in Bengal, but in Kolañca, a city of the superior middle country:

> Hear the truth concerning the generation of the great castes (*varṇas*). The Brāhmaṇ was born from the mouth for the purpose of spreading the injunctions of the Veda. The Kṣatriya arose from the arms for the purpose of exercising protection. The Vaiśyas were born from the thighs. The Śūdra was born from the feet and serving (*sevā*) was his duty (*karma*). The other three *varṇas* became devoid of virtue as the

[7]Though a Śūra dynasty apparently ruled in Dakṣiṇa-rāḍha in the eleventh century, a positive identification of Ādiśūra in the historical inscriptions has not yet been made. See Pramode Lāl Paul, *The Early History of Bengal* (Calcutta: Indian Research Institute, 1939), I, 82–83; II, 31–64. For other discussions on the historicity of Ādiśūra, see *History of Bengal*, I, 623–34; and D. C. Sircar, *Studies in the Society and Administration of Ancient and Medieval India* (Calcutta: Firma K. L. Mukhopadhyay, 1967), I, 10–30.

> Satya and Tretā passed and the Dvāpara age (*yuga*) drew near. By serving Kṛṣṇa,[8] he [the Śūdra] brought him into his control. Viṣṇu was in the city of Dvārikā sitting on a lion throne. With hands pressed together the Śūdra made a petition: "Listen, Lord God. What are the duties for us—praising the gods (*stava*), uttering *mantras* (powerful sounds) to the gods performing Vedic worship (*yajña*), and giving (*dāna*)?" Viṣṇu laughed and said, "I shall make an incarnation (*avatāra*) of you in the Kali age in order to show your respect." Thus was the command of Kṛṣṇa. Once again, this time in five parts, he went to Kolañca.[9] Kula-lakṣmī[10] moved swiftly, and he was born in five parts. All the Śūdras went to welcome the five men who were born in Kolañca once again to serve.[11]

The story then shifts to the country of Gauḍa or Bengal where the Śūdra king, Ādiśūra, engaged in an act of Vedic worship, finds that his own Brāhmaṇs, inferior in Vedic knowledge, cannot complete it. They urge the king to invite five superior Brāhmaṇs who can from Kolañca:

> The great king (*mahārāja*) Ādiśūra, born in the clan of Dhanvantari,[12] was the ruler of Rāḍha, Gauḍa,[13] and Vaṅga. He thought about the truth and performed endless acts of worship (*yajña*). His glory would always remain on earth. Having decided on the rules, he began a strange act of worship (*yajña*) enjoined in the Tantra and Veda (*āgama-nigama*). He assembled the Sapta-śati (700) Brāhmaṇs of his own country and asked them the rules for this act of worship. The Brāhmans petitioned the king with hands pressed together: "We do not know this information; but five good Brāhmaṇs dwell in the country of Kolañca-nagara. We have heard remarkable stories

[8]One of the human incarnations of Viṣṇu, the god who upholds proper order (*dharma*) in the world.

[9]In some texts, Kroḍañca (Kolañca or Kloñca) is given as the Brāhmaṇs' and Śūdras' place of origin; in others, Kānya-kubja (Kanauja) is given. It is not clear whether the two were the same place or not. Kānyakubja was the premier city of north India in the seventh to twelfth centuries. Kroḍañca was the source of learned immigrant Brāhmaṇs in the historical inscriptions. At any rate, it is clear that the texts identify both places with north India or Madhyadeśa, thought to be the superior home of the Veda. See Paul, *Early History of Bengal*, II, 37–39.

[10]The goddess of family and clan well-being. She is the wife of Viṣṇu.

[11]Nandarāma Mitra, Kulajī, Dacca University Library MSS (uncataloged), n.d., fol. 13a. Nandarāma, himself a Dakṣiṇa-rāḍhī Kāyastha, flourished around the end of the eighteenth and beginning of the nineteenth centuries.

[12]Ādiśūra is said to have been a member of the Ambaṣṭha or Vaidya caste which had medicine as its occupation. Dhanvantari, the physician of the gods, is thought to be the progenitor of the Vaidyas.

[13]Here the term "Gauda" appears to refer not to Rāḍha, Vaṅga, and Vārendra as a whole, but only to Vārendra.

about them. They are foremost masters of the four Vedas, like a second Brahmā,[14] and their austerity is great, sire. They have no equals on earth. Bring as priests, o king, the ones who seem appropriate." Hearing this, the lord of men carefully wrote a letter and swiftly dispatched a messenger with it. Starting his journey at an appropriate time, the messenger travelled day and night until he arrived at Kolañca. The five Brāhmaṇs were all in the same place, shining like the king of the twice-born, the moon. The messenger bowed and presented the letter. The sages read the letter and were pleased in their hearts. They therefore set out with great speed.[15]

When the five Brāhmaṇs and the five Śūdras arrive in Bengal in the guise of Kṣatriyas and claim only to perform inferior goat sacrifices, the king and his people panic. The day is saved, however, when the Brāhmaṇs demonstrate their superior life-giving power, and the king worshipfully invites them to stay:

Taking their families with them, they mounted horses and went to the kingdom of Gauḍa. They took with them their five beloved disciples (*śiṣya*) and arrived at the king's palace. Going up to the gate of the palace, they said, "We perform goat sacrifices." In this way the five Brāhmaṇs came to the gate. They came with hose on their feet and turbans on their heads; five elephants as well as troops were with them and formed a four-part battalion. When he heard this, the king bent his head and the women whose husbands were alive took vows. They felt great distress. When they saw the king's hesitation, the sages, while standing at the gate, blessed a dead piece of wood, on which new sprouts appeared. Then the Brāhmaṇs went away. When the king heard this he was startled, and the lord of men together with his ministers, went quickly after them, fell at their feet, and praised them. The sages, seeing this devotion, then returned and again entered the city. They sat on heavenly seats and the king, happy in his heart, asked, "What name is whose?"[16]

The king then examines the credentials of the divinely endowed Brāhmaṇs and Śūdras. All are accorded high rank as Kulīnas save Datta, who selfishly claims he is better than a Śūdra, and Guha, whose name sounds funny:

The five men with them truly appeared to have auspicious characteristics. It was as though the Gandharvas (heavenly musicians) were in the company of the gods. The sages spoke briefly: "We are

[14] Genitor of the universe.
[15] Mitra, Kulajī, fols. 13a–13b.
[16] *Ibid.*, fol. 13b.

Bhaṭṭanārāyaṇa, Dakṣa, Śrīharṣa, Chāndaḍa, and Vedagarbha. With us are the five best Śudras—Ghosh, Basu, Mitra, Datta, and Guha, whose minds are intent on enjoined conduct (*dharma*). All of us are filled with the results of good conduct (*puṇyavān*). Now that we have explained, honor (*māna*) us." The king said, "Who is with whom?" Makaranda Ghosh spoke: "Hear me, o king, I am with Bhaṭṭanārāyaṇa. He is Daśaratha Basu, conqueror of Madana (god of love) in handsomeness. He came with Dakṣa. Kālīdāsa in in the Mitra family shines as though born of the sun. He came with Śrīharṣa. Daśaratha Guha came with Vedagarbha." When they heard this, all the people at court laughed.[17] Puruṣottama Datta spoke, "I am not a servant, sire. I am superior to everyone in rank (*kula*) and conduct (*śīla*)." When the king heard such conceited words, he made him inferior (*hīna*) in rank (*maryādā*). Guha fell and went to Vaṅga; in that country he was honored as a Kulīna. Three houses here—Ghosh, Basu, and Mitra gained high rank (*kaulīnya*), prestige, and fame.[18]

Having successfully performed the worship, the Brāhmaṇs and Śūdras, who had brought their families with them, are worshipped by the king with gifts, settle in Gauḍa, and form new *jātis* by marrying. Nandarāma concludes his account of the origin of the Dakṣiṇa-rāḍhī Kāyastha Kulīnas thus:

After completing the act of worship, he gave those who were to become the Dakṣiṇa-rāḍhī Kulīnas lands (*bhūma*) and houses (*ghar-bāḍi*). And so, Ghosh, Basu, and Mitra made marriages (*kriyā-keli*) and united (*meli*).[19]

Perhaps the simplest and most common version of the Adiśūra story is that of the Rāḍhi Brāhmaṇs written in Sanskrit by Devīvara, their most famous genealogist at the beginning of the middle period. Just as the Kāyastha version gave prominence to their five Śūdra progenitors, so this Brāhmaṇ variant stresses the five Brāhmaṇs. Otherwise, the two versions do not vary except in one or two details.[20] The text translated below is, in fact, taken from a Vaṅgaja Kāyastha genealogy of the eighteenth century:

The lord of men (*nṛpeśvara*), Ādiśūra, was born in an Ambaṣṭha

[17] The word *guha* is similar to *guhya* which means "anus."

[18] Mitra, Kulajī, fols. 13b–13c.

[19] *Ibid.*, fol. 13c.

[20] Included among the credentials of the Brāhmaṇs and Kāyasthas in this variant are their Vedic *gotras*, the names needed in the performance of Vedic worship. Additionally, Guha's name here is Virāṭa, not Daśaratha, and neither he nor Datta are downgraded.

family and was the king of Rāḍha, Gauḍa, Vārendra, and Vaṅgadeśa, as well as the lord of the entire earth. One day, the king, who was attached to the Vedic code (*dharma-śāstra*), entered his own place together with his ministers, relatives, advisers, and Brāhmaṇs, and asked the Brāhmaṇs: "By what ritual, honored ones, is happiness attained. I want to hear all about this. Tell me, best of the twice-born." After hearing this, all of those Brāhmaṇs, whose bodies were dwarfed and whose minds were deformed, said to the king, "None of us knows by what rules this ritual is performed by the wise, what kind of rules they are or whence they come." When he heard these words, the king became filled with worry: "What shall I do, where shall I go?" he lamented again and again. By means of a messenger, he brought five Brāhmaṇs, learned in the Vedas and Śāstras, and skilled in all weaponry, from Kloñca.[21]

When he saw that the five Brāhmaṇs, who had been brought by a messenger from Kloñca as men learned in the Vedas and Śāstras, were Brāhmaṇs who were also learned in weaponry, mounted on bulls, and carrying swords and shields, despair arose in his heart. Knowing that lack of faith would arise in the king, the best of the twice-born placed the remains of a floral offering on top of a dead piece of wood. Then that piece of wood came to life covered with fruits and sprouts. The king, whose body trembled when he saw this, praised them profusely and with humility offered them seats and showed respect by washing their feet.

The five Brāhmaṇs and five Śūdras (who came with them from Kloñca) approached the king and proclaimed every benefit. He praised the Śūdras: "Today my birth is fruitful, alive, and well-lived, and my house is born pure through your coming." And he asked them, "What are your *gotras* and names and why are you with the twice-born? I want to hear all this." The Śūdras heard the words of the king and told their *gotras* and names: "Here is Dakṣa by name, great mind in the Kāśyapa *gotra*; his servant is Daśaratha Basu of the Gautama *gotra*. The clever Bhaṭṭanārāyaṇa, born in the Śāṇḍilya *gotra*, has as his servant Makaranda Ghosh in the Saukālina *gotra*. Śrīharṣa, best of sages and famed among the Bharadvājas, has as his servant Virāṭa Guha, remembered as Kāśyapa. This is Vedagarbha of Sāvarṇa *gotra*; his servant, named Kālīdāsa, is of the Mitra family, born in a Śūdra clan, and of the Viśvamitra *gotra*. And the one named Chandada is born in the Vātsya *gotra*." Puruṣottama Datta, born of Maudgalya *gotra* said, "I have come to your place to protect the others." The king heard all this and was pleased. After they had completed the act of worship as designated by the Vedic code for

[21]A variant of Kolañca.

> conduct (*dharma*) and in accord with the rules, the best of kings gave villages, gold, cows, clothes, and so forth to the twice-born as their honorarium (*dakṣiṇā*). And so all the Brāhmaṇs and Śūdras settled here in this country and many offspring resident in many regions were born to them. The offspring of those who, with minds of devotion cause their praise to be heard, will without doubt increase in the future.[22]

Let us now examine the significance of the Ādiśūra legends. Aparently the reordering of the Hindu community by King Pṛthu had been less than a total success, for the events portrayed in these Ādiśūra stories occur against a backdrop of misconduct and the confusion of coded substances which represent a new threat to the welfare of the community. Ādiśūra, the heroic, great king of Gauḍa is a Śūdra of the Vaidya or physician *jāti* and not a Kṣatriya. The seven hundred Brāhmaṇs who normally perform Vedic worship for him have dwarfed bodies and deformed minds and are not in full possession of the Veda. The five Brāhmaṇs invited to Bengal from the superior middle country where the four *varṇas* were first generated arrive on horseback and armed to the teeth, appearing to the Kṣatriya warriors and not Brāhmaṇ priest-preceptors. Finally, the five Śūdras who come with them as their disciples have combined themselves with the Vedic worship code of the higher twice-born *varṇas*. Despite this seeming confusion, however, values have not changed. The coded substance of the Veda and the performance of Vedic worship are still the ultimate sources of ordered welfare and prosperity, and the divinely endowed king is still responsible for the maintenance of proper order within the Hindu community.

How does the king, given the confused state of affairs in which he finds himself, solve the problem of maintaining proper order? The answer is, by putting people to the test and thereby discovering their "true" qualities. Consistent with the stress placed on the coded substance of worship, virtually all of these tests have to do with the Veda and worship. When his own Brāhmaṇs fail the test with respect to Vedic worship, he invites Brāhmaṇs said to be capable of performing it correctly. When they arrive in the guise of Kṣatriyas, however, the king refuses to worship them. This precipitates a crisis for the Hindu community of Gauḍa. This is resolved when the Brāhmaṇs, whose Vedic power is so great that they know in advance that the king will not recognize them, give evidence of their supreme

[22]Śarma, "Kula-dīpikā," fols. 4b–5b.

life-giving power by reviving a dead wooden column, something even the king, however great his coercive power (*daṇḍa*), cannot do. The king then honors them, yet the testing does not end here.

Worse even than the nonperformance of a Vedic worship was its incorrect performance; for if the correct performance brought about long life, happiness, and prosperity, its incorrect performance brought in its wake untimely death, sorrow, and hunger. Thus, before the Brāhmaṇs are asked to perform the worship desired by the king and settle in Bengal, he must examine their credentials in detail. Once satisfied that they and their Śūdra servants possess the true marks of the Vedic code, such as *gotras*, he asks them to perform the worship. They worship the gods on behalf of the king, and the king then worships the Brāhmaṇs and Śūdras on behalf of the Hindu community.

These acts of worship, the feeding of the gods by the Brāhmaṇs and the feeding of the Brāhmaṇs and Śūdras by the king, transform the immigrant Brāhmaṇs and Śūdras of the middle country into the highest Brāhmaṇs and Śūdras of Bengal. The five Brāhmaṇs become the ancestral seed-males of the fifty-nine clans of Rāḍhī Brāhmaṇs. The five Śūdras become the seed-males of five clans in the Dakṣiṇa-rāḍhī and Vaṅgaja Kāyastha subcastes. Three of these five Śūdras—Ghosh, Basu, and Mitra—become the progenitors of the three Kulīna clans in the Dakṣiṇa-rāḍhī subcastes, and Datta becomes the progenitor of a Siddha Maulika clan. Virāṭa Guha, who went to Vaṅga (east Bengal) becomes the progenitor of a Kulīna clan in the Vaṅgaja Kāyastha subcaste.

Thus, consistent with the ideology of worship, it is acts of worship which change the community just as it is acts of worship that sustain it. Order and prosperity depend on the correct possession of the Veda and the correct performance of enjoined acts of worship. By worshiping the immigrant Brāhmaṇs and Śūdras, whose power to sustain life and cause prosperity is recognized as superior to that of the indigenous Brāhmaṇs and Śūdras, that is, by feeding them, the king is able to transform them into Bengali Brāhmaṇs and Śūdras and thereby regenerate the Hindu community which makes up his kingdom. It is only after this royal act of worship that they combine their bodily substance with the territorial substance of Bengal by settling there and form *jātis* by making proper marriages and giving birth to children.

Yet all does not end well. Already there are indications of future problems and decline represented by Datta in the Dakṣiṇa-rāḍhī Kāyastha account. Considered to be lacking in one of the worshipful qualities appropriate to a Śūdra, humility (*vinaya*), he is "worshiped" by the king with a rank inferior to that of the other four Śūdras. Consequently, his standing in Bengal remains ambiguous. He settles there but does not become part of the new Kāyastha *jāti* because he does not intermarry with Ghosh, Basu, and Mitra.

King Vallāla Sena: Organization of the Brāhmaṇs and Kāyasthas into Territorial Jātis (Subcastes) and Ranked Worship Jātis (Grades)

Territorial Jātis

The third stage in the transformation of the Hindu community centers on the actions of two Śūdra king of the succeeding twelfth-century dynasty, Vallāla Sena (1158–1179), and his son Lakṣmaṇa Sena (1179–1206), during whose rule the Muslim invasions began.[23] These kings are credited with dividing the descendants of the Vedic Brāhmaṇs and Kāyastha Śūdras into subcastes, *jātis*, whose coded bodily substances were marked by the possession of their own distinct territories:

> The king Vallāla Sena, son in an Ambaṣṭha family, examined the Vedic codes of the families (*kula-śāstra*) with great care. He assembled all of the descendants of those Brāhmaṇs and Śūdras who had been brought by Ādiśūra in his own court. The Brāhmaṇs were assigned to the villages where they were settled and were divided into two subcastes (*śreṇī*) called Rāḍhī and Vārendra. In the same way that these two kinds of coded substance (*kula*) were made among the best of the Brāhmaṇs, so, four subcastes of Śūdras were made by the king: Udga (Uttara) and Dakṣiṇa-Rāḍha, Vaṅga, and Vārendra. These four designations were made according to the countries where they resided; and they now had four kinds of coded substance (*kula*), each according to their subcaste.[24]

More complicated than the transformation of the single Brāhmaṇs and Kāyastha *jātis* into sets of discrete territorial *jātis* was the

[23]Both of these kings have been identified in the historical inscriptions. See Paul, *Early History of Bengal*, I, 93–101. The genealogies identify them as Śūdras of the Ambaṣṭha or physician *jāti*; their own inscriptions identify them as Brahma-kṣatriyas or Kṣatriyas.

[24]Śarmā, "Kula-dīpikā," fols. 5b–6a.

transformation of the immigrant Brāhmaṇs and Kāyasthas, on the one hand, and the indigenous Brāhmaṇs and Kāyasthas, on the other, into persons of the same Brāhmaṇ and Kāyastha territorial *jātis* (subcastes). This was made especially difficult for two reasons. First, past acts of lowering conduct on the part of superior persons and of uplifting conduct on the part of inferior persons made it difficult to identify just what coded substances were possessed by whom. Second, since coded bodily substances were preserved first and foremost by those acts which controlled its perpetuation, proper marriage and reproduction, there was the danger that improper marriages of the upheld and superior with the fallen and inferior could, as in the days of King Veṇa, result in the lowering of the Hindu community, bringing disorder, hunger, and decline in their wake. The solution to this problem, attributed to Vallāla and Lakṣmaṇa Sena, was to organize the Brāhmaṇs and Kāyasthas into systems of ranked grades.

Worship Code and Kulīna *Rank*

The Brāhmaṇs and Śūdras brought by Ādiśūra were thought to have inherited in unbroken succession from the time of their progenitor's generation a superior coded substance (*kula*) distinguishing them from the non-Vedic Brāhmaṇs and Śūdras of Bengal. The actions enjoined by this embodied Vedic code were conceived of as inborn "attributes" (*guṇas*), which, taken together, formed the defining characteristics or marks (*lakṣaṇas*) of the Vedic Brāhmaṇs and their Kāyastha Śūdra servants. This superior form of coded bodily substance was referred to as *kaulīnya*, and persons who held this inherited rank were referred to, appropriately, as Kulīnas. Here, in a Dakṣiṇa-rāḍhī Kāyastha text, is a list of these nine inborn attributes:

> The Kulīna becomes purified (*śuddha*) in these nine attributes. He is endowed with good conduct (*ācāra*), humility (*vinaya*), and knowledge (*vidyā*). There are unending famous acts (*pratiṣṭhā*) and pilgrimages (*tīrtha-darśana*) on the part of his family. He has devotion (*niṣṭha*) for worship and marriages with Kulīnas (*kula-karma*). He is absorbed in the occupation (*vṛtti*) of his caste (*jāti*). He will be generous (*dātā*) and constantly purified through austerities (*tapasyā*).[25]

[25] Vācaspati, "Kula-sarvvasva," in Nagendranāth Vasu *Vaṅger Jātīya Itihāsa* (Calcutta: Viśvakosa Press, 1911–33), VI Pt. I, 115.

Save for one or two minor variations, the list of the Rāḍhī Brāhmaṇs is identical with that of the Dakṣiṇa-rāḍhī Kāyasthas:

> Whatever is practiced in accord with one's family (*kula*), caste (*varṇa*), and life-stage (*āśrama*) is declared to be good conduct (*acara*) so long as it arises out of the sounds (*śruti*) and memories (*smṛti*) of the Vedic code for conduct (*dharma*). Deference to preceptor, elder, and genealogist, and kind speech which is sweet-sounding, agreeable, and constant is viewed as humility (*vinaya*). Discrimination between the pure and impure and knowledge of the Vedic code (*dharmaśāstra*) are declared to be wisdom (*vidyā*). Deeds (*kīrtti*) done in distant regions which have arisen out of austerity and discipline and which are sung of by the foremost of the genealogists are considered to be famous acts (*pratiṣṭhā*). That which is done with reverence at pilgrimage places such as Gayā, and is visible, is to be known as pilgrimage (*tīrtha-darśana*). On the other hand, that firm faith which occurs in the mind that is intent on the Vedic code (*dharma*) through preseverance in the Vedic code (*dharma*) and knowledge of the Vedic code (*dharma*) is declared to be devotion (*niṣṭhā*). The equality of two parties arising out of the accepting and giving of daughters of equal rank to equals is considered to be reciprocal exchange (*āvṛtti*). Reflection on the eternal truth through control of the senses and worship of the family deity is declared to be austerity (*tapas*). That which is given for the assistance of others out of a desire for respect and that which is to be given from pure vessels are declared to be gifts (*dāna*).[26]

As can be seen from these two lists, the Kulīna code was primarily a worship code for conduct containing elements drawn from the Vedas and *śāstras*. What is significant here, of course, is that it was thought to be combined with the bodily substance of the Kulīnas. As coded bodily substance, *kaulīnya* was, therefore, perpetuated by proper marriage and reproduction. The Rāḍhī Brāhmaṇ list, which substituted *āvṛtti* for *vṛtti*, tells us that the marriages which best preserved *kaulīnya* were exchanges of daughters among the Kulīnas themselves. As we shall see, however, exchanges of daughters among Kulīnas and non-Kulīnas, initiated by indigenous Brāhmaṇs and Śūdras who wished to improve the quality of their coded bodily substance or rank, were already taking place. This was not, however, the only problem which confronted the Hindu community of Bengal with respect to the Kulīnas.

Though the coded bodily substance of a Kulīna, his rank, was

[26] Vācaspati, "Kularamā," in Chandrakānta Ghaṭaka-vidyānidhi, *Kulakalpadruma* (Calcutta: Bhavanipur Press, 1912), pp. 56–57.

perpetuated from one generation to the next by proper marriage and reproduction, the code had to be followed in between marriages if it was to be preserved. Failure to follow this divinely bestowed code was thought to result in the partial or even complete lowering of rank. Thus, judgment (*vicāra*) had to be exercised in order to determine who was a true Kulīna. During this formative period, such judgment was thought to be exercised not by subcaste assemblies and genealogists but by the paramount Hindu ruler conceived as the upholder of the moral order. So, Vallāla Sena, in pursuit of his inborn code as king, summoned the descendant of the five Brāhmaṇs and Śūdras to his court where he used the nine attributes of their code as a test in order to judge which of them were true Kulīnas and which not.

Ranked Worship Jātis: *Dakṣiṇa-Rāḍhī Kāyasthas*

The masters of three of the Kāyastha Śūdra families brought by Ādiśūra—Ghosh, Basu, and Mitra—were thought to be fully endowed with the nine attributes of the Vedic code in Dakṣiṇa-rāḍha. In relation to the other Śūdras they were, therefore, judged to be a pure, divine genus, possessed of superior generic rank (*kaulīnya*). So, Vallāla Sena properly recognized them as true Kulīnas.[27] Note here that the Dakṣiṇa-rāḍhī Kāyasthas see the formation of the territorial *jātis* of Kāyasthas as a consequence of an evil act of the king Lakṣmaṇa Sena. His improper intercourse with an inferior Ḍom woman, a symbolic threat to the maintenance of proper caste order, caused them to leave the court at Gauḍa and settle in the four regions of Bengal:

> The great king Vallāla Sena was born in the world after performing hundreds of austerities. By obediently serving Viṣṇu, he made clan prosperity (*kula-lakṣmī*) and caused the clans (*kula*) to rejoice. Just as Bhagīratha[28] brought the Gaṅgā and Viṣṇu appeared on earth as Indradyumna,[29] so the devotee Vallāla spread clan prosperity (*kula-lakṣmī*), the great power (*śakti*) of Viṣṇu. Having obtained this wealth

[27]Though sources independent of the genealogies do not confirm Vallāla's honoring of the Kulīnas, they do indicate that there were two subcastes of Vedic Brāhmaṇs, Rāḍhī and Vārendra. Several Brāhmaṇs having the surnames and *gotras* of the Rāḍhī and Vārendra Brāhmaṇs listed in the genealogies are also found in the inscriptions. See Paul, *Early History of Bengal*, II, 45–47.

[28]An heroic and powerful king born of the ocean (*sāgara*).

[29]A king born of the sun (*sūrya*) and an incarnation of Viṣṇu.

of family well-being, Vallāla, pleased in his heart, was worshiped in every house. Judging how to distinguish the castes (*jāti-bheda*) and upholding the purified clans (*vaṃśa*), he established the Kulīnas in their nine attributes. The Brāhmaṇ, the one who is served, and the Śūdra, the one who serves him, comprise the two major castes (*jāti*).

Three persons—Ghosh, Basu, and Mitra—were absorbed in the service of the Brāhmaṇs when the king Vallāla appeared. The Brāhmaṇ is an incarnation of Viṣṇu and these three persons are his servants. Seeing that they were endowed with the nine attributes, the king, whose great wisdom, actions, and powers are worshipped, no longer had any worries. He saw that their spotless offspring were his liberation, were an incarnation of clan prosperity (*Kula-lakṣmī*), and that their hearts were firm at the feet of the Brāhmaṇs. When he saw their nine attributes—good conduct (*acara*), humility (*vinaya*), and so forth—he knew the main reason. Those who do the service of the Brāhmaṇ, the preceptor and guest, whose worships (*pūjā*) and austerities are truth, and who serve with devotion; who follow the command of God and move on the path of the Veda; they obtain worship (*pūjā*) as worshipful Kulīnas. So he made these three persons the primary kings of clan rank (*kularāja*) [among the Śūdras] in Dakṣiṇa-rāḍha and pleased them with honorific marks of sandal-paste.

The three made marriages and caused their offspring to increase. And so everyone was in the country of Gauḍa. Then occurred the accusation of the king [Lakṣmaṇa Sena] and his defamation over the Ḍom maiden. So they left Gauḍa. All those who went to the east and west became known as Vaṅgaja and Vārendra, while those who went north became Uttara-rāḍhī. Six brothers in the three families settled in different places along the banks of the southern Gaṅgā, the source of Dakṣiṇa-rāḍha, built their houses before the Gaṅgā, and made their communities (*samāja*) recognized and superior. Prabhākara and Niśāpati Ghosh settled at Āknā and Bālī in the sixth generation. The uterine brothers Sukti and Mukti Basu settled at Bāgāṇḍā and Māhīnagara in the fifth generation and the Mitra offspring at Baḍiśā and Ṭekā. At that time they were in the ninth generation.[30]

A set of eighty Śūdras who did not possess the ninefold Vedic code for conduct as its generic code was transformed into the grade-designated Maulika within the Dakṣiṇa-rāḍhī Kāyastha subcaste during the Sena period. Only one of these eighty, the ambiguous Datta, was considered an immigrant Kāyastha from north India. The other seventy-nine were considered to be the Śūdras who were

[30] Mitra, Kulajī, fols. 2–3.

already settled in Bengal when the five Śūdras arrived from Kolañca. The genus formed by these persons was itself divided into two ranked grades usually referred to as Siddha and Sādhya.

The term "Siddha" means "cooked, purified, and completed, successful, and famous," suggesting that the Siddha Maulikas were the original Śūdras of Bengal, distinguished by their having undergone a process of transformation. Other synonyms such as San-maulika, "superior Maulika," and Maulika-rāja, "king among the Maulikas," were also used to describe these higher Maulikas. Eight persons were made into Siddha Maulika Kāyasthas by Vallāla Sena. One of these, the immigrant Datta, was a Kāyastha by birth. But he did not fully exhibit the Kulīna code for conduct. He was "defective in humility" (*vinaya*) and therefore had "only eight qualities left."[31] By lowering his substance and code in this way, Datta and his offspring lost their equivalence of rank with the other Kulīnas and with it the capacity to make reciprocal daughter exchanges and became equivalent in coded bodily substance to the other seven Siddha Maulikas.

These seven persons were indigenous Śūdras who had upgraded themselves by combining themselves with the coded substance of worship of the Kulīna Kāyasthas. Having approximated the Kulīna code for conduct, they acquired the capacity to make worshipful gifts of daughters and wealth to the Kulīnas, those who fully embodied the coded substance of *kaulīnya*. By making these exchanges, these Śūdras combined with the bodily substance of the Kulīna, formed a new genus, and gained the rank of Kāyastha from the Kulīna genus:

> Seven houses of Maulikas became successful (*siddha*). They were officers (*mutsuddis*) of the king. They became recognized [as Kāyasthas] by giving to the three [Kulīna families]. He (the Sena king) consented to this at the request of the Brāhmaṇs. Sen, Dās, Datta, Kar, Deb, Pālit, Sinha, and Guha are the eight Maulikas. These eight clans have become successful; they have risen in rank (*kula*) toward Ghosh, Basu, and Mitra by giving and taking with these three families. Thus, anyone who took from these three came to be a Kāyastha, though I think there is sometimes doubt with regard to them. They married with them and because of this, the coded substance (*kula*) of their offspring improved.[32]

[31] "Kula-pradīpa," Dacca University Library MSS (uncataloged), n.d., fol. 1.

[32] Baradākānta Basu Ghaṭaka, Kulajī, Dacca University Library MSS (uncataloged), n.d., fol. 2.

However, these two genera—Siddha Maulika and Kulīna—did not become equivalent in their substance and code. Though they approximated the Kulīna code, the Siddha Maulikas could not duplicate it, for the Kulīna code and rank had been generated by the gods themselves. Hence, the Siddha Maulikas, characterized as having only eight of the nine Kulīna attributes, were thought unable to make reciprocal exchanges of daughters with the Kulīnas. As a result, the two genera did not fully merge to form a single new genus. They remained as separate grades within the subcaste. And since the Siddha Maulikas were considered to be inferior to the Kulīnas in their substance and code, their generic rank was judged to be inferior to that of the Kulīna genus. So Vallāla Sena naturally and properly solved the problem of their classification by making them into a Siddha Maulika grade ranking beneath the Kulīnas in the Dakṣiṇa-rāḍhī Kāyastha subcaste.

The remaining seventy-two Śūdras were made into a Maulika genus designated as Sādhya. The term "Sādhya" means "potential," suggesting that the Sādhya Maulikas were indigenous Śūdras who had the inherent capacity to become successful but had not done so. Other terms used to describe these Śūdras—*kaṣṭa*, "troublesome," *sādhāraṇa*, "common," and *sāmānya*, 'ordinary, undistinguished,"—confirm this notion. A lustful king, Nityānanda, who, it may be inferred, appears temporarily to have usurped either Vallāla Sena or his son, Lakṣmaṇa, caused these Śūdras to come into being. Taking up where the wicked king Veṇa left off, he forced two beauteous maidens from each of the thirty-six *jātis* making up the Śūdra *varṇa* in Bengal to marry him and begat sons on them. The seventy-two sons born of these improper mixed marriages were, of course, inferior in coded substance or rank:

> The king Nityānanda was born in a Śūdra clan. His conduct (*vyavahāra*) was of the Āsurīya[33] type, but he was the paramount ruler of the kingdom of Gauḍa. That king Nityānanda became confused with desire; his mind immersed in badness, he married again and again the daughters of the thirty-six castes, having seen how worthy they were in quality and beauty. He accepted in marriage seventy-two daughters without judging which families were suitable and which not. From this were born sons who were called "sons of the king" (*rāja-puta*). They did not have the *gotras* and surnames that Ghosh, Basu, and Mitra had received. These three had settled on the banks of the

[33]The *asuras* were the enemies of the gods (*devas*); their power was great, but instead of bringing about order and prosperity, its exercise did just the opposite.

Gaṅgā and engaged in their particular code for conduct. Their communities and surnames were recognized and their *gotras* and *pravaras*[34] were distinct. The great king Lakṣmaṇa Sena did all of these things and gave the Dakṣiṇa-rāḍhī Kulīnas land and houses. Ghosh, Basu, and Mitra mixed (*meli*) and made marriages with each other.[35]

Texts of the Vaṅgaja Kāyasthas are similar in their accounts of the lowest grades in their subcastes:

And so they tell of the sons of the king (*rāja-putas*): the king Nityānanda was born in the clan of Mṛtyuñjaya. Fourteen castes (*varṇa*) came into being as a result of his marriages. On account of the origin of the stepmothers of the offspring of his marriages, the distinctness of the castes (*varṇa-bheda*) was not maintained. These fourteen sons of the king were Hor, Āditya, Sūr, Nandī, Brahma, Kuṇḍu, and Dām; Āic, Bhadra, Pāiñ, etc. There were twenty-four sons of the king in the view of some: Bad, Binda, and Lodh were born in the womb of a Tailaka (oil-presser) woman. Hoṛ, Hui, Añja, and Bhañja were born from the daughter of a Gopa (cowherd). Brahma, Barddhana, and Bhūta were the sons of a Kaibartta (cultivator-fisherman) daughter. Gaṇa and Pāiñ were born from the womb of a Kumbhakāra (potter) daughter. Sūr, Nandī, and Kuṇḍu were born from the womb of a Saṅkha-vaṇik (conch-dealer) daughter. Bhadra, Rāhut, Dām, and Āditya were born as well. Syām and Som were known as the sons of a Vāraja (betel-grower) daughter. The royal sons of these are designated (*rāja-putas*). Various designations are applied to the fourteen houses: Sīl is remembered as the Nāpita (barber) of the king, and Kuṇḍu as his slave (*bhṛtya*); Kar is known as a Rajaka (washerman) and Dhar is remembered as a Hāṛī (scavenger). "Avoid Dhar and Kar and ridicule their families. The rank of Sūr is in his skin only, just as iron is found only in the rim of a bell."[36]

Not all of the Kāyasthas of Bengal accepted Vallāla Sena's scheme for classifying "potential" or "troublesome" Kāyasthas, among them the Vārendra Kāyasthas. Their account of these persons is even more scathing:

In the course of time thirty-two houses of the king's domestic servants (*cākor*) and an additional forty houses of lower condition (*bhāva*) became independent. . . . Even though these seventy-two houses did not participate in the councils, they entered the Vārendra subcaste (*śreṇī*). Hear now about the conduct (*ācāra*) of the thirty-two houses of servants. Though they were all descendants of a Śūdra,

[34] *Pravaras* were Vedic names similar in their use to the *gotras*.
[35] Kāśīrāma Basu, Kulajī, Dacca University Library MSS (uncataloged), n.d., fol. 1.
[36] Śarmā, "Kula-dīpikā," fols. 13b–14a.

> they became bearers (*kāhār*) by occupation. Listen to the reason for this. The king used to chew betel constantly. The king used to travel about in a palanquin on their shoulders while eating *pān*. When the courtiers saw this they criticized them and for that reason those Śūdras became Kāhārs by caste. All of these unfit, unsuccessful, inferior Śūdras were devoid of wealth, devoid of good attributes, and absorbed in inferior acts of worship. Those who seized Nandī [daughters] by force began to mix in the Kāyastha caste. The king thought to raise them all and arranged their marriages with prominent Kāyasthas. They entered the caste (*paṭi*) more and more and began to mix, but in the Vārendra Subcaste (*paṭi*) they became persons to be avoided.
>
> Listen now to the distinct features of the forty houses; some are censured and to be avoided, while others are superior. Hear now the reason for this. There was once a prominent king named Nityaśūra. He began to make marriages that were acts of pleasure and one by one he made seventy-two marriages. The king made marriages in this and other countries and moreover made them in inferior families and inferior clans. In the course of time offspring were born. They became known as "sons of the field." When he heard this he became angry and summoned them. In his rage he fearlessly began to cut them down. So they fled to Vallāla and he arranged their marriages with superiors.[37]

Clearly, these grades of Sādhya Kāyasthas were thought to be identical with the lower castes of Śūdras. Some were thought to be the descendants of Kāyastha Śūdras whose embodied ranks had become "troublesome" (*kaṣṭa*) by following the inferior occupational codes of the lower Śūdra castes. Most, however, were believed to be the offspring of inferior Śūdras and an evil king. Characterized as devoid of wealth, devoid of good attributes, and absorbed in inferior acts of worship, their codes for conduct were thought to be not an approximation of the Vedic code of the Kulīnas but the very negation of it. These Śūdras were, therefore, properly judged to have a rank inferior to that of the "actualized" or "successful" (*siddha*) Śūdra. Yet because they were Śūdras and often claimed to be Kāyasthas, they were recognized as forming "latent" (*sādhya*) genera within the Kāyastha subcastes. They had the inborn capacity to become successful by emulating the code for conduct of the successful and then making worshipful exchanges of daughters with the higher genera. The Dakṣiṇa-rāḍhī story of Nityānanda concludes on an optimistic note: "Those of the seventy-two who make the

[37]Yadunandana, *Mūla Ḍhākur o Samalocanā; arthāt, Kāyastha Samājer Vivaraṇa* (Calcutta: Bharat Mihir Press, 1891), pp. 31–32.

ādyarasa and *pratisāri* marriages with the Kulīnas become Maulika-rājas and among these, he who protects the nine grades of Kulīnas becomes the council-master (*goṣṭhī-pati*)."[38] In a similar vein, the Vaṅgaja text states: "by worshiping the high clans over the generations, they become Mahāpātra in rank; thus, one born in an inferior clan may become pure over the generations."[39]

Thus, King Vallāla Sena attempted to solve the problem of mixing and confusion among the Śūdras of Bengal by devising what I have called a "dual" or "alternate" organization scheme for them. According to it, Śūdras who clustered around the coded substances defining the inferior occupational *jātis* were classed as persons of those *jātis*. On the other hand, Śūdras who clustered around the coded substances defining the Kulīna Kāyasthas, the highest of the Śūdras, could be classed as belonging to the "latent" or even "actualized" grades of the Kāyastha *jātis*.

Ranked Worship Jātis: *Rāḍhī Brāhmaṇs*

The transformation of the Brāhmaṇs' caste organization paralleled that of the Kāyasthas' though differing in some details. All fifty-nine of the clans in this subcaste were thought to be descended from the five Vedic Brāhmaṇs brought to Bengal by Ādiśūra. According to their genealogies, the fifty-six sons of these five Brāhmaṇs were invited to Vallāla Sena's court where he gave each of them a village (*grāma*) to settle in. The names of these clans were referred to as *gāñi* or *grāmika* after these villages.[40]

Vallāla Sena also judged the ranks of these persons. He declared that of the nine "attributes" of a Kulīna, the reciprocal exchange of daughters in marriage was the distinguishing one. Twenty-two of the fifty-nine Rāḍhī Brāhmaṇs accepted this ruling of the king and agreed to follow this marriage code. Hence, they were judged to be Kulīnas. Of these twenty-two, eight were judged to be Mukhya or "primary" Kulīnas because they were "endowed with the full attributes."[41] Fourteen persons were judged to be Gauṇa or "secondary" Kulīnas because they were "somewhat less in the nine attributes."[42] The remaining thirty-seven persons disagreed with

[38]Basu, Kulajī, fol. 2.
[39]Śarmā, "Kula-dīpikā," fols. 6b–7a.
[40]Vasu, *Vaṅger Jātīya Itihāsa*, I, Pt. I, 112.
[41]"Kula-mañjarī," in Vasu, *Vaṅger Jātīya Itihāsa*, I, Pt. I, 145.
[42]*Ibid.*

the king and refused to follow the marriage code enjoining reciprocal exchanges. Because they were thus defective in this distinguishing attribute, they were judged to be inferior in coded bodily substance or rank and declared to be Śrotriyas, Brāhmaṇs who were learned in the Vedas but lacked the highest rank.

Later, on account of their departure from the Kulīna marriage code, the descendants of the Gauṇa Kulīnas became divided into three ranked grades of Śrotriyas all of which were ranked below the original grade of thirty-four Śrotriyas. Some attribute this reorganization to a later Hindu king, Datta-khāsa: "The Gauṇas, who had a rule enjoining reciprocal exchanges of Gauṇas with Gauṇas and the occasional gift of a daughter to a Mukhya, were made Śrotriyas by the king Datta-khāsa by virtue of their assuming the same nature as the Śrotriyas."[43] Others attribute it to the famous fifteenth-century genealogist, Devīvara.[44] At any rate, the Śrotriya Rāḍhīs of the middle period came to be organized into four grades ranked high and low. The clans descended from the original thirty-seven Śrotriyas are "free of defects" in the marriages of their daughters to the Kulīnas and come to be designated the Susiddha or "very successful Śrotriyas." Three clans descended from three of the Gauṇas "always succeed" in marrying daughters to the Kulīnas and come to be designated Siddha or "successful" Śrotriyas. Four who "sometimes succeed and sometimes not" come to be known as Sādhya or "latent," and seven who are "destroyers of high rank" are named the Ari or "enemy" Śrotriyas.[45] The latter are also referred as Kaṣṭa or "troublesome" Śrotriyas, as among the Dakṣiṇa-rāḍhī Kāyasthas.

As these characterizations suggest, the Susiddha, Siddha, and Sādhya Śrotriyas were all grouped together and sharply distinguished from the Ari Śrotriyas. The former grades, because their coded bodily substances were similar to that of the Kulīnas, were all thought capable of giving suitable daughters to the Kulīnas, and the Kulīnas were thought to be capable of accepting these daughters and transforming them into proper Kulīna wives. Even though they were said to have originated from the same superior coded substance as the other Rāḍhī Brāhmaṇs, the Ari Śrotriyas were held to be so

[43]Devīvara, "Kula-kārikā," in Vasu, *Vaṅger Jātīya Itihāsa*, I, Pt. I, 172.

[44]Ghaṭaka-vidyānidhi, *Kulakalpadruma*, pp. 20–21.

[45]Vācaspati, "Kularamā," in Mahimāchandra Majumdār, *Gauḍe Brāhmaṇ* (Calcutta: B. L. Chakravarti, New School-Book Press, 1886), p. 201.

different and inferior that they were thought incapable of giving daughters to a Kulīna without inferiorizing the Kulīna's generic code and rank. Their inferiority arose because they are thought to have merged their coded bodily substances with those of the non-Vedic Saptaśati Brāhmaṇs:

> Listen to a judgment (*vicāra*) on the Rāḍhīs, Vārendras, and Saptaśatis. Some came earlier and others later; this is the essence of the matter. The Saptaśatis say that they have obtained the Brāhmaṇhood of the Rāḍhīs and Vārendras through the marriage of Saptaśati daughters to those from Kānyakubja; and, therefore, the Saptaśatis say they are not inferior, they are to be respected. But others, because of their good sense, do not take heed of their words.[46]

As among the Kāyasthas, these Saptaśatis were thought capable, by combining with the lower Śrotriyas, of becoming masters of the assembly among the Śrotriyas:

> In those successful (*prasiddha*) Śrotriya clans which, because they were contemptible, never had given daughters to the [Kulīna] unions (*melas*), the crest-jewels of the Saptaśatis have gone from purified to very purified, and become respected as council-masters (*goṣṭhī-pati*). However, just because the Saptaśati Brāhmaṇs say they are purified, does that mean that one ever forgets who has high rank and good character? Many who were begotten by non-Kulīna Rāḍhīs were in the end born in the wombs of Saptaśati daughters. . . . Those who were born in the Śāṇḍilya *gotra* said they were descendants of Bhaṭṭanārāyaṇa; those of the Kāśyapa *gotra* said they were the descendants of Dakṣa, and Sāvarṇas called themselves the descendants of Vedagarbha. Those born of the Vatsya *gotra* said they were the offspring of Chāndaḍa, and Bharadvājas said they were the descendants of Śrīharṣa. They all introduce themselves as Śrotriyas and some say they are successful or purified.[47]

Thus, the Sena kings, by summoning the Brāhmaṇs and Śūdras to his court, testing their conduct, judging which was high and low, and organizing them into ranked worship *jātis*, had inaugurated a dual or alternate organization which was capable of maintaining order within the Hindu community in the face of confusion over caste identities. As organized by the Senas, these grades of clans in each subcaste were thought to hold ranks synonymous with their inherited substances and inborn worship codes. The Kulīna grades

[46]Nula Pañchānana, "Goṣṭhī-kathā," in Vasu, *Vaṅger Jātīya Itihāsa*, I, Pt. I, 90.
[47]Śrīnāth Bandya, "Saptaśati-kārikā," in Vasu, *Vaṅger Jātīya Itihāsa*, I, Pt. I, 98–99.

of clans were the descendants of the Brāhmaṇs and Śūdras brought from Madhyadeśa by Ādiśūra. They were thought to have inherited a ninefold Vedic code for conduct from their progenitors in unbroken succession. The rank synonymous with this inherited code, referred to as *kaulīnya*, was thought of as divinely superior to all other forms of inherited rank. The prosperity of the entire community was thought to depend upon their continued possession of this coded substance of Vedic worship.

The *kaulīnya* code and rank were thought to be acquired by a person through birth and maintained through good conduct. Once lost through misconduct, this inherited *kaulīnya* could never be fully regained. Hence, among those immigrant Brāhmaṇs and Śūdras who had inherited this Vedic code, only those who were judged by Vallāla Sena to follow the code were recognized by him to hold the superior rank of true Kulīnas. These male persons and their families, recognized as equivalent in their generic codes and ranks, were thought to have the capacity to make reciprocal exchanges of daughters among themselves. By doing this, these families of the same code and rank united their substances to form the Kulīna grades.

The non-Kulīna clans consisted of persons who did not possess this coded substance of the Veda in its fullest form. Some of these persons, like the progenitors of the Datta and Guha clans in the Dakṣiṇa-rāḍhī Kāyastha subcaste and the progenitors of the thirty-four Susiddha Śrotriya clans in the Rāḍhī Brāhmaṇ subcaste, were descendants of the immigrant Vedic Brāhmaṇs and Śūdras who had ruined their inherited Vedic code and rank through misconduct. So they were naturally and properly judged by Vallāla to rank below the Kulīnas. Others were the descendants of the indigenous non-Vedic Brāhmaṇs and Śūdras. Those persons who had purified their substance and code by emulating the Vedic code for conduct, even though they could never duplicate it, were made into actualized (*siddha*) Śrotriyas or Maulikas and recognized to have ranks just beneath the Kulīnas. Because the codes and ranks of the Kulīnas and successful non-Kulīnas were nonequivalent, they were thought unable to make reciprocal exchanges with each other. Their proximity in code and rank, however, did endow the successful non-Kulīnas with the capacity to make nonreciprocal exchanges of both daughters and wealth with the Kulīnas. By worshipping the Kulīnas with gifts of daughters, the successful non-Kulīna genera mixed their coded substance with the Kulīnas to form grades within the Vedic Brāhmaṇ and Kāyastha Śūdra subcastes.

The remaining Brāhmaṇs and Śūdras of Bengal, those who had the inborn capacity of emulating the Vedic code of the Kulīnas but were judged not to have actualized it yet, were made into latent (*sādhya*) or troublesome (*kaṣṭa*) Śrotriyas and Maulikas and recognized to rank below the actualized grade. Though these latent Śrotriyas and Maulikas were thought unable to exchange daughters with the Kulīnas, they were considered capable of making nonreciprocal exchanges with the actualized non-Kulīnas and becoming actualized. Thus, the latent Śrotriyas and Maulikas formed only potential genera within the Vedic Brāhmaṇ and Kāyastha Śūdra subcastes.

MUSLIM CONQUEST: MIDDLE PERIOD REORGANIZATION

Marriage Alone Comes to Define Rank

The Muslim conquest of Bengal initiates the fourth and final stage in the transformation of the Hindu community of Gauḍa. Muslim armies, which began their conquest of Bengal in 1200 A.D., ultimately destroyed the Hindu king of Gauḍa and replaced him with a Muslim ruler. Their conquest of Bengal did not, however, make them members of the community of Gauḍa so far as the Hindus were concerned. To the contrary, the presence of these powerful non-Hindu, who were characterized as "thieves" (*dasyu*) and "foreigners" (*yavana*), was thought initially to bring about misconduct and disorder. This was especially so because Brāhmaṇs and Śūdras, motivated by greed, availed themselves of opportunities proffered by the Muslim conquerors and ruined their coded substance by improperly mixing with them:

> During the period of Hindu sovereignty (*rājatva*), happiness (*sukha*) and wisdom (*vidyā*) were complete and Brāhmaṇhood was more important than anything else. When the Hindu sun set, ignorance and darkness appeared and conduct enjoined by the Veda (*śruta-śilatā*) departed. The country (*deśa*) became devoid of good conduct (*sadācāra-śūnya*) and the Brāhmaṇ and Śūdra, both of whom had excessive greed for wealth (*artha*), became one and the same. In this way, priest and servant entered together on the straight path of a dog's life and did not even cry "Alas!" at the ruin (*nāśa*) of the Vedic code (*dharma*). Under the influence of wealth (*dhana*) and separated

from good conduct, everyone became Kulīna or Śrotriya in name only. People of every clan (*gotra*), void of wisdom, made marriages among the Kulīnas and became fond of calling themselves Śrotriyas. Barely a trace of wise men remained and only matters of wealth were held worthy of consideration. The lowest passions became especially strong. The gain of wealth (*artha*) and enjoyment (*kāma*) became the goals of mankind; liberation (*apavarga*) was considered inappropriate and acts of worship in accord with the Vedic code (*dharma-karma*) were excessively weak.

Some became high ranking ministers and officials of the Muslims (Yavana), trustworthy salts they! Those who accepted important service came to be called Rāy-rāyan and became the source of trouble. The Rāy-rāyans together with their brothers and affines spread out over the country and engaged in work for the Muslims (*dasyu*); they were heroes on the waterways and land routes. They freely provided supplies for the armies of the Muslim king (*pātśā*) and became pleased, even though they were involved in the slaughter of cows and Brāhmaṇs. In this way, the Brāhmaṇs became the experts of the Muslims.[48]

Under such circumstances, the niceties of the Kulīna code were cast aside and improper marriages, exchanges of daughters which did not bring about welfare and prosperity, were made. The result was a new round of mixtures and confusion. Now, only a few persons were left who had preserved their Vedic codes and substances:

In this way, pure clans obtained the results of impure marriages, and became absolutely devoid of knowledge. Once their knowledge had gone, all of them became absorbed in bad actions; the Brāhmaṇ became the expert of the Muslim. In order to dissolve their faults, Some of these men invited the sons of Kulīnas and made gifts of daughters together with cows and gold. In the Kali age, reparations (*prāyaścitta*) undo evil acts and mere giving (*dāna*) becomes good conduct (*sad-vṛtta*). So they hid their faults by giving away food. The impure sons of Kulīnas, like weakened cows, remained stuck in the mud of evil deeds for a long time. In order to get out of the mud of evil deeds, they made marriages in the houses of Muslims (*dasyus*), and, through these, became even more sunk in ignorance.

Those born of Kulīnas who adhered to the Vedic code (*śruta-śīla*) and had not in this way become lacking in strength, accepted the daughters of the faultless. Devoid of greed, fortunate and respected, they were foremost in rank, remaining with their own proper wives for

[48]Nula Pañchānana, Goṣṭhī-kathā, in Lālmohan Vidyānidhi, *Sambandhanirṇaya* (Calcutta: M. C. Bhaṭṭāchārya, 1949), I, 297–98. An important text of the Rāḍhī Brāhmaṇs, probably composed in the seventeenth century.

> the sake of having pure sons. Pure Śrotriyas who adhered to the Vedic code worshipped the Kulīna gods with incense and flowers and made offerings of their daughters to them. They held their wives' hands and uttered "svasti" so that they would bear immortal sons; and while blessing them, they said, "Become the equal of Sāvitrī." Those Śrotriyas and Kulīnas who spent their days in happiness for the sake of the birth of pure sons gave birth to the two grades, each favorably inclined toward the other.[49]

The Muslim conquest and the subsequent upsurge of misconduct, and especially of improper marriages, confronted the Brāhmaṇs and Kāyasthas with new problems. True, the problem of how to classify persons and maintain order when caste identities were not clear had already been solved by the former Sena kings, and, as we shall see, their solution remained in use until the nineteenth century. But there were three new problems which aggravated the old and recurring problem of caste mixture and confusion.

First, interaction with the Muslim rulers, as a source of personal wealth, was desirable; yet because contact with them ruined the coded bodily substance of Hindus, it was also an undesirable source of community decline and disorder. This problem was resolved by narrowing the range of acts by which the coded substance of the Veda was to be preserved. During the initial period of conquest, almost any contact with the Muslims was considered to ruin a Hindu's rank, especially if he were a Kulīna. Gradually, during the two centuries following the first conquest, marriage with a Muslim came to be considered the only act by which a Hindu would ruin his rank. This meant that Hindus could work for the Muslim rulers and interact with them in a variety of ways and still preserve their coded bodily substance as Hindus so long as they did not make marriages with the Muslims.[50]

This change in value with respect to Vedic conduct made it possible, by the fifteenth century, for Muslims and Hindus to honor or respect one another instead of using one another merely for gain. Muslim rulers began to show respect to Hindus by giving them offices in their revenue administration and landed estates (*zamindārī*) as well

[49] *Ibid.*, I, 298–99.

[50] M. A. Rahim also views the reorganizaton of the Kulīnas as a response to the Muslim conquest of Bengal and correctly sees it as an effort to maintain "orthodoxy" while interacting with the Muslims, though he is wrong in claiming this to be a result of the "liberal" and "egalitarian" ideas introduced by Muslims into Bengal. See his provocative *Social and Cultural History of Bengal* (Karachi: Pakistan Historical Society, 1963), I, 312–17.

as titles such as Khān.[51] Reciprocally, Hindus began to show respect to the Muslim king of Bengal and to attribute to him the power to do good. Like the former Hindu king, he becomes characterized as a "great king" (*mahārāja*) and he "lord of the earth" (*kṣiti-pati*) who, "like Rāma takes care of (*pāle*) the people (*prajā*)," and "protects the earth through the impartial application of coercive power (*daṇḍa*)."[52] Consistent with the power ascribed to acts of worship, these worshipful acts of honor or respect were seen to transform the Hindus and Muslims of Gauḍa into persons of a single community, bringing about their mutual well-being and prosperity.[53]

A second problem faced by the Brāhmaṇs and Kāyasthas had to do with the sustenance of the Veda within the Hindu community itself. The new stress placed on proper marriage as the sole act of worship by which embodied Vedic rank was to be maintained had its positive side within the Hindu community and especially among the Brāhmaṇs and Kāyasthas. From now on, marriage, which had been considered the necessary but not sufficient act by which embodied rank was sustained, becomes in and of itself the primary act of worship by which rank is to be sustained. At the same time, marriage also becomes the act by which wealth is distributed to deserving and needy Kulīnas. The Hindu king had done this in the past. Now, the Brāhmaṇs and Kāyasthas, by giving the Kulīnas with whom they marry wealth and food, take on this royal function. The genealogies of the Brāhmaṇs and Kāyasthas bear witness to the new centrality of marriage. The space they devote to land and office holding or the manifestation of the nine attributes of the Kulīna code is marginal when compared with the space devoted to marriage gifts and their marvelous effects.

Still another problem confronted by the Brāhmaṇs and Kāyasthas was how to maintain orderly rank relationships among themselves in the absence of a single powerful Hindu king. The new Muslim ruler my have taken on the responsibility of ordering relationships among Muslims and between Hindus and Muslims, but he did not take up the responsibility of ordering Vedic rank relations among the Hindu castes and clans.

[51] *Ibid.*, I, 255.

[52] *Ibid.*, I, 241.

[53] Most interesting in regard to Hindu-Muslim relations is the fact that both unite to form a single community though neither apparently gives up the primacy placed on the worship of divine beings as the ordering act yielding prosperity. Obviously, this is a problem calling for further research.

Councils Form to Uphold Rank

This problem was solved in the fourteenth and fifteenth centuries after about two hundred years of disorder and, perhaps, of experimentation by the formation of subcaste councils (*samāja*). These were the agencies by which the Brāhmaṇs and Kāyasthas agreed to place new emphasis on marriage, reformulated and specified the marriage rules that appear in the genealogies, and, after improvising on the organizational schemes of Vallāla Sena, reclassified the Brāhmaṇs and Kāyasthas according to these new criteria. Operating as structural replacements for the Hindu king, these councils were guided in their work of judging marriage conduct and recognizing ranks by newly generated specialists—genealogists—and by a local notable of the subcaste who acted as "council-master" (*samāja-pati*). The famous genealogist, Devīvara, himself led the council of the Rāḍhī Brāhmaṇs.[54] Udayaṇācārya,[55] Danuja-marddana De,[56] and Purandar Khān Basu,[57] all of whom were local "kings" (*rāja*), convened councils in their respective subcastes—Vārendra Brāhmaṇ, Vaṅgaja Kāyastha, and Dakṣiṇa-rāḍhī Kāyastha.

The formation of these councils represents a significant change in the Hindu community. Previously, the single Hindu king of Gauḍa had performed tasks of this kind without the aid of genealogists and only the most passive concurrence of the persons summoned to his council. Now, after his destruction, the relationship between king and council is reversed. The local notables, no longer entitled "great king" (*mahārāja*), but merely "king" (*rājā*), receive their power to act from the council. As one text succinctly puts it, "Look, the power (*śakti*) of the council (*samāja*) sits on the head of royal power (*rāja-śakti*)."[58]

The first council of the Dakṣiṇa-rāḍhī Kāyasthas is said to have met during the lives of those who were the thirteenth generational descendants of the Kāyastha brought by Ādiśūra. The master of this council (*goṣṭhī-pati*) was Gopīnāth Basu, a Dakṣiṇa-rāḍhī Kāyastha Kulīna who was a minister of the Muslim ruler of Bengal

[54] Majumdār, *Gauḍe Brāhmaṇ*, pp. 206–9.

[55] *Ibid.*, pp. 101–8.

[56] Braj Sundar Mitra, *Candradvīper Rāja-vaṃśa o Vaṅgaja Kāyasthagaṇer Vivaraṇa* (Bariśāl: Kumudakānta Basu, 1913), pp. 6–24.

[57] Vasu, *Vaṅger Jātīya Itihāsa*, VI, Pt. I, 99–112.

[58] Nula Pañchānana, "Goṣṭhī-katha," in Vidyānidhi, *Sambandhanirṇaya*, I, 300.

in the last quarter of the fifteenth century and held the title Purandar Khān:[59] "Purandar came from heaven to earth and brought the Kulīnas together in order to convene a council (*sabhā*)."[60] He acted to stay the decline of proper order by making the clans and grades in his subcaste into units ranked by their marriage codes:

> For some time in this way [after the progenitors of the Kulīnas had left Gauḍa and settled on the banks of the Gaṅgā] the clans increased equally and persons of equal clans made marriages with each other. There were no high or low families and marriages were firm; generations were not fixed, they were approximate. In the thirteenth generation, Purandar, the regulator of the clans, was born in the house of Īśāna in the Basu clan. This great king filled the world with famous acts and began the arrangement of the clans (*kula*).[61]

Modifying the organization scheme inherited from Vallāla Sena, Purandar organized the persons of the Ghosh, Basu, and Mitra clans into ranked families, using the seniority of their birth as the criterion: "He recorded in proper order the six great communities (*samāja*) of the three clans, their six respective Prakṛtas (progenitors) and their younger ranked brothers . . . according to the principle of the seniority (*jyeṣṭhatā*) of the eldest."[62] Having done this, he and the council then formulated a revised marriage code for the Kulīna clans, enjoining them to worship each other by making reciprocal exchanges of daughters, thereby uniting them in an alliance or union of equals: "The king convened a council of Ghosh and the others and shone as he tied the alliance (*mela*)."[63] He also formulated a marriage code enjoining the Maulikas to make nonreciprocal exchanges with the Kulīnas in every generation: "Purandar Basu generated high rank through the following: the fixing of the generations, the *ādyarasa* [gift of an eldest daughter of a Maulika to a Kulīna], and the *pratisāraṇa* [gift of a younger daughter of a Kulīna to a Maulika]."[64] Finally, the council instituted the practice of keeping genealogical records and brought in genealogists to assist it in testing and judging conduct: "From now on people would make judgments after first consulting genealogies."[65]

[59] *Ibid.*, VI, Pt. I, 103.

[60] Nandarāma Mitra, "Ḍhākurī," in Vasu, *Vaṅger Jātīya Itihāsa*, VI, Pt. I, 105.

[61] Nandarāma Mitra, "Dakṣiṇa-rāḍhīya Kārikā," in Vasu, *Vaṅger Jātīya Itihāsa*, VI, Pt. I, 106.

[62] *Ibid.*

[63] Ghaṭakāchārya, "Kārikā," in Vasu, *Vaṅger Jātihāsa*, VI, Pt. I, 107.

[64] Nandarāma Mitra, Kulajī, fol. 1.

[65] *Ibid.*

The shift to marriage as the primary criterion of rank and the organization of the Kulīnas into newly devised grades also took place in the Rāḍhī Brāhmaṇ subcaste:

> Kulīnas and Śrotriyas had made marriages in all directions; all were equal in clan rank, there were no distinctions. The Kulīnas and Śrotriyas who had been made separate by Vallala afterwards became high (*ucca*) and low (*nīca*). Among the Śrotriyas, three different grades—high, middle, and low—came into existence. Today, there are Kulīnas and Śrotrīyas in the same *gotras*; even those of the same *gotra* are not equal in prestige. Now the Kulīnas are divided into thirty-six unions (*mela*). They are ranked in high and low clans (*vaṃśa*) according to their good and bad marriages.[66]

These subcaste councils, which were innovations of the fourteenth and fifteenth centuries, met repeatedly throughout succeeding centuries and in every Brāhmaṇ and Kāyastha *jāti*. They tested and judged marriage conduct and maintained Vedic rank order in their own terms among the persons who claimed to be Brāhmaṇs and Kāyasthas, using the modified classification scheme first conceived by Vallāla Sena. Just how these councils operated will be taken up in Chapter IV.

To sum up, the Bengali Brāhmaṇs and Kāyasthas viewed their middle period system of castes and clans neither as changeless nor as a deviant with respect to the ancient and universal four-*varṇa* concept of society depicted in the *śāstras* and *purāṇas*. Rather, they saw it as a particular, regional variant of the latter, containing within it the coded bodily substances of the four *varṇas* but in a transformed state.

Jātis and *kulas* were all defined by the possession of their particular, distinct, and inherited coded bodily substances, but they were also defined by their proper combination with other coded substances, those of territory, occupation, and worship. The Brāhmaṇs and Kāyasthas of middle period Bengal placed the highest value on the coded substance of Vedic worship as that which provided order, well-being, and prosperity for their society. Hence, for them the maintenance of a unified, orderly, and prosperous community, while requiring the maintenance of the integrity of the coded bodily substances by which castes and clans were defined, called above all for the uninterrupted preservation of the Veda as differentially embodied in the castes and clans of the Hindu community.

[66]Nula Pañchānana, "Goṣṭhī-kathā," in Vidyānidhi, *Sambandhanirṇaya*, I, 299–300.

Three kinds of conduct were of central importance in sustaining the embodied Veda: the worship conduct of the Brāhmaṇ, the fullest embodiment of the Veda among men and the performer of Vedic acts of worship; the protective conduct of the king, the par excellence worshiper and feeder of the Brāhmaṇ; and, finally, the marriage conduct of the castes. Improper conduct on the part of the Brāhmaṇ worshiper, the king, or the castes was held to cause the improper mixing of the coded substances defining the community of castes and clans, ruining or inferiorizing the Veda immanent in them.

Since the quality of conduct in these three areas was seen to oscillate between good and bad over time, there were periods of order and prosperity in which the integrity of coded bodily substances was maintained. These alternated with periods of disorder and want in which coded bodily substances were mixed and inferiorized, precipitating systemic changes in the morphology of the Hindu community. The changes which resulted in the generation of the Hindu community of middle period Bengal occurred in four stages.

Stage one, initiated by the improper conduct of King Veṇa, who caused the four *varṇas* to intermarry, saw the transformation of the four *varṇa* community into a two-*varṇa* community. After the remaining pure Brāhmaṇs killed Veṇa with Vedic *mantras* and replaced him with his son, Pṛthu, he and the Brāhmaṇs restored order and prosperity by classifying the mixed offspring into two *varṇas*, the Brāhmaṇ, consisting of Vedic Brāhmaṇs and fallen Brāhmaṇs, and the Śūdra, consisting of the Kāyastha and other *sat* occupational *jātis* partially possessed of the Veda and of the *asat*, not so endowed, making a total of thirty-six.

Stage two was initiated by ignorant Brāhmaṇs who could not perform a Vedic act of worship for King Ādiśūra who then invited five Vedic Brāhmaṇs and their trusty Kāyastha servants, the ancestors of the Kulīnas, the fullest Brāhmaṇ and Śūdra embodiments of the Veda in middle period Bengal. After completing the worship and receiving worshipful gifts of wealth from the king, they settle in Bengal, thereby regenerating its two-*varṇa* community.

A subsequent king, Vallāla Sena, acted in stage three to transform the Brāhmaṇs and Kāyasthas of Bengal into subcastes containing grades ranked with respect to their embodiment of the Veda. The descendants of the Brāhmaṇs and Kāyastha imported from Kanauja, settled in the different countries making up the kingdom of Gauḍa, had begun to intermarry with the local and inferior Brāhmaṇs and Śūdras of Bengal, threatening thereby to ruin their superior embodied ranks. So, Vallāla Sena, in order to preserve the integrity of the community, summoned them to court. He solved the problem of regional variations that had arisen by dividing them into territorial *jātis* or subcastes, for example, Dakṣiṇa-rāḍhī Kāyastha and Rāḍhī Brāhmaṇ, each with its own territorially distinct substance and code. More important, he tried to solve the problem of generic mixing by generating a dual or alternate scheme which was capable of classifying the population of Gauḍa either into the already existing ranked occupational *jātis* or into new ranked worship *jātis* or grades within the Brāhmaṇ and Kāyastha subcastes. Testing and judging the conduct of the Brāhmaṇs and Śūdras invited to court, he declared the descendants of the imported Brāhmaṇs and Śūdras who had sustained their embodied Vedic ranks, so crucial to the well-being and prosperity of the entire community, by following their superior ninefold worship code, to be Kulīnas; those who had not, he classed as lower Vaṃśajas. The fallen and indigenous Brāhmaṇs and Śūdras who had purified themselves by associating with the Kulīnas he classed as Siddha or "actualized" Śrotriya Brāhmaṇs or Maulika Kāyasthas; those who had, not he dubbed Sādhya or "latent." This system of ranked worship *jātis*, which accommodated social mobility and at the same time maintained order, was adhered to by the Brāhmaṇs and Kāyasthas throughout the middle period.

The fourth stage in the transformation of the Hindu community began with the Muslim conquest of Bengal. Considered at first as barbarians, contact with whom ruined Vedic rank, the new Muslim conquerors removed the Hindu king of Gauḍa and replaced him with their own king. Many Brāhmaṇs and Kāyasthas, including even the Kulīnas, began, out of need or greed, to seek wealth under this new king and so ruined their embodied ranks. Moreover, unrestrained by the firm hand of a Hindu king, Hindus began once again to make improper mixed marriages.

The Brāhmaṇs and Kāyasthas met these new threats to the integrity of the Veda in two ways. First, so that they might establish a proper community relationship with the Muslims, the Brāhmaṇs and Kāyasthas narrowed their standard of good conduct to marriage alone. This new stress on marriage had a profound effect. Previously, Brāhmaṇs and Kāyasthas had sustained their inherited ranks and gained fame and respect not only by making proper marriages but also by adhering to their manifold Vedic codes. Now, the way to sustain rank and the path to fame was to be through marriage alone. Second, the Brāhmaṇs and Kāyasthas moved to replace the Hindu king by reorganizing themselves within their local communities. Collectively taking up the royal functions of the Hindu king, the Brāhmaṇs and Kāyasthas formed their own councils in order to judge their own conduct, organized the Kulīnas into ranked grades, and placed the other Brāhmaṇs and Kāyasthas in proper order according to the newly codified marriage criteria so that prosperity might return. This transformation, which placed stress on marriage and on the acts of caste councils, persisted down into the nineteenth century.

Chapter III

WORSHIP AND THE TRANSMUTATION OF RANKS

Feeding the Gods Improves Embodied Rank

The sharing of coded bodily substance was the feature that defined the relationships of persons belonging to the same *jāti* or *kula*. The purpose of this chapter is to show how exchanges of coded substances or gifts related persons of different *jātis* and *kulas* belonging to the same community. In particular, the argument here will be that gifts of wealth (*dhana*) and food (*khādya*), which had as their purpose the nourishment of the gods, were characterized as acts of worship (*yajña*, *pūjā*) and were considered to be the actions that maintained, developed, or even improved the embodied ranks of persons, castes, and clans in middle period Bengal. Hence, I shall refer to these acts of worship as "defining actions."

Acts of worship were actions involving offerings to the gods and were considered to bring about the well-being (*maṅgala*, *hita*, etc.) and prosperity (*śrī*, *lakṣmī*, etc.) of the community in general and of the persons and genera participating in them in particular. As such, acts of worship were both general and complex. Their larger, more diffuse purpose encompassed within it many specific purposes, only one of which was to maintain and transform coded bodily substance in its inherited rank aspect. Since our primary concern is the study of rank, we shall refer only to those purposes of worship which directly deal with rank.

Central to an understanding of how worship affected rank and consistent with the notion that embodied ranks, as coded bodily substances, were living entities is the process which I shall refer to as "transmutation." The embodied ranks of genera and persons, conceived of as living entities, were thought to undergo one of two life processes during a person's lifetime, the one a kind of "growing" or "maturing" and "uplifting" process, the other a kind of "decaying," "degenerating," and "lowering" process.

Inherited rank (*jāti*, *kula*), whether generic or personal, was thought to undergo one of these two opposed processes of transmutation during a person's lifetime. Each particular substance or entity was thought to have an inborn, coded capacity to undergo actions having as their purpose the transmutation of that substance into its subtler "fruit." The Bengali saying, "As is the action (*karma*), so is the fruit (*phala*),"[1] succinctly states this cultural concept. Through the proper actions of refinement (*saṃskāra*), heating (*tapas*), cooking (*pāka*), purification (*śuddhi*), realization (*siddhi*), increase (*vṛddhi*), preservation (*rākhā*), and so forth, a substance was transmuted into its higher fruits. Conversely, through the improper actions of decrease (*hrāsa*), breaking (*bhaṅga*), ruin (*nāśa*), destruction (*kṣaya*), and so forth, a substance was transmuted into its lower fruits. Thus, by refining, purifying, increasing, preserving, strengthening, and realizing his inherited rank, a person was able to transmute it into its superior fruits—fame (*yaśa*), reputation (*kīrtti*), respect (*sanmāna*), name (*nāma*), praise (*praśaṃsā*), greatness (*mahimā*, *gaurava*), prestige (*maryyādā*), luster (*śobhana*), and so forth. Conversely, by decreasing, ruining, destroying, lowering, and causing it to fall, a person transmuted his inherited rank into its inferior fruits—disrespect (*apamāna*), shame (*lajjā*), rebuke (*nindā*), bad name (*durnāma*), disgrace (*kalaṅka*), scandal (*apavāda*), and so forth.

A person as a casteman or clansman was believed to transform his inherited corporate rank into its superior fruits by performing those acts and, in particular, the acts of worship enjoined by the code of his caste or clan. Conversely, a person was thought to transmute his inherited corporate rank into its inferior fruits by not acting according to the inborn moral code of his genus. To follow his generic code and transmute his inherited rank into superior fruits was, of course, considered to be the proper goal of a person defined as a casteman or clansman. The pursuit of other goals at the expense of worship was considered an improper goal.

All actions were conceived of by Bengali Hindus as belonging to four categories (*catur-varga*) defined by the goals (*artha*) of these actions. The first three of these were *kāma*, the "desire for enjoyment" (*bhoga-vāsanā*); *artha*, the "*gain* of wealth" (*dhanārjana*); and *dharma*, the "realization of one's code for conduct" (*dharma-sādhana*). What this latter meant in middle period Bengal, of course,

[1]Sushīl Kumār De, *Bāṃlā Pravāda* (Calcutta: A. Mukherji, 1952), p. 686.

was the proper performance of acts of worship, upon which the ordered well-being and prosperity of the community depended. And the par excellence act of worship was one involving the gift of wealth and food for the purpose of nourishing a divine being.

These three goals (*tri-varga*), the ones appropriate to the class of living beings, those defined by the possession of bodies, were, in turn, sharply distinguished from the fourth and ultimate goal (*apavarga*) of a person, *mukti*, or "liberation," the separation of a person's pure, irreducible coded substance (*ātman*) from his body (*śarīra*) and its permanent reabsorption into *brahman*, the coded substance out of which the entire universe was generated. Pursuit of each the first three of these goals by appropriate action was though to be necessary for every person belonging, by virtue of his possession of a body, to the domain of birth (*janma*) and action (*karma*), the world of perpetual flux (*saṃsāra*). Thus, without the desire for enjoyment a person could not gain wealth, and without wealth, a person could not perform acts of worship, could not feed the gods.

Though pursuit of all three of these goals was required, it was thought that each preceding goal in the series had to be properly subordinated to the succeeding goal in order that the latter could be attained. Thus, the goal of *kāma*, the desire for enjoyment, was to be subordinated to the goal of *artha*, the gain of wealth, and both of these were in turn to be subordinated to the goal of *dharma*, the performance of worship. The inborn worship code (*dharma*) of a genus, the actions by which its persons sustained and nourished themselves and others, thus encompassed the goals and actions of enjoyment and wealth.

While the worship codes of the castes and clans varied in the particular actions they enjoined, all of them subordinated the desire for enjoyment to the gain of wealth and both of these to the proper performance of worship. No matter what his particular code, therefore, a person as a casteman or clansman was believed to transmute his inherited rank into its superior fruits by subordinating desire and gain to the worship conduct enjoined on his genus. Conversely, a person was thought to transmute his inherited corporate rank into its inferior fruits by subordinating the worship conduct enjoined on his genus to desire or gain.

Variations in action and in the fruits obtained through action are explained by variations in a person's capacity to subordinate personal enjoyment and gain to worship. Every person was born under different circumstances, the product of many discrete past births and actions. Accordingly, every person had his own discrete, composite, inborn code for conduct (*svadharma*). Thus, in some persons the goal of worship predominated whereas in others the goal of gain predominated. The progenitors of the Kulīnas, who properly fed the Vedic gods, and Kings Ādiśūra and Vallāla Sena, who fed the divinely endowed Kulīnas, are models of persons in whom the proper goal of worship predominated. So, too, are the indigenous Śūdras who worshiped the Śūdra Kulīnas with wealth and food and intermarried with them. As the results of their moral actions, the progenitors of the Kulīnas obtained superior respect and fame; as a result of theirs, Ādiśūra obtained happiness, and Vallāla Sena, liberation itself.

The indigenous Śūdras obtained as the fruit of their acts of worship the transmutation of their inferior Śūdra rank into superior Kāyastha rank. Puruṣottama Datta, the Madhyadeśa Śūdra who became a Maulika instead of a Kulīna, is a model of a person in whom the goal of selfish desire (*abhimāna*, *ahaṃkāra*) for superior rank predominated over the proper goal of worship. The kings Lakṣmaṇa Sena and Nityānanda are models of persons in whom passionate desires (*moha*) predominated. Finally, the Brāhmaṇs who abandoned the Veda and Vedic worship after the coming of Muslim rule are models of persons in whom greed for wealth (*artha-lobha*) predominated. All of these persons who subordinated the goal of worship to those of desire and gain obtained inferior fruits as the results of their actions. The selfish Datta became devoid of high rank, the lustful Lakṣmaṇa Sena lost his kingdom, passionate Nityānanda obtained seventy-two inferior sons, and the greedy Brāhmaṇs lost their superior ranks as Vedic Brāhmaṇs.

Let us now turn to an examination of how acts of worship maintained and transmuted embodied ranks in middle period Bengal, looking first at caste ranks and then at clan ranks.

Worship of the Brāhmaṇ and Caste Rank

Gods and Brāhmaṇs

The actions by which caste ranks were thought to be sustained and transmuted in the middle period were acts of worship involving the exchange of wealth, the source of food, and food, the source of a genus' bodily substance and rank. The various kinds of wealth and food were thought to have higher and lower values for a genus according to their capacity to sustain and transmute the genus' rank. In general, more valuable substances appear to have been those requiring the greater number of transmutations before they turned into coded bodily substance or rank. Wealth (*dhana*, *sampatti*)—land, cash, jewelry, and so forth—were considered to be substances more valuable than food (*khādya*, *khābār*, *bhakṣya*) because they had to be converted into food before they could be eaten and transmuted into bodily substance. Among the types of food, uncooked refined foodstuffs (*āma-vastu*, *sidhā*) were considered more valuable than cooked (*pakva*, *siddha*) foods. Of cooked food, special foods marked by their being cooked in clarified butter (*ājya-pakva*, *ghṛtānna*, *ghī-bhāt*), in a pan (*kandu-pakva*), sugar (*miṣṭānna*, *miṣṭ*), oil (*taila-pakva*, *tele-bhājā*), and milk (*payaḥpakva*, *pāyasānna*, *paramānna*) were all considered to be higher in nutritional value than more quickly digested, ordinary, umarked food (*anna*, *bhāt*) such as rice (*cāul*) and lentils (*dāl*) boiled in water. Cooked food uncontaminated by its mixture with human bodily substances was in turn considered to be more valuable than leavings (*ucchiṣṭānna*, *ẽṭo*), food contaminated with saliva and so forth, and therefore ruined.

The act of worship (*yajña*, *pūjā*), properly executed, was the act of "proper order" (*dharma*) par excellence. As we have already seen, the inherited ranks of the occupational *jātis* within the Hindu community were synonymous not with the relative values or qualities of the coded substances of Vedic worship they embodied. Hence, the castes were thought to sustain and transmute their embodied ranks by the exchanges of wealth and food made on the occasion of a Vedic act of worship. It was not only a statement of high and low rank in which the lower honored the higher; it was also an act requiring the subordination of enjoyment and gain to the maintenance of proper order in the community.

The inborn code for conduct of the Vedic Brāhmaṇ enjoined him to worship the gods with Vedic *mantras*. The gods (*deva*) were considered to be higher than the Brāhmaṇ because whereas the Brāhmaṇ worshiped them, they did not worship the Brāhmaṇ. Exchanges of food enacted this high and low relationship. Brāhmaṇs could offer both uncooked and cooked food to the gods. If properly prepared so as not to be ruined, even his boiled rice was considered suitable as life-sustaining food (*bhoga*) for the gods. The gods were more powerful and higher, however, because their leavings, food which from their point of view was ruined, were considered to be "benefits" (*prasāda*) by the Brāhmaṇ, having a higher value than any food which he himself could prepare and eat:

> After purifying himself with the evening worship (*sandhyā*), a Brāhmaṇ should constantly serve me and eat my leavings (*prasāda*). A thing not offered to me is considered inedible (*abhakṣya*). Food not offered to Viṣṇu is like feces and water like urine. That Brāhmaṇ who constantly eats the leavings of Viṣṇu is liberated while alive (*jīvan-mukta*).[2]

> A Brāhmaṇ who eats the leavings of Viṣṇu is liberated while alive and purifies all pilgrimage places, the earth, and mankind. Without a doubt, he gains at every step the fruit of bathing at all the pilgrimage places, observing all the vows, and performing the Aśvamedha sacrifice. He is pure like fire and wind and as bright as the sun. He never has to see the world of Yama, the messenger of Yama, or Yama himself, even in a dream. He becomes an attendant of Viṣṇu and spends his time in great happiness in the world of Vaikuṇṭha with Viṣṇu. A Brāhmaṇ who is the servant of Viṣṇu never falls.[3]

Thus, by giving away all his food to the gods and then eating whatever they left, the Vedic Brāhmaṇ of the middle period was thought to not only honor the gods but also to subordinate his own enjoyment and gain to the maintenance of proper order in the community. As a result, his embodied rank was transformed into its superior fruits.

Brāhmaṇs and Śūdras

The inborn code for conduct of the Śūdra enjoined him to serve the Brāhmaṇ. The Vedic Brāhmaṇ was considered higher than the Śūdra because while the Śūdra served him, he served only the gods, not the Śūdra. Exchanges of food enacted this high and low relationship. The Śūdra offered wealth, uncooked food, and, in some cases, even special cooked food to the Brāhmaṇ; these, if properly prepared and offered under proper circumstances, were thought to be suitable

[2] *Brahma-vaivartta Purāṇa*, trans into Bengali by Pañchānana Tarkaratna (Calcutta: Natavar Chakravartti, 1925), pp. 695–96.

[3] *Ibid.*, p. 696. The Aśvamedha is one of the more elaborate Vedic sacrifices; Yama is the god of death; Vaikuṇṭha is a heaven particular to Visnu.

as nourishing food for the Brāhmaṇ. Yet the Śūdra was not as powerful or high as the Brāhmaṇ. First, the Śūdra could offer wealth and uncooked foods to the Vedic gods, but he could not, like the Brāhmaṇ, offer cooked food, either special or ordinary. These were considered to be leavings, a decaying food substance unsuitable as nourishment for the gods: "How will the Śūdra give boiled rice (*rādhā-bhāt*) to the gods? Food cooked by him is [considered by the gods to be] leavings (*ucchiṣṭa*) while his uncooked foods (*āma*) are [considered to be] cooked foods (*pakva*)."[4]

Second, the Śūdra could offer wealth and uncooked food to the Brāhmaṇ, but he could not usually offer cooked food to the Brāhmaṇ: "The uncooked foods (*āma-vastu*) given by a Śūdra are considered to be cooked (*pakva*) and the cooked food (*pakvānna*) of a Śūdra is proven to be leavings (*ucchiṣṭa*). There is a saying in the code-book (*śāstra*), 'That which is unasked for is nectar (*amṛta*).' Thus, [accepting] unrequested uncooked foods from a Śūdra is not an impure act."[5] On the other hand, the Brāhmaṇ could give the Śūdra ordinary cooked food and even his leavings in exchange for services rendered. These foods were considered by the Śūdra to be greater in life-sustaining power than even the uncooked food of the Śūdra. Hence, by making proper offering to the Brāhmaṇ of wealth and uncooked food, the Śūdra of the middle period in Bengal was believed not only to subordinate his enjoyment and wealth to the maintenance of proper order but to transmute his rank into its superior fruits—"life" (*jīvana*) and the "attainment of all desires" (*sarvva-kāmāpti*).[6]

A distinction was made in middle period Bengal between the higher (*sat*, "good, pure") Śūdra castes and the lower (*asat*, "not good, ordinary") Śūdra castes. The inborn code for conduct of the higher Śūdra, and especially of the highest Śūdra, the Kāyastha, enjoined him to serve the Vedic Brāhmaṇ with devotion (*bhakti*) and to induce him to perform Vedic worship on his behalf (without the Vedic *mantras*) and to eat his special cooked food by giving him offerings of wealth ranging from land grants (*brahmottara*) to cash honoraria (*dakṣiṇā*): "The Kāyastha is a higher Śūdra having mastery in cooked food (*pāka*) and the Vedic act of worship (*yajña*). By the words, 'the cooked food of a Śūdra,' I mean cooked in clarified

[4]Nula Pañchānana, "Goṣṭhī-kathā," in Lālmohan Vidyānidhi, *Sambandhanirṇaya* (Calcutta: M. C. Bhaṭṭāchārya, 1949), I, 275.

[5]*Ibid.*, 203.

[6]Raghunandana Bhaṭṭāchārya, *Śūdra-kṛtya-vicāraṇa-tattva*, in his *Institutes of the Hindoo Religion* (Śrīrāmpur: Srirampur Press, 1834–35), pp. 361–62.

butter and so forth (*ājya-pakvādi*)."[7] The higher Śūdra was higher than the lower because while both served the Brāhmaṇ, the higher Śūdra served only the Vedic Brāhmaṇ and not the lower Śūdra. As usual, exchanges of food stated this high and low relationship. The special cooked food of a higher Śūdra was considered to be suitable food for a Brāhmaṇ, but that of a lower, ordinary Śūdra was not: "The cooked food of an [ordinary] Śūdra taken in the house of an ordinary Śūdra is like blood (*śoṇita*) to a Brāhmaṇ, but in the case of the pure Śūdra, who is devoted to the Brāhmaṇ, it is otherwise."[8]

Since the acceptance of cooked food from a Śūdra was, however, considered to lower the rank of the Brāhmaṇ, the higher Śūdra had to induce the invited Brāhmaṇ to take his food by offering him a cash honorarium for the increase of the Brāhmaṇ's prosperity. The manner in which his honorarium was offered and accepted was important. If the Brāhmaṇ accepted the wealth as a favor from the Śūdra so that he could realize his code for conduct, then it was an act conducive to the Śūdra's welfare. If, however, the Brāhmaṇ indicated his desire for the wealth by asking for it, then it was considered to be an act in which the well-being of the Śūdra was subordinated to his own enjoyment and gain:

> The high caste and well-to-do Śūdras never eat in the house of a Brāhmaṇ without paying for the honour a *praṇāmī*, or salutation fee, of at least one rupee. The Brāhmaṇ host never insists on such payment, and in fact it is usually forced upon him. But when a Brāhmaṇ eats in the house of a Śūdra on a ceremonial occasion, the payment of a fee by the host to the guest is a *sine qua non*. This fee is called *bhojana dakṣiṇā*, and ordinarily varies from one anna to one rupee.[9]

When the higher or "orthodox" Śūdra was invited to a Brāhmaṇ's house, he was additionally favored with the leavings of the Brāhmaṇ whereas, again, the lower Śūdra was not:

> When a Brāhmaṇ invites a Śūdra, the latter is usually asked to partake of the host's *prasāda*, or favour, in the shape of the leavings of his plate. Orthodox Śūdras actually take offence if invited by the use of any other formula. No Śūdra is allowed to eat in the same room or at the same time with Brāhmaṇs. While the Brāhmaṇ guests eat, the Śūdras have to wait in a different part of the house. It is not, however,

[7] Nula Pañchānana, "Goṣṭhi-kathā," in Vidyānidhi, *Sambandhanirṇaya*, I, 203.
[8] *Ibid.*
[9] Jogendra Nāth Bhaṭṭāchārya, *Hindu Castes and Sects* (Calcutta: Editions Indian, 1968), p. 17. First published in 1896.

> to be supposed that the Śūdras take any offence at such treatment. On the contrary, they not only wait patiently, but, in some places, insist upon eating the leavings of the Brāhmaṇs, and refuse to eat anything from clean plates.[10]

The Brāhmaṇ also favored him with water dirtied by his big toe. This was considered to be "nectar," higher in value than any food prepared by the pure Śūdra:

> The more orthodox Śūdras carry their veneration for the priestly class to such an extent, that they will not cross the shadow of a Brāhmaṇ, and it is not unusual for them to be under a vow not to eat any food in the morning, before drinking *Vipra-caraṇamṛta*, i.e., water in which the toe of a Brāhmaṇ has dipped. On the other hand, the pride of the Brāhmaṇ is such that they do not bow even to the images of the gods worshipped in a Śūdra's house by Brāhmaṇ priests.[11]

Thus, by offering the Brāhmaṇ an honorarium of wealth as an inducement to perform Vedic worship or eat his special cooked food and by eating his leavings or drinking his foot nectar, the higher Śūdra was believed to transmute his inherited rank into its superior fruits.

Originally, exchanges of wealth and food had merely accompanied the elaborate Vedic worship of the gods and the personal service of the Brāhmaṇ. Now in the ever declining Kali age of the middle period when many Vedic Brāhmaṇs do not perform Vedic worship and many Śūdras do not earn their livelihood by rendering personal service to the Brāhmaṇs, the exchanges of wealth and food made on the occasion of a Tantric act of worship (*pūjā*) are often equated with Vedic worship (*yajña*) and service. The mere offering of food to the gods is seen to be equivalent to Vedic worship by the Brāhmaṇ; inducing a Brāhmaṇ to eat special cooked food by giving him an honorarium is seen to be the offering of Vedic worship by the Śūdra; and gifts to Brāhmaṇs are seen as service. Conversely, the leavings of the gods accepted by the Brāhmaṇ and the leavings of the Brāhmaṇs accepted by the *sat* Śūdra come increasingly to be equated with the powerful coded substances of the Veda itself. Thus, exchanges of wealth and food themselves come to be seen as the defining actions by which a person or caste transmutes his inherited rank into its higher or lower fruits: "In the Kali [age] life (*prāṇa*) depends on

[10] *Ibid.*, p. 16.
[11] *Ibid.*

food (*anna*); [hence] fasting is not praised. Instead of fasting, giving (*dāna*) alone is prescribed. O great queen [Kālī]! In the Kali [age] giving causes the realization of everything (*sarvva-siddhi-kara*)."[12]

By making those exchanges of wealth and food enjoined in their generic codes, persons were thought to transmute their inherited caste ranks into their superior fruits. On the other hand, persons who departed from these minimum norms because of their particular circumstances were thought to improperly subordinate the well-being and prosperity of the community to their own enjoyment and gain. They thereby transmuted their inherited rank into an inferior form and separated themselves from their share in the community's prosperity. This is, for example, what happened to Brāhmaṇs who, out of ignorance of the Vedic code improperly desired and accepted cooked food from ordinary Śūdra:

> When in difficulty, or in the position of a guest (*atithi*), goods given by a Śūdra are not to be despised; and the uncooked food of a pure Śūdra is not undesirable to a Brāhmaṇ. However, ignorant Brāhmaṇs, making many excuses, repeatedly ate the cooked food (*pakvānna*) of the ordinary Śūdras. When they saw this, the virtuous one whispered it among themselves and gradually informed each other of all these faulty acts (*doṣa*). The faulty ones became obstacles in the community in connection with acts of worship; fallen (*patita*), suspended (*sthakita*), and inferior in acts of worship (*kriyā-hīna*), they stand isolated.[13]

Worship of the Kulīna and Clan Rank

Marriage: Seed and Field

Proper marriage (*vivāha*, *biyā*), the gift (*dāna*, *pradāna*), or acceptance (*grahaṇa*, *ādāna*) of a daughter was the chief of the ten-*saṃskāras* or "refining acts of worship" causing the purification of a person's body (*śarīra-śuddhi*).[14] These *saṃskāras* were, in turn, included among the enjoined acts of worship of a clan (*kulācāra*).

One of the specific purposes of marriage was to provide a caste and its clans with children, and especially sons, embodying the coded substance of their parents' caste and clan. Only children

[12] *Mahānirvāna-tantra*, ed. Jībānanda Vidyāsāgara (Calcutta: New Valmiki Press, 1884), p. 182.

[13] Pañchānana, "Goṣṭhī-kathā," in Vidyanidhi, *Sambandhanirṇaya*, I, 205–6.

[14] Sures Chandra Banerji, *Smṛtiśāstre Bāṅgālī* (Calcutta: A. Mukherji, 1961), pp. 47, 74–85.

having the same substance and code as their parents were considered capable of taking up the caste's particular livelihood, and only children so qualified were considered able to transform their parents into benevolent ancestors (*pitṛ*) after death and to worship them with offerings of food (*śrāddha*) on appropriate occasions.

Castes and clans contained in their codes complementary marriage rules, which, it is supposed, operated to ensure the birth of proper offspring. The occupational, territorial, and worship *jātis* and, particularly, the universal *varṇas* contained in their codes a rule enjoining men to marry women "sharing the same coded bodily substance" (*savarṇa*). The complement of this rule, contained in the clan codes of a particular caste, enjoined men to marry women "not sharing the same coded bodily substance" (*asagotra*). These two rules are the well-known rules of caste "endogamy" and clan "exogamy."

The reason for these rules and, especially, the endogamy rule, as stated in much of the sociological literature, is that "status" or "membership" in a caste, viewed in Western dualistic terms either as a legal, religious, or cultural thing, or, by contrast, as a natural, racial thing, a matter of blood purity, was transmitted by bilateral descent. On the surface, this reason appears to be correct. We have, in fact, already seen that intercaste marriages were seen to lead to the mixing of the castes (*varṇa-saṅkara*) and that the offspring of such marriages were inferior hybrids or anomalies. There is, however, a problem with this explanation and one that is crucial to this study of marriage and rank.

Scholars have long noted that many castes, including the Brāhmaṇs and Kāyasthas of Bengal, are organized into ranked grades of clans, the higher of which "are regarded as of purer blood"[15] than the lower. According to the theory of bilateral descent, these grades should be endogamous if they are to retain their integrity over the generations. Yet castes organized into ranked grades almost invariably have rules enjoining, or at least permitting, the gifts of daughters of the lower grades to the higher (hypergamy, "marrying up") or the gifts of daughters of the higher grades to the lower (hypogamy, "marrying down"). Since the lower grades of Brāhmaṇs and Kāyasthas in Bengal included persons of the lower Brāhmaṇ and Śūdra castes, the making of hypergamous and hypogamous marriages

[15] J. H. Hutton, *Caste in India. Its Nature, Function, and Origins* (Oxford: University Press, 1961), p. 54.

among the ranked grades in these castes would mean, in effect, that persons were making intercaste marriages. Yet in Bengal (and in other regions of North India as well), the children of such marriages were in no way considered anomalous and invariably acquired the rank of their father.

Similar problems also arise in connection with the clan membership of the women themselves. According to the Bengalis, a *kula* or clan properly included all of the male descendants (*santāna-santati*) of the clan's ancestral male as well as the unmarried daughters of the clan (*kula-kanyā*). Once these daughters were properly given away in marriage to men of other clans, however, they ceased to be persons of their fathers' clan. On the other hand, the wives of the clan (*kula-vadhū*), persons not usually considered to be members of a "patrilineal descent group" by anthropologists, were, when properly accepted from other clans, included in the clan. Among the Brāhmaṇs and Kāyasthas of middle period Bengal, even wives taken from other clans of higher or lower ranked grades were included along with offspring of such marriages. What is more, all of the persons belonging to the clan, in consonance with the assumed nonduality of substance and code, were thought to be related not only by the same shared code for conduct but also by the same shared bodily substance.

It should be obvious at this point that these "problems" were not really problems at all for the actors in the social system. They are problems for Europeans, Americans, and anthropologists only because Hindu ideas about heredity and marriage differ from Western ones. If we can specify what these cultural differences are, then these problems can be solved.

Bengali Hindu ideas about heredity and marriage are expounded metaphorically in the "seed and field" theory of human reproduction, a theory which is old and widespread in Hindu India.[16] This theory holds that conception takes place as a result of the mixing of the semen (*śukra*) of a genitor (*janaka*) with the uterine blood (*śoṇita*) of a genetrix (*jananī*) in her womb (*garbha*) during sexual union (*saṅga*). According to this theory, the coded bodily substance of a genus can be transmitted to a child in the reproductive substances of both parents.

So far this theory seems similar to the bilateral theory of Euro-

[16] *Sāradātilakatantram*, ed. Arthur Avalon (Calcutta: Sanskrit Press Depository, 1933), pp. 3–33; and Manu, *Manu-smṛti* [Dharmaśāstra], ed. Ganganātha Jhā (Calcutta: Asiatic Society of Bengal, 1932–39), X.59–61, 65–72.

American culture. There are, however, a number of important differences which arise, once again, out of the assumed nonduality of "man" and "nature" in Hinduism, permitting men as "moral" actors both to shape and be shaped by "natural" substances. Of the two reproductive substances, semen was considered to be more powerful, to have a greater capacity to maintain an ordered society endowed with well-being and prosperity. Consequently, it was thought that the coded substance which defined a caste or clan should properly be transmitted from one generation to the next through the semen of men and not the uterine blood of women. It is precisely here that the seed and field metaphor comes into play, giving this bilateral theory its unique Hindu twist. Semen or "seed" (*bīja*) should carry in it the distinctive generic attributes and code for conduct while the womb or "field" (*kṣetra*) should grow and nourish the seed without, of course, transmitting any of the plant's generic features to it. If these complementary functions are performed, the resulting offspring will inherit their father's and not their mother's coded bodily substance.

The act which transformed the semen and womb of a man and woman into seed and field was marriage. During the marriage ceremony a man and the previously unrelated woman who was to become his wife were transformed into a "single body" (*eka-deha*) by changing the woman's clan code and substance into those of her husband and his clan. Before marriage, a man was considered to be an incomplete person incapable of performing those acts of worship (*dharma*) enjoined by his code for conduct. The act of marriage completed him as a person by providing him with a "partner for acts of worship" (*saha-dharmiṇī*), a "wife for the purpose of worship" (*dharma-patnī*), his "half-body" (*ardhāṅga*). At the same time that marriage made a man and woman into one person, however, it also made them into two complementary persons, transforming the woman into the provider of the field for her husband's seed.

The specific portion of the marriage ceremony which wrought this transformation among Bengali Brāhmaṇs and Kāyasthas was that segment of the whole referred to as the "concluding marriage" or *uttara-vivāha*.[17] It was performed by the groom and his family

[17]For accounts of the Brāhman or Kāyastha marriage ceremony, see Raghunandana Bhaṭṭāchārya, *Udvāhatattvam*, ed. Heramba Nāth Chatterji (Calcutta: Sanskrit College, 1963), p. 27; Herbert H. Risley, *Tribes and Castes of Bengal* (Calcutta: Bengal secretariat Press, 1891), I, 148–52; and Krishnaballabh Ray, *Vaṅgīya Kāyastha Samāja* (Calcutta: B. Palit, 1903), pp. 67–70, 77–79, 87–88, 108–12.

priest (*kula-purohita*) and employed Vedic *mantras* asking the gods to do such things as exchange the hearts of the bride and groom and provide them with sons. Food offerings were also made to the Vedic gods through a fire (*homa*). The crucial part of this segment, however, was the "seven steps" or *sapta-padi* whereby the groom made the bride into his half-body. Once completed, the marriage of the two was considered indissoluble. After this followed the change of clan name or *gotra-parivarttana* and the "gift of a vermilion mark" or *sindūra-dāna* onto the forehead of the bride by the groom, again symbolizing the change of her substance and code, her transformation into her husband's half-body and field. The *uttara-vivāha* concluded with the "wife's boiled rice" or *bou-bhāt* in which the new bride cooked and served boiled rice to her husband's relatives in his house. Their acceptance of it transformed her into a woman sharing the coded bodily substance not only of her husband but of his clan (*kula*) as well.

Thus, the problems of clan membership for women are solved. A clan or *kula* consisted, in the Bengali view, of persons who shared the body of the same ancestral male. The role played by marriage in Bengali culture makes this definition both simple and accurate with respect to both men and women, for an out-marrying daughter, who shared the coded bodily substance of her father's clan was transformed by marriage into a woman sharing the coded bodily substance of her husband's clan. This marriage transformation also solves the problem of membership for the children of hypergamous or hypogamous marriages, for the transformation of the wife "neutralized" her capacity to transmit the coded bodily substance of caste and clan to her children by making her uterine substances into a field for her husband's seed.

This transformational view of marriage did not open the way for intercaste marriages on a regular basis. There was a catch in it: The woman accepted for marriage had to possess coded bodily substance considered to be suitably transformable by her husband and his clan. As we have already seen, a daughter who possessed coded bodily substance marked by the same Vedic *gotra* or clan name as the groom (*sagotra*) was considered unsuitable for marriage. So, too, was a daughter who was more generally related by blood (*svajana*, *sapiṇḍa*), was older in age (*vayojyeṣṭha*), belonged to a disparate generation (*viparyāya*) or to a different country (*deśāntara*), possessed the same personal name as his mother (*mātṛ-nāma*), was already betrothed to another (*anya-pūrvā*), or, having reached puberty, possessed menstrual blood (*rajasvalā*).[18] The latter was especially important; daughters who had not yet menstruated were, apparently, considered more easily transformable than those who had.

While the application of these criteria had as their purpose avoiding the improper or ineffective mixture of coded bodily substances, the application of other bodily criteria had to do with the daughter's capacity to give birth to pure, whole offspring. A woman whose husband was dead (*raṇḍikāgamana*), who had had an abortion (*bhrūṇahatyā*), who was blind at birth (*janmāndha*), suffering from leprosy (*kuṣṭha-rogī*), crippled (*khañja*), defective of limb (*aṅgahīna*), blind in one eye (*kāṇa*), hunchbacked (*kubja*), faulty in conduct (*duṣṭa*), or defective in speech (*vākyejaḍa*) was believed to be unsuitable for marriage in this respect.[19] Families which made marriages that improperly mixed coded bodily substances or combined good bodily substances with the defective caused the embodied ranks of the clans which they possessed to become "ruined" (*naṣṭa*), "fallen" (*patita*), and "inferior" (*hīna*).

Finally, we come to the question of caste and clan rank as criteria of suitability. Generally, it was assumed in the *kulajīs* that a daughter who was not of the same *varṇa* was not transformable into a field suitable for growing a man's seed. Aside from this, a daughter who appeared to be equivalent or similar in embodied caste or clan rank was also considered suitable for transformation into a proper wife. A Kulīna Kāyastha or Brāhmaṇ could, for example, accept the daughter of a Kulīna (equivalent in rank) or of a Siddha Maulika or Śrotriya (similar but inferior in rank) and transform both of these into Kulīna wives. He could not, however, accept the daughter of a Sādhya Maulika Kāyastha or, in the case of a Brāhmaṇ, a Sādhya or Ari Śrotriya (dissimilar and inferior in rank). Persons of these clans were considered to contain in their embodied ranks the attributes of the inferior lower Śūdra castes or non-Vedic Brāhmaṇs of the *asat* Śūdras. The acceptance of such daughters, though they need not lead to the generation of inferior, hybrid *jātis*, would

[18]Rāmānanda Śarmā, "Kula-dīpikā," Dacca University Library MSS (uncataloged), n.d., fol. 13a; Nandarāma Mitra, "Dakṣiṇa-rāḍhīya Kula-kārikā," in Nagendranāth Vasu, *Vaṅger Jātīya Itihāsa* (Calcutta: Viśvakoṣa Press, 1911–33), VI, Pt. I, 79; and Yadunandana, *Vārendra Ḍhākur* (Calcutta: Viśvakosa Press, 1912), p. 17.

[19]Vācaspati, "Kularamā," in Chandrakānta Ghaṭaka-vidyānidhi, *Kulakalpadruma* (Calcutta: Bhavanipur Press, 1912), pp. 19–20.

inferiorize the embodied rank of a Kulīna and his children.

Thus, while the transformational aspect of marriage opened the way for marriages among men and women of different clans and even different caste ranks, the power of a man to transform a woman into a proper wife was limited. He might, for example, be able to transform a woman of the same clan rank but having minor bodily defects into a proper wife, or he might be able to transform a woman of lower clan rank into a proper wife if she were suitable in every other respect, but he probably could not transform a woman inferior in both ways into a good wife. In any case, there was general agreement that a woman of one *varṇa* could not be transformed into the proper wife of a man of another. After all, the field had to be suitable for the seed which was to be planted in it.

Marriage: Hypergamy and Hypogamy Need Not Transform Rank

We turn now to a discussion of the two forms of marriage associated with differences in family or clan rank and known in the anthropological literature as hypergamy and hypogamy. Hypergamy involves the gift of a daughter along with a gift of wealth or "dowry" to a groom of higher rank. Its opposite, hypogamy, entails the gift of a daughter to a groom of lower rank in exchange for wealth or a "bride-price" given to the bride's father. Most important, these forms of marriage, and especially hypergamy, are supposed to involve the "trading" of wealth for "status" or "prestige" among high and low grades of clans. As I have already argued, the view of marriage as an act of worship generating and sustaining high and low clan ranks and transmuting those embodied ranks into fame, respect, and so on, arose in the middle period in Bengal after the Muslim conquest. Before then, proper marriages were necessary but not sufficient to transmute a person's rank. He had also to perform other acts of worship such as those enjoined in the ninefold Kulīna code for conduct. Yet marriage patterns before this change took place could also be characterized as either hypergamous or hypogamous. What I shall argue here is that hypergamy and hypogamy were used by Bengali Hindus for different purposes in different historical contexts.

The *dharmaśāstras* distinguish eight forms of marriage, two of which are the ones designated as hypergamy and hypogamy. The best of these, the *brāhma*, considered most appropriate for the Brāhmaṇ, is the one described as hypergamous; a lower form, the *āsura*, deemed proper for the Vaiśya and Śūdra, is the one described as hypogamous. The marriage codes of the Vedic Brāhmaṇ *jātis* of middle period Bengal enjoined only the *brāhma* form; the codes of the Kāyastha *jātis*, consistent with their partial combination with the Veda, exhibited a clear preference for the *brāhma* form, but also permitted the *āsura* form.

Like the other acts of worship we have discussed in examining caste rank, these marriages were conceived of as acts of worship involving the offering of wealth and food to deities. According to the medieval Bengali interpretation of the *śāstras*, the *āsura* marriage was an act of worship (*dharma*) in which the father of the bride, "should accept wealth (*paṇa*) in the house of the groom (*vara*) and in exchange for that wealth, he should make a gift of his daughter to that groom."[20] The *brāhma* marriage, conceived of as the opposite in form to that of the *āsura*, was an act of worship in which the father of the bride "should bring a groom endowed with good clan and good conduct (*kula-śīla*) to his own house and he should adorn his daughter with valuable clothes and ornaments. Then, he should pronounce their personal names and *gotras* and give her to him."[21] The gift of wealth to the groom, which was supposed to follow his acceptance, was called a *dakṣiṇā*, the same term applied to the honorarium given to the Brāhmaṇ priest after he performed an act of worship for someone, the gift of which transferred the benefits gained from the priest to the worshiper.

As acts of worship, both of these forms imply an inequality of rank between the father of the bride and the groom. In the *āsura* form, the groom worshipfully invites the bride's father to his house and offers him a gift of wealth, receiving in exchange the more valuable gift of a daughter. Hence, in this transaction the bride's father ranks higher than the groom. In the *brāhma* form, the bride's father invites the groom to his house, worships him, and humbly asks him to accept not only his daughter but also a gift of wealth. This is a strange exchange, for it appears that the groom is accorded higher rank in this transaction, yet appears to give nothing in return. This is not really so, however. Once the daughter had been accepted by the groom's family and transformed into a wife, the giver of the

[20]Nibandha, Dacca University Library MSS (uncataloged), n.d., fol. 7.
[21]*Ibid.*

daughter, who had subordinated his own family's desire for the gain of wealth to the concern for the well-being of the groom and his family by "feeding" them a healthy, ornamented daughter and accepting nothing in return, gained such intangible benefits as "immunity from the effects of improper acts (*paritrāna*) for twenty-nine generations,"[22] benefits more valuable than the gifts he gave the groom. Note, however, that the giving of these gifts did not in and of itself transmute the rank of the worshiper into wordly fame, respect, and glory. Nor did the giving of other gifts made on the occasion of a marriage.

The groom or the bride's father were not the only deities worshiped with gifts of wealth and food on the occasion of a marriage. Other deities were similarly worshiped because they, too, participated in transforming the groom and bride into man and wife. The bride and groom, divine because they would perpetuate the clan with sons, were given presents of clothes, household utensils, etc., called *yautūka*, by both sets of relatives. The groom made worshipful gifts of clothes, and so on, called *namaskārī*, to the bride's relatives after being welcomed in her house. She, having been welcomed at his, gave *namaskārī* gifts to his relatives. The guests invited to feast at both houses were given small departure gifts, called *vidāya*, by the groom's and bride's fathers. The Brāhmaṇ and gods at each house were given worshipful offerings, called *praṇāmī*, and each father gave an honorarium (*dakṣiṇā*) to his priest. Finally, the community (*samāja*) servants such as the barber who played a part in the ceremony were given community gifts, called *sāmājikatā*.

What is significant about these latter gifts is that they could be given by persons of both sides and in roughly equal amounts and qualities if both families were equal in embodied rank. Thus, both families in effect worshiped each other, providing each other with wealth and food on the one hand and with well-being and prosperity on the other. Once again, though, these gifts did not necessarily bring the givers fame, respect, and glory.

This pattern of symmetrical giving contrasts sharply with the pattern of gifts given to the bride's father in the hypogamous or *āsura* marriage and the gifts given to the groom in the hypergamous or *brāhma* marriage. These exchanges, both of which were asymmetrical, generated a temporary relationship of inequality between two families because of the relative values of the items exchanged even

[22] *Ibid.*

if their embodied clan ranks (*kula*) were not inherently different. They did not, however, generate or sustain a permanent relationship of inequality in clan rank. Nor, to repeat, did these asymmetrical gifts of wealth bring the worshiper fame, respect, and glory. In other words, hypergamy and hypogamy did not, according to Hindus, necessarily entail the trading of wealth for status or prestige on the part of persons belonging to high and low clans.

Among the Brāhmaṇs and Kāyasthas of middle period Bengal, however, these two forms of marriage exchange, along with the other gifts of wealth just listed, did. They were systematically used not only to state and sustain the inherently high and low ranks of and non-Kulīna clans but also to transmute embodied ranks into fame, respect, and glory.

Marriage: Feeding the Kulīna Gods Transforms Clan Rank

Let us turn now to see how these patterns of worship and gift-giving operated in marriages made among persons of clans having high and low embodied ranks (*kula*), namely, the Brāhmaṇs and Kāyasthas of middle period Bengal.

An action by which a person defined as a clansman was considered to achieve the goal of transforming his inherited clan rank into its superior fruits was referred to as an "action of clan rank" (*kula-karma*). Originally, a Kulīna was thought to transmute his inherited rank into its superior fruits by performing all of the actions of rank enjoined in his full ninefold Vedic code for conduct; and a non-Kulīna was thought to transmute his by following his lesser Vedic code. Hence, the term *kula-karma* originally referred to the wide range of actions embodied in these codes. Now, in the declining Kali era of the middle period, the clan rank of a Vedic Brāhmaṇ or Kāyastha Śūdra is thought to be transmuted into its superior fruits simply by performing the actions of rank enjoined in the narrower marriage codes of the clans, the codes adopted by the Brāhmaṇ and Kāyastha councils at the beginning of the middle period:

> The root of everyone's clan rank is gift and acceptance.[23]

> The primary roots of the seven clans are the distinctions in marriages;

[23]Yadunandana, *Vārendra Ḍhākur*, p. 18.

> through these, you should understand, the clan ranks were formed. You should judge the rank of a clan by the significance of its marriages. Through the giving and taking of daughters you will know a clan is superior.[24]
>
> It is as though acceptances are the roots of ranks and gifts the branches and shoots.[25]
>
> Listen, everyone, Nandarāma Mitra says that clan rank is maintained through gift and acceptance.[26]
>
> High and low rank is the real gain of marriage.[27]

As a result, the term *kula-karma* comes during this period to be restricted in its meaning to one defining action of rank, marriage.

While the Brāhmaṇs and Kāyasthas of middle period Bengal believed that the transmutation of inherited rank into its higher fruits was achieved by marriage, they did not believe that it was attained through just any marriage. The Kulīna alone was thought to have the divine power (*śakti*) to make this transmutation. He was considered to be the king of clan rank (*kula-rāja*), the master of clan rank (*kula-pati*), the ornament of rank (*kula-bhūṣaṇa*), and the lamp of rank (*kula-dīpaka*), a god (*ṭhākura*) in relation to the non-Kulīna. Hence, every person, whether Kulīna or non-Kulīna, was believed to obtain the superior fruits of fame, respect, fortune, greatness, and so forth by marrying with the Kulīnas. Marriage with a Kulīna not only transformed one's inherited rank into its superior fruits; it also "repaired" past mistakes. It could even transform the inferior rank ("iron") of a fallen Brāhmaṇ or ordinary Śūdra into the superior rank ("gold") of a Vedic Brāhmaṇ or Kāyastha Śūdra:

> The rank of him is in the marriage he makes with a Kulīna, for the Kulīna is the increaser of everyone, the source of all fortune.[28]
>
> Some write of Kulīna rank, but everyone sings of it when he sees it. The rank of the great Kulīna was born out of his embodied code for

[24] *Ibid.*, p. 57.

[25] Nandarāma Mitra, "Kārikā," in Vasu, *Vaṅger Jātīya Itihāsa*, VI, Pt. I, 234.

[26] *Ibid.*, 251.

[27] Rajanikara Ghaṭaka, "Dakṣiṇa-rāḍhīya Kula-kārikā," in Vasu, *Vaṅger Jātīya Itihāsa*, VI, Pt. I, 109.

[28] Mitra, "Dakṣiṇa-rāḍhīya Kula-kārikā," in Vasu, *Vaṅger Jātīya Itihāsa*, VI, Pt. I, 78.

> conduct (*guṇa*). Because rank was first born in these clans, there are Kulīnas in the world, but now that it is born, rank moves from one generation (*puruṣa*) to the next. Whatever other embodied code may go with him, he obtains the code for high rank, the great code, in every generation. The removal of bad through good acts is called "reparations" (*prāyaścitta*) in the Veda. But in the Veda of rank marriages with Kulīnas (*kula-karma*) are the reparations. It is the code for conduct (*dharma*) of a Kulīna to make the impure (*asat*) pure (*sat*), just as it is the code (*karma*) of a touchstone to make iron into gold.[29]

> One born in an inferior clan becomes purified (*śuddha*) in each generation when he gives and accepts daughters in the Kulīna clans. Through marriage one gains superiority as well as inferiority.[30]

Thus, the term "action of rank" (*kula-karma*) comes to be further restricted, for in the Vedic Brāhmaṇ and Kāyastha Śūdra subcastes it means not simply "marriage" but "marriage with a Kulīna."

While marriage with a Kulīna was believed to be the defining action by which clan rank was transformed into its superior fruits, not all marriages with Kulīnas were thought to have the same efficacy in doing so. During the middle period, the subcastes placed varying stresses on gifts and acceptances and, in some cases, by distinguishing between first marriages of eldest daughters and sons from subsequent marriages of younger offspring. Three subcastes—Rāḍhī and Vārendra Brāhmaṇ and Vaṅgaja Kāyastha—believed that the successful transformation of inherited rank depended on the marriage of the daughter (*kanyā-gata-kula*). Accordingly, the gift of a daughter was thought to be the decisive action by which inherited rank was transmuted in these subcastes. According to a Rāḍhī Brāhmaṇ text, "Where the daughter is given, there is one's rank."[31] Hence, among these Brāhmaṇs and Kāyasthas the gift of a daughter to a Kulīna was thought to be the decisive action by which all persons of their subcastes transformed their inherited ranks into their higher fruits. Such a belief encouraged the making of hypergamous or *brāhma* marriages (gifts of daughters to superiors) while discouraging the making of hypogamous or *āsura* marriages (gifts of daughters to inferiors).

Two subcastes—Dakṣiṇa-rāḍhī and Uttara-rāḍhī Kāyastha—

[29]Bṛhaspati, "Ḍhākur," in Vasu, *Vaṅger Jātīya Itihāsa*, VI, Pt. I, 97.
[30]Śarmā, "Kula-dīpikā," fol. 7a.
[31]Vasu, *Vaṅger Jātīya Itihāsa*, I, Pt. I, 193.

believed that the transmutation of inherited rank depended on the marriage of the eldest son (*putra-gata-kula*). Accordingly, the acceptance of a daughter for marriage with the eldest son was thought to be the decisive action by which rank was transmuted in these subcastes. A Dakṣiṇa-rāḍhī text states succinctly: "Acceptance is the life of rank."[32] Similarly, an Uttara-rāḍhī text asserts: "Though good acts (*guṇa*) of acceptance rank becomes pure, through faulty acts (*doṣa*) of acceptance, rank becomes broken; thus, through the strength of acceptance, the waves of rank fluctuate."[33] Hence among these Kāyasthas the acceptance of a daughter from a Kulīna (to be married with the eldest son) was thought to be the decisive action by which all persons of these subcastes transformed their ranks as Kāyasthas into their superior fruits. As we shall see, such a belief encouraged the making of hypogamous or *āsura* marriages in the case of eldest sons without discouraging the making of hypergamous or *brāhma* marriages in the case of younger sons. Finally, one subcaste—Vārendra Kāyastha—believed that the transformation of rank rested equally on gifts and acceptances.[34]

Because of the Kulīna's superior capacity to transform inherited rank into its superior fruits, he was considered to be a human deity. An action of rank (*kula-karma*), marriage with a Kulīna, was thought, therefore, to take the form of worship (*pūjā*, *arccanā*) in which a daughter was given to a Kulīna or accepted from him after wealth and food were offered to that Kulīna in order to induce him to make this transforming marriage: "Look, if the wealth (*dhana*) that a man spends on acts of worship is spent truthfully, he certainly attains liberation (*mukti*). But the great happiness that he obtains in this life is through the making of marriages. He who becomes the receptacle of wealth is able to attain that happiness, for the expenditure of wealth is the source of rank (*kula*) and rank is the source of fame (*yaśa*)."[35] So strong was this belief that a marriage with a Kulīna which did not involve a gift of wealth was not considered efficacious in transforming a person's inherited rank: "Without wealth (*kara*) there is no transmutation of rank."[36]

The distinctive gift of wealth that was given to the Kulīnas was

[32] Dīnabandhu Kulabhūṣaṇa Ghaṭaka, *Kāyastha-kārikā* (Calcutta: n.p., 1886), I, 19.

[33] Vasu, *Vaṅger Jātīya Itihāsa*, III, Pt. I, 54.

[34] Yadunandana, *Vārendra Ḍhākur*, pp. 18–20.

[35] Sukadeva Sinha, "Uttara-rāḍhīya Kula-kārikā," in Vasu, *Vaṅger Jātīya Itihāsa*, III, Pt. I, 69.

[36] Bṛhaspati, "Ḍhākur," in Vasu, *Vaṅger Jātīya Itihāsa*, VI, Pt. I, 96.

referred to as *paṇa*, a word meaning wealth (*artha*, *dhana*), value (*mūlya*), or tax (*śulka*, *kara*). Another term, *kula-maryādā*, meaning "clan prestige," pointed to the purpose for which the wealth was given. Though similar both to the *dakṣiṇā* given to the groom in a *brāhma* marriage and to the gift of wealth made to the father of the bride in an *āsura* marriage, the gift of *paṇa* differed from both in that its purpose was not to gain intangible benefits after death, as in the *brāhma*, nor to gain the benefit of a bride, as in the *āsura*, but to transmute one's embodied rank into the fruits of fame, glory, and prestige in the here and now. Given in the form of coins (*mudrā*) either to the Kulīna father of the groom or bride and paid before the marriage took place, the *paṇa* appears to have been conceived of as a kind of tax or toll which one had to give or pay to the king of clan rank in exchange for the benefits of rank that flowed from a marriage with him. Thus, the hypergamous or *brāhma* gift of a daughter to a superior Kulīna entailed the gift of wealth to the groom's father. It was considered to be "that gift of a daughter to a groom (*vara*) of equivalent generation and pure to both families whom one invited for worship (*āhvāna*) with a gift of full wealth (*pūrṇa-paṇa*), that is, whom one invites to one's own house where one convenes the council and brings one's daughter after adorning her with jewels and worshiping her with gifts."[37] On the other hand, the hypogamous or *āsura* acceptance of a daughter from a superior Kulīna entailed the reverse flow of wealth to the bride's father. It was considered to be, "that gift in which one accepts wealth (*paṇa*) from an inferior and gives the daughter."[38]

As we shall see in the following chapter, marriage with a Kulīna affected the symmetry of the other gifts given on the occasion of a marriage. The family higher in clan rank gave less wealth and food; the family lower in clan rank gave more.

Before the changes that occurred at the outset of the middle period, marriages with the Kulīnas had been seen as necessary acts by which the Brāhmaṇs and Kāyasthas sustained their inherited ranks, but these marriages had not been viewed as sufficient for them to gain respect, fame, and so on. In order to transmute their embodied Vedic ranks into wordly fame, respect, and glory, the Brāhmaṇs and Kāyasthas had to perform the acts of Vedic worship (*ācāra*) enjoined in the *śāstras*, show humility (*vinaya*) to their preceptors,

[37]Śarmā, "Kula-dīpikā," fol. 8b.
[38]*Ibid.*, fol. 8a.

make gifts (*dāna*), go on pilgrimages (*tīrtha-darśana*), and perform the other acts enjoined by their Vedic codes. Now, in the middle period, marriage with a Kulīna in and of itself becomes the act by which the Brāhmaṇs and Kāyasthas gain wordly fame and prestige. As we have shown here, the mere gift or acceptance of a daughter with a Kulīna, whether of the *āsura* or the *brāhma* type, was not enough to make this happen. One had also to worship the Kulīna with offerings of wealth and food. The embodied Vedic rank of the Kulīna was seen as the subtle and superior source of a Brāhmaṇ's or Kāyastha's well-being. But this coded bodily substance needed wealth and food for its nourishment. By giving the Kulīnas suitable wealth and food, the Brāhmaṇ or Kāyastha nourished the embodied rank of the Kulīna. In return, the divine Kulīna transmuted the embodied rank of his Brāhmaṇ or Kāyastha worshiper into fame, respect, and prestige.

Thus, marriage with a Kulīna had two purposes. One was to provide the Kulīna with needed wealth and food; the other was to provide his worshiper with the fame, respect, and prestige he deserved. The next chapter shows how these marriage exchanges operated to distribute wealth and transform inherited rank among the ranked grades of Brāhmaṇs and Kāyasthas.

Let us summarize. The rank of a caste (*jāti*) in the Bengali Hindu conception was the coded bodily substance possessed by persons of the same *jāti*. The relative ranks of occupational *jātis* or, more accurately, of sets of occupational *jātis*—Brāhmaṇ, Śūdra, *sat* Śūdra, *asat* Śūdra, etc.—were defined in terms of the degree to which they were marked by the presence of the coded substance of Vedic worship. This is the "attribute" often referred to as the relative degree of "purity" possessed by a *jāti*. However, to treat of coded bodily substance as a passive attribute denoting a degree of spiritual or ritual cleanliness misses a major cultural point. Bengali Hindus conceived of the relative rank of a *jāti* as its relative embodied power (*śakti*) or potential to transform the coded substances of wealth and food into well-being, prosperity, long life, and so on.

If rank was a matter of inherent attribute, it was also a matter of demonstrated interaction. What we have shown in this chapter is that the relative ranks implicit in the divine powers of *jātis* were sustained and demonstrated by acts of worship, asymmetrical interactions involving the selfless feeding of the gods. Thus, the

Brāhmaṇs worshiped and fed the gods, and the Śūdras worshiped and fed the Brāhmaṇs, considered to be gods on earth.

Turning to the question of clan rank, we saw that marriage, the gift or acceptance of a daughter, was considered to be an act of worship that related persons of different clans. Marriage was, perhaps, the transformative act par excellence. It transformed a daughter into a wife, changing her bodily substance and code for conduct into those of her husband and his clan and making her reproductive substances the "field" in which her husband planted his "seed."

Originally, the two forms of Hindu marriage, the *brāhma* (hypergamy), appropriate to the Brāhmaṇ, and the *āsura* form (hypogamy), appropriate to the Śūdra, did not sustain higher and lower clan ranks and did not transmute these into fame, glory, and respect. During middle period Bengal, however, with the new stress placed on marriage, both of these forms came to have these purposes. By making a worshipful gift of wealth (*paṇa*) to a Kulīna, the Brāhmaṇs and Kāyasthas, both Kulīna and non-Kulīna, were thought to sustain their clan ranks and transmute them into fame, respect, glory, and so forth. Thus, just as the Brāhmaṇs and Śūdras gained prosperity and well-being by worshiping and feeding Brāhmaṇs, so Kulīnas and non-Kulīnas alike gained fame and respect by worshiping and feeding Kulīnas.

Chapter IV

KULĪNA WORSHIP

KULĪNAS WORSHIP KULĪNAS

Reciprocity

The Kulīna clans of each territorial *jāti* or subcaste of Brāhmaṇs or Kāyasthas were thought to be the highest in clan rank. Their inborn code for conduct enjoined them, during the middle period, to maintain their superiority and transform their inherited ranks as Vedic Brāhmaṇs and Kāyasthas by marrying among themselves. The progenitors of the Kulīnas in each subcaste, equally endowed at birth by the gods with their superior ranks as Vedic Brāhmaṇs or Kāyasthas, had demonstrated their equality and transformed their inherited ranks by worshipping each other with gifts of daughters, wealth, and food and performing the other actions enjoined in their codes for conduct. The Rāḍhī Brāhmaṇ Kulīnas, for instance, had been asked to make the following promise: "Make return gifts (*pratidāna*) of honor, and so forth (*mānādi*) by pairs. If there are exchanges (*parivartta*) of daughters through gift and acceptance, then there will be equivalence on both sides, each of which has the code for conduct of a superior clan (*kula-dharma*)."[1] In a similar vein, a passage from an Uttara-rāḍhī Kāyastha text summarizes the exchanges made among the Kulīnas and their results:

> When these four features are present—the gift of food, good speech, promise of marriage, and humility—they call it a worshipful invitation (*ḍāka*) to marry. The defining mark of the proper cooking (*pāka*) of rank is the mutual gift and acceptance of daughters. The receipt of wealth (*paṇa*) in the house of a man who owes it is known as binding the debtor to pay his debt (*khātaka-bandī*). Worshipful invitation

[1] "Kula-mañjarī," in Nagendranāth Vasu *Vaṅger Jātīya Itihāsa* (Calcutta: Viśvakoṣa Press, 1911–33), I, Pt. I, 144.

to marry, the proper cooking of rank, and binding the debtor to pay his debt are the features of high rank.[2]

By making these exchanges with each other, the progenitors of the Kulīna clans in each subcaste generated a kind of "marriage alliance" among themselves which they referred to as the "relationship of reciprocity" (*paryāyatva*): "Because the natures of their ranks (*kula-bhāva*) are equivalent (*samāna*) and there is giving and acceptance and the two are equivalent in clan origin, reciprocity is declared."[3] Now, according to the values of the middle period, the Kulīnas acquired their rank solely by birth and transformed it into its superior fruits not by following the ninefold code for conduct but solely by reenacting past reciprocal exchanges in each generation:

> The nature of one born in a clan having a particular superior code for conduct is Kulīnahood, and "particular superior" means characterized by the nine enjoined acts. It is not meant by this, however, that if the nine enjoined acts arose in an ordinary person of the present that he would be a Kulīna; for Kulīnahood is the uninterrupted reciprocity of exchange.[4]

> Reciprocal exchange (*āvṛtti*), as distinguished from *ācāra* and the other eight kinds of conduct in Kulīnahood; and reciprocal exchange is a transaction in the form of acceptance, and so forth. . . .[5]

Because of this stress placed on marriage, the highest norm in a Kulīna's marriage code was the one urging him to make all of his marriage exchanges with other Kulīnas: "That gift or acceptance is best which is in accord with the relationship of reciprocity."[6] The Kulīna who made such exchanges exclusively was thought to transmute his inherited rank into special rank among the Kulīnas: "He who both accepts the daughters of Kulīnas and given daughters to Kulīnas is a lamp of high clan rank (*kula-dīpaka*)."[7] On the other hand, the lowest norm a Kulīna could adhere to and still

[2]Uttara-rāḍhī Kāyastha Kulajī, Dacca University Library MSS (uncataloged), n.d., fol. 4a.
[3]Śarmā, "Kula-dīpikā," fols. 7a–7b.
[4]*Ibid.*, fol. 7a.
[5]Chandrakānta Ghaṭaka-vidyānidhi, *Kulakalpadruma* (Calcutta: Bhavanipur Press, 1912), p. 57.
[6]Rāmānanda Śarmā, "Kula-dīpikā," Dacca University Library MSS (uncataloged), n.d., fol. 7b.
[7]*Ibid.*

transform his rank into its superior fruits was to marry either his eldest daughter or eldest son with a Kulīna. Among the Dakṣiṇa-rāḍhī Kāyasthas, where the transmutation of rank depended on the eldest son, a Kulīna had, at the very least, to accept the daughter of a Kulīna and marry her to his eldest son. Among the Rāḍhī Brāhmaṇs and Vaṅgaja Kāyasthas, where rank depended on the daughter, a Kulīna had to give at least one daughter, (preferably his eldest) to a Kulīna. Rāmānanda, genealogist of the Vaṅgaja Kāyasthas, asserts that in the middle period the following of this lower norm was proper and sufficient. He states that the rule, "A Kulīna attains superiority by both gifts and acceptance in marriage," is, "an ancient view," and that, "in the present the realization (*siddhi*) of rank comes about through gifts alone."[8]

A Kulīna could realize his rank in these daughter-dependent subcastes even if he had no daughter: "And so, he should complete marriages (*kula-karma*) through gifts and acceptances; however, in the absence of a daughter, he should give away a grass daughter (*kuśa-tyāga*) or make the mutual promise of marriage (*pratijñā*)."[9] The first of these "ritual substitutions" involved giving a daughter made of *kuśa* grass to another Kulīna. The second, the mutual promise of marriage, is described as follows in a nineteenth-century account:

> Those Kulīnas between whom there should be reciprocal exchange go to the bank of a tank or river with appropriate clansmen and other relatives as well as the genealogists, and they together, each holding either an earthen or brass pot full of water, recite the promise (*pratijña*) of exchange according to the rules of betrothal and immerse the vessels full of water; this is promise of marriage in the case of reciprocal exchange.[10]

Reciprocity among the Kulīnas at the clan level was important, for it meant that in terms of embodied Vedic rank they were independent of other men. Kulīna Brāhmaṇs and Kāyasthas, in relation to the Śrotriyas and Maulikas, could, if they were able to give to other Kulīnas, cause their own inherited ranks to be transmuted into worldly fame, respect, and glory. As we shall see, the Śrotriyas and Maulikas were unable to do this by giving among themselves, no matter how much wealth they had.

[8] *Ibid.*, fol. 9b.

[9] *Ibid.*

[10] Mahimāchandra Majumdār, *Gauḍe Brāhman* (Calcutta: B. L. Chakravarti, New School-Book Press, 1886), p. 157.

While a Kulīna could substitute one action (*karma*) for another in order to preserve his rank, no Kulīna was able to substitute an action for birth (*janma*). Generated by the gods, the embodied rank of a Kulīna was obtainable only by birth: "A Kulīna is a person born in a special superior clan."[11] Hence, the action of adopting a son, even if he were the son of another Kulīna, was declared to be ineffective in making him a Kulīna son. A Vaṅgaja Kāyastha text states that, "Should the son of a Kulīna become the adopted (*poṣya*) son of another Kulīna, the inferiority of that Kulīna's rank is not purified by action. His son has no high rank. Should the son of a Madhyalya or Mahāpātra become the adopted son of a Kulīna, then he has no rank at all; he is a Vaṃśaja."[12] A Dakṣiṇa-rāḍhī Kāyastha text concurs in this view: "An adopted son (*dattaka-putra*) has no high rank. The adopted son of a Kulīna will not be a Kulīna and even though he possesses sonhood in all other matters, in the matter of high rank, he has no sonhood. He will be only a Vaṃśaja."[13] So, while a Kulīna was believed capable of perpetuating his embodied rank without a born daughter, he was believed incapable of perpetuating it without a born son.

The transformational power of even the Kulīna was, thus, limited. The power he exercised through marriage could transform the inherited ranks of other Kulīnas and non-Kulīnas into fame, respect, and glory. He could transform non-Kulīna women into Kulīna wives, and he could make "latent" Brāhmaṇ or Kāyastha men, persons who appeared to be of inferior Brāhmaṇ or Śūdra rank, into "actual" Brāhmaṇs or Kāyasthas, but he could not make them into Kulīnas. Only through the act of birth could Kulīna men make other Kulīna men.

Nonreciprocity

Though the Kulīna clans in a subcaste were equivalent in code and rank and were thought to have the capacity to reciprocate the gifts exchanged among them, the grades into which the Kulīnas of a subcaste were organized were considered to be similar but not equivalent in codes and ranks. The higher grades were higher and more powerful because they were able to purify and refine, preserve

[11]Śarmā, "Kula-dīpikā," fol. 7a.
[12]*Ibid.*, fol. 15a.
[13]Dīnabandhu Kulabhūṣaṇa Ghaṭaka, *Kāyastha-kārikā* (Calcutta: n.p., 1886), I, 22.

or increase, the inherited ranks of the lower grades by making exchanges with them. The lower grades were lower and less powerful because, by reciprocating these exchanges, they were thought to break and endanger, ruin or lower, the inherited ranks of the higher grades. Hence, the exchanges enjoined in the marriage codes of the ranked grades were conceived of as necessarily nonreciprocal, allowing the higher grades to make exchanges which purified the ranks of the lower grades without endangering their own higher ranks.

The marriage codes of these ranked grades were quite complex and included a wide range of rules or norms, each of which applied to particular, individual circumstances and each of which entailed particular consequences for a person's rank when followed. In general, however, the pattern which nonreciprocal exchanges took depended on whether gifts or acceptances were decisive in transforming inherited rank. Among the Dakṣiṇa-rāḍhī Kāyastha Kulīnas, who were differentiated according to the order of their birth into nine ranked seniority grades (Mukhya, Kaniṣṭha, etc.), the transmutation of rank was believed to depend primarily on thë marriage of the eldest son. Hence, by giving his eldest daughter to an inferior, a Kulīna of this subcaste preserved his inherited rank but temporarily "dipped" (*majjā*) it, changing it into a grosser form having "shame" (*lajjā*) or "rebuke" (*nindā*) as its inferior fruits: "A gift to an inferior is declared to have dipping as its nature."[14] On the other hand, by accepting a daughter from an inferior, junior grade and marrying her to his eldest son, he endangered or even ruined his inherited rank instead of strengthening it: "Acceptance from an inferior (*anuja*) endangers one's rank."[15] Accordingly, the minimum norm by which a Kulīna preserved his inherited rank, strengthening (*śaurya*) it and turning it into respect, fame, and so forth, was one enjoining him to give his eldest daughter to an equal: "By a gift to an equal, rank is strengthened."[16] More important, this minimum norm enjoined him to accept the younger daughter of a superior for marriage with his eldest son: "Acceptance from a superior strengthens."[17]

If we look behind these explicily stated norms, we wee the same

[14]Ghaṭakāchārya, "Kārikā," in Vasu, *Vañger Jātīya Itihāsa*, VI, Pt. I, 107.
[15]*Ibid.*
[16]*Ibid.*
[17]*Ibid.*

logic of exchange operating here that operated in the exchanges of food among the ranked castes. The daughters of a Mukhya were designated, according to the order of their gift in marriage, as "foremost daughter" (*āg-chei*), "second daughter" (*do-chei*), and so forth. The daughters of a non-Mukhya were similarly designated as "proper bodily shape" (*ākṛti*), "she who moves in the opposite direction" (*pratisāriṇī*), and "inferior" (*jaghanya*).[18] As this terminology suggests, first gifts ("cooked food") were considered to be higher in value than the second or subsequent gifts of a grade ("leavings"). The former were properly to be given in acts of worship whereas the latter were properly to be given as favors or benefits.

Thus, the Mukhya, for example, was considered to be higher in rank than the Kaniṣṭha because while the Kaniṣṭha worshipped him, he did not worship the Kaniṣṭha. The exchanges of daughters enacted this high and low relationship. Kaniṣṭhas could offer their first gifts as worship to the Mukhyas. If these were properly marriageable daughters, they were considered to be suitable as second acceptances by the Mukhyas. The Mukhya was, however, more powerful and higher than the Kaniṣṭha because his second gift, not needed by him to transmute his own rank and given to the Kaniṣṭha as a favor, was considered to be the "root" (*mūla*) of the Kaniṣṭha's rank,[19] better suited as a first acceptance for transmuting his inherited rank than even the first gift of another Kaniṣṭha. Thus, by following the norms in their marriage codes, the Kulīnas of the high and low grades not only maintained their relative corporate ranks; they also transmuted their inherited ranks as persons into their subtle, superior fruits—fame, respect, greatness, and so forth.

By making other kinds of marriages included in the codes of higher and lower grades, an individual Kulīna could transmute his lower corporate rank into a higher corporate rank, or, conversely, he could transmute his higher rank into a lower one. Social mobility was institutionalized among the Kulīnas of the Brāhmaṇ and Kāyastha subcastes. Among the Dakṣiṇa-rāḍhī Kāyasthas, a Kulīna who acquired a rank lower than that of his father by birth as a younger son was thought able to attain by marriage the rank of his father or elder brother. Accordingly, a distinction was made between the rank a man acquired by birth (*janma*) and by increase (*bāṛi*).

[18] Vācaspati, "Kula-sarvvasva," in Vasu, *Vaṅger Jātīya Itihāsa*), VI, Pt. I, 112.
[19] *Ibid.* 113.

For example, the second son of a Mukhya, a Kaniṣṭha by birth, was also a Mukhya by increase. By obtaining the eldest daughter of a Mukhya as a favor (she was normally to be given in worship to the eldest son of a Mukhya) and marrying her to his eldest son, the Kaniṣṭha became a Mukhya.[20] Thus, the result of such hypogamous marriages was upward social mobility.

On the other hand, the result of hypergamous marriages was downward social mobility. A Kulīna of a higher grade who married his eldest son with the inferior daughter of a lower grade was thought to decrease (*hrāsa*) rather than increase his rank and transmute his inherited rank into that of the lower grade: "If a Mukhya makes a first acceptance from a Madhyāṃśa, he will become a Madhyāṃśa; if a Teoja makes a first acceptance from a Madhyāṃśa Dvitīya-po, he will become a Madhyāṃśa Dvitīya-po. This is the rule in all marriages of rank (*kula-sambandha*)."[21]

The exchange of a daughter with a superior in an action of rank could not, of course, proceed without an honorific offering of wealth given in order to induce the superior to transmute one's rank either by accepting or giving a daughter. The value of the wealth to be given to the father of the superior bride or groom was calculated along two dimensions. First, the value of the wealth given was supposed to be in proportion to the differences in rank between the higher and lower. The greater the difference, the greater the amount of wealth. Second, the value of the wealth was to be in proportion to the act of transmutation desired. The amount of wealth given to induce a superior to transmute one's inherited rank into its superior fruits was determined according to a schedule of fixed payments. On the other hand, the amount of wealth given to induce a superior to transmute lower rank into higher rank was not fixed but determined in accord with the receiver's "needs."

Since the differences in rank or acts of transmutation among the Kulīnas, no matter how great, were never thought to be as great as the differences between a Kulīna and a non-Kulīna, the wealth given by one Kulīna to another as an inducement to transmute rank was never as much as that given by a non-Kulīna to a Kulīna. One commentator says in regard to the amounts of wealth given: "There was no strain on the part of Kulīna Kāyasthas when Kulīnas gave and accepted with each other."[22] Still, the wide range of marriage

[20]Dīnabandhu, *Kāyasta-kārikā*, I, 18–19.

[21]*Ibid.*, 22.

[22]Rājendrakumār Ghosh, *Kāyastha-samāja-tattva* (Calcutta: By the Author, 1931), p. 98.

norms involving exchanges of varying amounts of wealth as inducements to transmute rank among the Kulīnas allowed them to pursue three different strategies in making marriages, each, of course, in accord with the codes and economic circumstances of the persons involved.

By marrying with equals or near equals, which entailed neither giving nor receiving large amounts of wealth, a Kulīna of moderate wealth was able to maintain a proper balance between the goal of "selfless" worship achieved by giving wealth away, and the goal of personal gain achieved by receiving wealth, and thereby preserve both rank and his wealth; for it is clear that the amounts of wealth given in such transactions were thought properly to be small and were determined according to a fixed schedule of rates. Unfortunately, detailed information on the amounts of wealth given to the father of the bride or groom of equal or higher rank is not available for the Dakṣiṇa-rāḍhī Kāyasthas during the middle period. The wealth or *paṇa* given by a Siddha Maulika to a Kulīna (rank unspecified) was fixed at 50 rupees.[23] Among the Kulīnas of the Vaṅgaja Kāyastha subcaste, where data on the amounts of *paṇa* is available for the eighteenth century, the highest amount given was either 24 or 40 rupees, depending on the area in which a person was settled.[24] Among the Rāḍhī Brāhmaṇ Kulīnas the highest amount fixed was reported to be even lower, 16 rupees.[25] Hence, it is quite likely that the amount of *paṇa* given in a marriage which had as its purpose the preservation of rank was probably not more than 25 rupees among the eighteenth-century Dakṣiṇa-rāḍhī Kulīnas. Similarly, the value of marriage presents (*yautūka*) offered to the bride and groom in such a marriage was usually low and the contributions of both sides usually equal.[26]

By pursuing a strategy of marrying all his offspring with those of the higher grades, which involved giving away large amounts of wealth and receiving great fame, prestige, and so forth in return, a Kulīna of great wealth strengthened or even raised his rank but lost wealth. For example, the amount of bride-wealth (*kanyā-paṇa*) that had to be given to induce a superior Kulīna to give his eldest daughter and thereby raise one's rank was many times greater than

[23]Shib Chunder Bose, *The Hindoos As They Are* (Calcutta: W. Newman & Co., 1881), p. 49.

[24]Śarmā, "Kula-dīpikā," fols. 10a–10b.

[25]Brindāban Chandra Putatuṇḍa, *The Manners and Customs in Bengal in the Seventeenth and Eighteenth Centuries* (Bariśāl: Bariśāl Śākhā-Pariṣad, 1916), p. 114.

[26]B. C. Bose, *Hindu Matrimony* (Calcutta: J. N. Ghose & Co., 1880), pp. 6–7.

25 rupees. One Kaniṣṭha, Jīvankrishna of the wealthy Mitra family of Darjīpāṛā in Calcutta, gave a bride-wealth of 801 rupees in 1848 in order to obtain the eldest daughter of Jaygopāl Basu, a Mukhya, and rise one grade to Mukhya rank. Jīvankrishna's brother, Gopālkrishna, a Madhyāṃśa by birth, gave even more—1,301 rupees—in order to obtain the eldest daughter of Maheshchandra Ghosh, another Mukhya, and rise two grades to Mukhya rank.[27]

The greatest power to transform inherited rank either into its superior fruits or even into higher rank was thought to be the innate property of the highest or Mukhya grade, senior-most in birth. By demonstrating his inborn prowess in a series of nine (!) marriages, a Mukhya of great wealth was thought to strengthen or refine his inherited rank to the maximum extent possible for any Kulīna in the subcaste. This he did by marrying his four younger daughters to the eldest sons of lower grades and marrying his three younger sons with the eldest daughters of the lower grades:

> Of all the seniority grades (*kula*) high and low, the Mukhya is the king (*rājā*); everyone worships (*pūjā*) him and gains the wealth of his rank. His first daughter is to be given to an equal, his second to a Kaniṣṭha, his third to a Chabhāyā, his fourth to a Madhyāṃśa, and his fifth to a Teoja; these are the main gifts. It is his duty to make his first acceptance with one equal in birth. When he takes the [eldest] daughter of a Kaniṣṭha, his second acceptance is virtuous. His third acceptance is with a Madhyāṃśa, I tell this to the council. The fourth acceptance is with a Teoja. When the Mukhya completes all these acceptances up to this point, he is perfectly formed of nine colors.[28]

Since the Mukhya was already highest in rank of the nine grades by birth, he did not, of course, make offerings of wealth (*paṇa*) to the fathers of the brides and grooms of lower rank. Even so, it was necessary to expend large sums of wealth in order to obtain "nine-colored" rank. In their competition for rank, other Kulīnas apparently resisted the attempts of prolific, wealthy Mukhyas to complete this set of transactions. As a result, poor Kulīnas were often the only ones available, and they apparently agreed to make such marriages only if their daughters or sons were given large marriage presents (*yautūka*). Thus, for Rāmnārāyaṇ Basu Sarbādhikārī (1746–1826), one of the five Mukhyas to succeed

[27]Bimal Chandra Mitra, *Darjjī-pāṛā-Mitra-vaṃśa-paricayer Kayeka Adhyāya* (Calcutta: By the Author, 1953), p. 23.

[28]Vacaspati, "Kula-sarvvasva," in Vasu, *Vaṅger-Jātīya Itihāsa*, VI, Pt. I, 112–13.

in this Herculean labor, "it was necessary to spend a great deal of wealth on this activity. Suppose a proper Kulīna became available but he was poor. Since the gift of a daughter to this kind of groom was considered very improper, he gave money and land for the maintenance of grooms. For this, 150,000 rupees were spent."[29]

The third strategy a Kulīna could pursue was the inverse of the second. By marrying his offspring, especially his eldest daughter and son, with inferiors, a Kulīna of little or no wealth gained wealth. But by subordinating the goal of selfless worship to that of personal gain, he turned his rank into the inferior fruits of rebuke (*nindā*), disrespect (*apamāna*), and shame (*lajjā*), or even lowered his rank altogether.

This social mobility which was seen to occur within the closed Kulīna genera was not considered to be the result of any fundamental conflict or tension between the position a person acquired by "ascription" (birth) in an unchanging social order and the position he acquired by "achievement" (conduct). It would be wrong to assume that the Brāhmaṇs and Kāyasthas viewed their caste and clan order as a static or absolute one. In the superior times, places, and circumstances of the past, every Kulīna, fed by the powerful Hindu king, might have been able to pursue the higher goal of worship, refining and preserving his embodied clan rank and transforming it into its superior fruits—fame, respect, and so forth, by following the ninefold code for conduct. In the present Kali age of the middle period, however, times, places, and circumstances were such that the goals pursued necessarily varied. Kulīnas now had to be their own kings and feed each other. Hence, only those who had the wealth could pursue the higher goal of worship (*dharma*), refining their embodied ranks; others, however, had to pursue the lower goal of gain (*artha*) in order ultimately to return to the pursuit of the higher. And in the middle period, marriages were seen to be the decisive acts by which men pursued these goals.

Thus, the Brāhmaṇs and Kāyasthas viewed the Kulīnas as persons whose wealth and rank were in perpetual flux, changing in response to time, place, and circumstances. Keśarī, genealogist of the Uttararāḍhī Kāyasthas, vigorously articulates this view of the Kulīna, who is seen to alternate his pursuit of these two goals. When he is in need of wealth,

[29]Saurīndra Kumār Ghosh, *Kriḍā-samrāṭ* (Calcutta: N. P. Sarvādhikārī Smaraka Samiti, 1963), pp. 17–18.

His acceptances decrease and his gifts stay the same, while he wanders about eating at the invitation of others. Called a touchstone (*nikaṣ*) of rank, he stops inviting others to marry with offerings of wealth and, because he purifies (*śuddha*) and cooks (*pāka*) rank through marriage, he receives money for accepting a daughter as well as for receiving one, and travels from house to house feasting. When he again prospers by making wealth, once again he invites others to marry with gifts of wealth. . . . The giving of wealth (*artha-dāna*) is the root (*mūla*) of everyone. Without it, his root and rank go away. By strength of wealth, once again his rank rises. Therefore, Keśarī says that the invitation to marry with an offering of wealth is the root of high rank.[30]

Another Uttara-rādhī text states this view from the point of view of the ranked grades themselves: "In three generations, embodied rank (*kula*) becomes pure (*nirābil*), in three generations broken (*bhaṅga*). In three generations the waves of the grades move up and down. Defects by marriages made over three generations remain for three generations, while increases by marriage made over three generations purify for three generations."[31]

Fallen Kulīnas

The lowest ranked grade of Kulīnas in the Brāhmaṇ and Kāyastha subcastes, referred to as Vaṃśaja, Kulaja, or Bhaṅga Kulīna, contained persons who, though descended by birth (*-ja*) from a Kulīna clan (*kula*, *vaṃśa*), had, in terms of their embodied ranks and inborn codes, become "broken" (*bhaṅga*, *bhraṣṭa*), "inferiorized" (*hīna*), "ruined" (*naṣṭa*), or "suspended" (*sthakita*). A Kulīna was thought to break his coded bodily substance or rank during the middle period not by departing from the general activities enjoined in the ninefold Kulīna code but by failing to maintain his relationship of reciprocal exchange with the other Kulīnas of his through marriage. Thus, the Vaṃśaja is defined in terms of his marital exchanges: "He who, though born of a good Kulīna and attached to his code (*dharma*), does not have successive reciprocal exchanges with the Kulīnas, is proclaimed a Vaṃśaja."[32] And: "The nature of a Vaṃśaja is the abandonment (*rohitatva*) of the

[30]Ghaṭaka-keśarī, "Kula-kārikā," in Vasu, *Vaṅger Jātīya Itihāsa*, III, Pt. I, 51.
[31]"Uttara-rāḍhīya Kula-pañjikā," in Vasu, *Vaṅger Jātīya Itihāsa*, III, Pt. I, 54.
[32]Vācaspati, "Kularamā," in Vasu, *Vaṅger Jātīya Itihāsa*, I, Pt. I, 157.

uninterrupted relationship of reciprocity when rank is suspended (*sthakita*)."[33]

The marriage codes of the Kulīnas in each subcaste, no matter how wide the range of marriage norms they contained, included a minimum norm for preserving rank. In the Dakṣiṇa-rāḍhī Kāyastha subcaste, where the preservation of Kulīna rank depended on the marriage of the eldest son, the minimum norm enjoined acceptance of a Kulīna daughter. A Kulīna who did not and accepted the daughter of a Vaṃśaja or Maulika instead was said to ruin or lower his inherited rank and became similar in rank to persons of these lower grades: "Listen carefully to how one becomes a Maulikānta; it happens if he does not make a first acceptance with a Kulīna and accepts from a Maulika instead. In every clan Maulikāntas come into existence in this way. Through the breaking of rank (*kula-bhaṅga*), disrespect arises, this is the fruit. If he makes his first acceptance with a Vaṃśaja, he comes to resemble him."[34]

Conversely, in subcastes where the preservation of Kulīna rank rested on the marriage of a daughter, the gift of a daughter to a Kulina was the minimum norm. Among the Vaṅgaja Kāyasthas, a Kulīna who did not adhere to this norm was thought to fall from his rank and become a Kulaja whereas his descendants eventually became Vaṃśaja: "If just one gift of a daughter in marriage remains, he is considered a Kulīna; otherwise, he is a Kulaja, fallen through the ripening of his act. By the fifth generation there is no trace of Kulīna rank left and he becomes a Vaṃśaja having that particular prestige. Higher than the Maulika by virtue of his clan (*vaṃśa*), he stands shamed at the door of the Kulīna."[35]

Though Kulīnas were thought capable of preserving their divinely generated rank by their own actions, it was believed that no human was capable of generating Kulīna rank who did not receive it at birth. Thus, a Kulīna who broke his rank was considered unable to regain it: "Even though there is a rise of one who has been ruined, and even though he is descended of a Kulīna, no matter how much giving and taking he does with Kulīnas, he is declared to be a Kulaja."[36]

A Kulīna was believed to depart from his generic marriage code as

[33]Śarmā, "Kula-dīpikā," fol. 16b.
[34]Vācaspati, "Kula-sarvvasva," in Vasu, *Vaṅger Jātīya Itihāsa*, VI, Pt. I, 115.
[35]Bṛhaspati, "Ḍhākur," in Vasu, *Vaṅger Jātīya Itihāsa*, VI, Pt. I, 96.
[36]Śarmā, "Kula-dīpikā," fol. 16b.

a Kulīna because his lower personal code, conditioned by poverty or greed, enjoined him to acquire wealth. A Kulīna of high Kulīna rank could exchange his rank for the wealth of a lower Kulīna, but a poor or greedy Kulīna of low rank could not readily pursue this strategy. He was forced by his own circumstances to pursue a strategy of subordinating the goal of worship to that of gain, exchanging his rank for the wealth of the inferior Vaṃśajas and non-Kulīnas. Thus,

> Achu Ghosh, the son of Chā̃ni Ghosh, on account of poverty (*durbhakṣa*) and in order to maintain his dependents, married the daughter of Byuran Dey and became inferior. . . . On account of poverty, Achu Ghosh went to the house of Byuran Dey and asked, "Where is Byuran Dey?" His slave said, "He is ploughing in the fields." He went there and asked, "Whose name is Byuran Dey?" He said, "It is my name." Then Achu Ghosh said, "I am not able to feed and maintain my dependents; my poverty is great. Give your daughter in marriage to me." He said, "You are Kulīna, I am ordinary (*sāmānya*). Nonetheless, I shall marry my daughter with you if you will live in my house until my daughter has a son." Achu Ghosh said, "Good, I will live [in your house], but you must support my dependents." In this way, the two reached an agreement and the marriage took place.[37]

> The honour of the house of a pure Kulīna is generally tarnished through one main reason of poverty or avarice. In the event of a pure Kulīna being in straitened circumstances, the inducement of pecuniary gain would, on the occasion of his daughter's marriage, incline him to resort to a family who are Bhaṅga Kulīnas or Maulikas; for, then the Bhaṅga Kulīnas or Maulikas will, in consideration of the diminished honour of their house, pay a certain sum of money or property to him at the time of the marriage, and his acceptance of this offer renders his house less illustrious and brings it down a degree below its actual rank; and thence forward all his successors will feel the consequences of such degradation, while, on the other hand, the glory of the Bhaṅga Kulīna's or Maulika's house is enhanced by this alliance.[38]

Kulīnas who subordinated the goal of worship to the goal of gain by accepting wealth from the Maulikas out of greed instead of need were held to "buy and sell" (*biki-kini*) their sons and daughters. As a result, they ruined the superior prestige, pride, and so forth

[37] *Ibid.*, fols. 22a–22b.
[38] Bose, *Hindu Matrimony*, p. 5.

inherent in their rank even if they did not ruin their rank outright. Nandarāma, genealogist of the Dakṣiṇa-rāḍhī Kāyasthas, states that, "Buying and selling (*biki-kini*) is not in the code for conduct (*kulācāra*) of a Kulīna. What pride is there in selling a daughter to a Maulika? Those who live by selling their sons and daughters lose their greatness and prestige and have no pride in the council. Nandarāma Mitra says, 'Listen, Maulikas, not taking is in the code for conduct of the Kulīna.'"[39]

The Kulīna, superior in rank to the Vaṃśaja, was thought able to purify the rank of the Vaṃśaja by making marriage exchanges with him. The inferior Vaṃśaja, however, was believed to ruin or lower the rank of the Kulīna by reciprocating these exchanges. Hence, exchanges which the Kulīna made with the Vaṃśaja were conceived of as nonreciprocal, allowing the Kulīna to purify and preserve the rank of the Vaṃśaja without endangering or ruining his own rank. Thus, among the Dakṣiṇa-rāḍhī Kāyasthas, the Kulīnas of the nine ranked grades, all of whom were considered higher and more powerful than the Vaṃśajas, had to marry their eldest sons with the daughters of other Kulīnas. However, they were able to marry their inferior, younger daughters to the eldest sons of the Vaṃśajas, for these were considered to have greater capacity to transmute Vaṃśaja rank into respect than even the eldest daughters of other Vaṃśajas: "Listen to the code for conduct of the Vaṃśaja. A Kulīna may give his eldest daughter to him in a *prāmāṇika*. The Kaniṣṭha may give his fourth daughter, the Mukhya his fifth. The Madhyāṃśa and Teoja Doja-pos may give their second daughters. Even from the gift of the Madhyāṃśa Doja-po, a Vaṃśaja gains [respect.]."[40]

In order to induce the Kulīna to preserve his rank, the Vaṃśaja, of course, had to make offerings of groom-wealth or bride-wealth considered suitable for the Kulīna's nourishment. The amounts given were apparently considered to be quite large, especially when the Vaṃśaja involved was wealthy and, presumably, of dubious birth: "The rich and ambitious Vaṃśajas are very desirous of giving their daughters in marriage to Kulīna Brāhmaṇs and I know instances in which very heavy *paṇas* (dowries) were given to the bridegroom's parents for inducing them to give their sons in marriage with the

[39] Nandarāma Mitra, "Maulika Ḍhākuri," Dacca University Library MSS (uncataloged), n.d., fol. 1b.

[40] Nandarāma Mitra, "Vaṃśaja Ḍhākuri," Dacca University Library MSS (uncataloged), n.d., fol. 1a.

daughters of Vaṃśajas."[41] The offering of large amounts of wealth indicated the difference between the Kulīna and Vaṃśaja and the inferiority of the latter, for whereas the Kulīnas were obliged to marry other Kulīnas in order to preserve their rank, they were under no obligation to marry with the fallen Vaṃśajas. Hence, like the Śrotriya or Maulika, the Vaṃśaja had to offer a large inducement.

The inferiority of the Vaṃśaja was also marked in food exchanges. Kulīnas were not only able to accept the wealth of other Kulīnas; they were also able to accept and eat the ordinary cooked food, boiled rice, at the feasts of other Kulīnas of their subcaste, whatever their rank. The ordinary food of the Vaṃśaja, however, was considered unsuitable as a source of nourishment for the Kulīnas. Among the Rāḍhī Brāhmaṇs, "The Kulīnas regard the Vaṃśajas as very inferior in rank, and on ceremonial occasions, particularly in marriages, the Kulīnas will not interdine with them, and are therefore rarely invited on occasions of marriage of Vaṃśajas who are practically outcastes of Kulīna Brāhmaṇs."[42] Thus, the Vaṃśaja genus was viewed as a kind of interstitial genus. Though persons of this genus had originally possessed the embodied rank and code of the Kulīnas, they had, through misconduct, come to possess ranks and codes more like those of the Śrotriyas or Maulikas than of the Kulīnas. One Dakṣiṇa-rāḍhī text sees the Vaṃśaja as suspended between the Kulīna and Maulika like the king Triśaṅku, who, after improperly performing a sacrifice in order to ascend to heaven, remains suspended in the sky in the form of the Southern Cross constellation.[43]

Śrotriyas and Maulikas Worship Kulīnas

Siddhas: Par Excellence Feeders of the Kulīnas

Bengali Brāhmaṇs and Kāyasthas saw their own past as one characterized by periods where embodied Vedic ranks were upheld by correct conduct by the proper combining and separating of coded substances, only to be followed by periods in which those embodied ranks became confused and inferiorized by improper mixtures of

[41] Basanta Coomar Bose, *Hindu Customs in Bengal* (Calcutta: Book Company, 1928), p. 32.

[42] *Ibid.*

[43] Vācaspati, "Kula-sarrvasva," in Vasu, *Vaṅger Jātīya Itihāsa*, VI, Pt. I, 114.

coded substances. Hence, the Hindu community was believed to contain persons and families whose original, superior ranks had become latent and troubled. Families which appeared to belong to lower occupational *jātis* often claimed to belong to the higher, and families which belonged to the higher occupational *jātis* often behaved as though they belonged to the lower.

The problem of how to maintain an orderly and unified community under such circumstances had been solved before the middle period by Vallāla Sena. He ingeniously established a dual or alternate organization scheme for classifying families into *jātis*. According to his scheme, all Śūdras, for example, could be classed, as they had been, into sets of ranked occupational *jātis*. Or, alternatively, the same Śūdras, and especially those who declared they were really Kāyasthas and not inferior Śūdras, could be classed as Kāyasthas.

The axial *jāti* in this scheme was the Maulika Kāyastha *jāti*. This *jāti* said to consist of persons drawn from all thirty-six Śūdra *jātis*, contained two ranked *jātis*, Siddha, or actualized Maulika Kāyasthas, and Sādhya, "latent" or "troubled" Maulika Kāyasthas. Those families which "actualized" their embodied ranks by worshiping the Kulīnas were classed as Siddha whereas families of the lower Śūdra *jātis*, who said they had the capacity to marry and feed the Kulīnas but had not done so, were classed as Sādhyas. Let us first discuss the middle period relations of the Siddha Śrotriyas and Maulikas to the Kulīnas and then turn to a consideration of the Sādhyas and the process of upward caste mobility.

The Kulīna clans of the middle period, endowed since their divine generation with their ninefold Vedic code for conduct, had acquired their ranks as Vedic Brāhmaṇs or Kāyastha Śūdras by birth, and they were thought of as continually refining and preserving their ranks over time by making reciprocal exchanges among themselves. The non-Kulīna clans, descended from Brāhmaṇs and Śūdras who ruined their embodied Vedic ranks and had come to belong to inferior occupational *jātis*, were believed to have "actualized" (*siddha*) their "latent" (*sādhya*) or "troubled" (*kaṣṭa*) ranks as Vedic Brāhmaṇ and Kāyasthas once again by making purificatory marriages with the Kulīnas in their respective subcastes. It was considered necessary for their descendants to continue purifying their ranks in succeeding generations not by marrying among themselves but by repeating the purifying marriages made by their progenitors. Hence, just as the Kulīnas were considered to be inferior to the Vedic gods who had generated them, so the Śrotriyas and Maulikas were held to be inferior to the human gods who had generated them, the Kulīnas.

Thus, the Śrotriya and Maulika clans formed separate, ranked worship *jātis* or "grades" similar in substance and code to the Kulīnas but inferior. The similarities of the Kulīnas and non-Kulīnas made it possible for them to exchange daughters. Their differences in rank, however, meant that their gifts and acceptances had different consequences. The gifts and acceptances made by the higher Kulīnas with the lower non-Kulīnas were seen to purify and preserve the inherited ranks of the latter; yet if these gifts and acceptances were reciprocated by the non-Kulīnas, they were believed to ruin or even lower the ranks of the Kulīnas. Thus, if the Kulīna was to preserve his own rank, the exchanges he made with the Śrotriya or Maulika had necessarily to be characterized by the "absence of reciprocity."[44]

The particular marriage codes of the non-Kulīna clans varied from one subcaste to the other, just as did the marriage codes of the Kulīnas and Vaṃśajas. Among the Dakṣiṇa-rāḍhī Kāyasthas, where rank was maintained by the marriage of the eldest son, the Siddha Maulika, by virtue of his gifts to the Kulīna in the past was thought to have the power in the present to offer his eldest daughter as a first gift to the Kulīna. Unlike the eldest daughter of a Kulīna, however, she was not considered to be acceptable as a Kulīna's first wife, or *dharma-patnī*, "the wife for the purpose of performing acts of worship." To the contrary, she was acceptable only as a second wife or *kāma-patnī*, "a wife for enjoyment," as the name of this gift, *ādyarasa-dāna* or "gift of erotic sentiment," indicates. Accordingly, the acceptance of such a gift was held capable of bringing a Kulīna only personal enjoyment; it could not transmute his embodied rank into its subtle superior fruits. Only the acceptance of a proper daughter from another Kulīna could do this.

The Kulīna's transformational power was much greater than that of the Siddha Maulika. Not only could he make his daughters, whether eldest or younger, into a bride considered acceptable as first wife, *dharma-patnī*, for the eldest son of the Siddha Maulika; more important, by making these gifts, which would have ruined the rank of a Kulīna if he had accepted them from a Maulika, he could transmute the inherited rank of the Siddha Maulika into its superior fruits—fame, greatness, luster, and so forth. Thus, the

[44]Ghaṭaka-vidyānidhi, *Kulakalpadruma*, p. 57.

gift of a Kulīna's eldest daughter to a Siddha Maulika of the same generation was referred to as a *prāmāṇika-dāna*, a "gift causing perfection" of the Siddha Maulika's rank. Maulikas who obtained this gift were said to transmute their rank into greatness (*mahimā*).[45] Similarly, acceptance of the daughter of a Kulīna of inferior generation, referred to as the "acceptance of a son's daughter (*pautrī-grahaṇa*), was held to bring "luster" (*śobhana*) to a Siddha Maulika's rank.[46] While the acceptance of these two gifts was optional, the acceptance of a younger daughter (*pratisāraṇa*) of a Kulīna was obligatory, for it was the "establisher of life" (*prāṇa-pratiṣṭhatā*), the gift which transformed the "latent" Maulika Śūdra into an "actualized" (*siddha*) Maulika Kāyastha.[47]

Like the Mukhya Kulīna, the Siddha Maulika could polish his rank even further by making additional or better marriages than those already described—a second *ādyarasa*, acceptance of a Mukhya's sixth daughter (instead of the younger daughter of a lower Kulīna), and acceptance of a son's son's daughter:

> Listen to the marriages of the Maulika who becomes absorbed in increasing his fame (*yaśa*) and reputation (*kīrtti*), I speak of them all. The rule is first to make the *ādyarasa* gift of a daughter, by which he obtains the treasure of the nine seniority grades beginning with Mukhya. Next, he makes a second *ādyarasa* gift and, according to the rule, properly becomes a very successful (*prasiddha*) Maulika. He accepts a younger daughter (*pratisāraṇa*) of the same generation from one of the eight seniority grades beginning with Kaniṣṭha, this is the rule recorded by the learned. The new practice of accepting the sixth daughter (*gaṛ-chei*) of a Mukhya has also become the rule; in this way he obtains full view (*sandarśana*) of the Mukhya and a great reputation (*atiśaya nāma*). Then he makes the acceptance of a son's daughter (*pautrī*), a son's son's daughter (*prapautrī*), or a son's son's son's daughter (*atiprapautrī*) of a Kulīna. Through these actions with the nine seniority grades he becomes very lustrous (*suśobhana*).[48]

Nonreciprocal exchanges among the Rāḍhī Brāhmaṇs, where rank was believed to be decisively transformed by the gift rather than the acceptance of a daughter, were supposed to be exclusively hypergamous. Śrotriyas were enjoined to give daughters to the

[45] Vācaspati, "Kula-sarvvasva," in Vasu, *Vaṅger Jātīya Itihāsa*, VI, Pt. I, 114–15.
[46] *Ibid.*, 114.
[47] Nandarāma Mitra, "Maulika Ḍhākuri," fol. la.
[48] Vācaspati, "Kula-sarvvasva," in Vasu, *Vaṅger Jātīya Itihāsa*, VI, Pt. I, 115.

Kulīnas, daughters considered to be "fully acceptable" (*saṃgrāhya*) to the Kulīnas, even as first wives (*dharma-patnī*). Their acceptance did not prevent the Kulīna Brāhmaṇ from refining and preserving his own superior rank so long as he gave all his daughters to other Kulīnas. If, however, he gave even a single daughter to a Śrotriya, he ruined his Kulīna rank: "Having given a daughter to a Śrotriya, a Kulīna becomes a Vaṃśaja."[49]

The making of these nonreciprocal exchanges allowed a Kulīna, whether Kāyastha or Brāhmaṇ, to marry with a non-Kulīna without ruining or lowering his inherited rank, provided, of course, that he also made at least one appropriate marriage with other Kulīnas. In subcastes such as the Dakṣiṇa-rāḍhī Kāyastha, this meant marry-his eldest son with the daughter of another Kulīna whereas in subcastes such as the Rāḍhī Brāhmaṇ, this meant marrying a daughter to another Kulīna. Still, a Kulīna did suffer the loss of fame, respect, prestige, and so forth by marrying with non-Kulīnas. Hence, such marriages were appropriate only for a Kulīna whose personal code and circumstances enjoined him to acquire wealth and food.

Appropriately enough, it was necessary for the Maulikas and Śrotriyas to worship the divine but needy Kulīnas in their respective subcastes with suitable offerings of wealth and food in order to induce them to make marriages so that the Maulikas and Śrotriyas could purify and preserve their inherited ranks and transmute them into their superior fruits: "When he makes a marriage with a Kulīna, he will worship him with great wealth and show him humility (*vinaya*), for the Kulīna is indeed a god (*ṭhākura*), great in rank."[50] Thus, cash offerings (*paṇa*) were made to the father of the Kulīna groom or bride as inducements to marry his children with non-Kulīnas:

> Thousands and thousands of rupees are spent in securing the favors or alliance of the Kulīnas—the great arbiters of caste—and he who by the power of his purse can enlist on his side a larger number of these pampered Kulīnas generally takes away the palm.[51]

> Kulīna fathers take money from Maulikas and marry their daughters in well-established Maulika houses.[52]

[49] Ghaṭaka-vidyānidhi, *Kulakalpadruma*, p. 57.
[50] Bṛhaspati, "Ḍhākur," in Vasu, *Vaṅger Jātīya Itihāsa*, VI, Pt. I, 95.
[51] Bose, *Hindoos As They Are*, p. 170.
[52] Rājendrakumār Ghosh, *Kāyastha-samāja-tattva* (Calcutta: By the Author, 1931),

The amount of wealth (*paṇa*) given in worship to a Kulīna by a non-Kulīna in a marriage which maintained rank was fixed, though, of course, at a higher rate than that paid by one Kulīna to another. Unfortunately, however, there is little detailed evidence in the genealogies on this. A later secondary account of a Dakṣiṇa-rāḍhī Kāyastha marriage, written in 1881, states that the amount was then fixed at 50 rupees.[53] Another account, written in 1897, states that the highest amount given by a Maulika to a Kulīna in any of the subcastes was 101 rupees.[54] Both of these are considerably higher amounts than those recorded as the highest fixed rates—24 or 40 rupees—to be given by one Kulīna to another in the Vaṅgaja Kāyastha genealogies. Since similar rates for this subcaste were still current in eastern Bengal in the latter part of the nineteenth century,[55] it is likely that the rates mentioned in the secondary sources were also current in the late eighteenth and early nineteenth centuries.

The marriage presents (*yautūka*) offered to the bride and groom, which were supposed to be of equal value on the part of intermarrying Kulīnas, were supposed to be greater in value on the part of a Śrotriya or Maulika when he married with a Kulīna. Among the Dakṣiṇa-rāḍhī Kāyasthas,

> the Bhaṅga Kulīna or Maulika should give his daughter the greater portion of personal ornaments, or a certain sum of money in lieu thereof amounting to their total value, also gifts to the intended son-in-law; and the Kulīna will present only one or two ornaments to the bride. This is according to what is called the general rule; and it is optional to the parties to increase or decrease the number or value of the presents. Besides the above, the parents of the girl must, directly the marriage is accomplished, offer other presents for the use of the couple. They must give a bed with all its accompaniments to sleep upon, brass and other metallic utensils for domestic use, and clothes of greater and less value for extraordinary and ordinary use of the girl. The bridegroom also will receive some personal ornaments, such as a ring, a necklace, as well as some new apparels to dress himself with. Presents of this description and value are generally given and received by persons not in affluent condition, and wealthy men create novel presents on these occasions which their sufficiency of wealth admits of.[56]

[53]Bose, *Hindoos As They Are*, p. 49.

[54]Mohinīmohan Gupta, *Pās Karār Ḍākāti* (Calcutta: S. Bhattacharya, 1897), p. 19.

[55]James Wise, *Notes on the Races, Castes, and Trades of Eastern Bengal* (London: Harrison & Sons, 1883), p. 315.

[56]Bose, *Hindu Matrimony*, p. 6.

The Śrotriya or Maulika also was required to make gifts ranging in substance from cash to special cooked foods (sweets) to the Kulīna kinsmen of the bride or groom. Among the Dakṣiṇa-rāḍhī Kāyasthas, "the Maulika family sends presents of clothes, sweetmeats, fishes, sour and sweet milk and some money, say about twenty-five rupees, to the house of the Kulīna family, as a mark of honor to the latter, to which, from his superior caste he is fairly entitled."[57]

Among the Vaṅgaja Kāyasthas, "If a Kulīna gives his son or daughter in marriage with a Maulika, his kinsmen are entitled to have *bidāy* and in all cases each house gets some cash payment which varies from rupees two to five, in our family, besides mustard oil, betel leaves, *dahi* (curds) and fish."[58] Other gifts required of the Śrotriya or Maulika were highly particularistic and, of course, varied from one *jāti* to the other. At the conclusion of the wedding ritual in the Dakṣiṇa-rāḍhī Kāyastha subcaste, "the officiating priests of both sides must have their *dakṣiṇā* or pecuniary reward. If the boy be of the Maulika caste and the girl of the Kulīna caste, the former must give double what the latter gives, i.e., 16 rupees and 8 rupees. Here, as in every other instance, the superiority asserts its peculiar privileges."[59]

The prestations required of Maulikas, here referred to pejoratively as Bāṅgāls, after the Vaṅgaja Kāyastha wedding were more elaborate:

> Kulīnas extort money from Bāṅgāls in East Bengal in various ways. When they go the house of the latter on the occasion of a marriage, they will demand and get some money for *grāmadarśanī* or seeing the village, then for *culā-khuḍāni* or digging the ground for making a hearth to cook their food. Before marriage they had extorted some money for attending the *pati-patra* ceremony when the marriage is finally settled. After the marriage when they leave the place, the Kulīnas get *bidāy*, or leave money, which varies from ten to twenty-five or more for each Kulīna. The Brāhmaṇs, *gomastās*, servants, the barber, the washerman who usually accompany them all get money, and the Bāṅgāl has to pay the cost of the food and the hire of the boat or railway fare both ways. Kulīnas who usually travel third class travel second class, or even first class when attending a marriage

[57]Bose, *Hindoos As They Are*, p. 54.
[58]Bose, *Hindu Customs in Bengal*, p. 52.
[59]Bose, *Hindoos As They Are*, pp. 64–65.

at a Bāṅgāl's house. As already stated the Bāṅgāl must give a pot of *dahi*, one of mustard oil, 80 betel leaves and a fish to each Kulīna kinsman of the bridegroom before he starts for the marriage.[60]

While gifts ranging from cash through special cooked food items were considered suitable for acceptance or consumption by the Kulīna, the ordinary cooked food (boiled rice) of a non-Kulīna was considered unacceptable, especially on the occasion of a wedding feast (*bhojana*) where equals were expected to sit in the same room or row (*paṅkti*) and eat together. B. C. Bose, writing of the Vaṅgaja Kāyasthas, states that: "In East Bengal Kulīnas do not allow any Maulika to partake of the marriage feast sitting in the same room with them. The Maulikas must sit in a separate room. This rule is strictly observed. In this marriage feast the bridegroom's party and the bride's party sit to breakfast in the same room if they are Kulīnas."[61] The refusal of the Kulīnas to eat Maulika boiled rice was apparently so strong in this subcaste that Rāmānanda even included it among the nine enjoined acts for a Kulīna: "*Niṣṭhā* is the avoidance of eating the boiled rice of inferiors."[62] Statements in other texts state of the Kulīnas that, "Those who eat boiled rice in their houses become lower in rank."[63] Among the Dakṣiṇa-rāḍhī Kāyasthas, Kulīnas, would accept the boiled rice of the Maulikas but only if additional gifts of higher value were made: "Even among equals of the same caste, and much more among inferiors, boiled rice is not taken without mature consideration, and some sort of compensation from the inferior to the superior for condescending to eat the same. The compensation is made in money and clothes according to the rank of the Kulīnas."[64]

The acceptance of boiled rice was an important transmutational unit in the marriage ritual. The marriage of the daughter was thought to transform her bodily substance and code into those of her husband and his clan, and the *bou-bhāt* or "wife's boiled rice" feast which took place after she was taken to her husband's house was believed to complete this change. The refusal of the Kulīna to accept boiled rice from non-Kulīnas required the non-Kulīna bride of a Kulīna to undergo an additional act of transmutation so that she could

[60]Bose, *Hindu Customs in Bengal*, p. 70.
[61]*Ibid.*, p. 42.
[62]Śarmā, "Kula-dīpikā," fol. 16a.
[63]Ghaṭaka-keśarī, "Kula-kārikā," in Vasu, *Vaṅger Jātīya Itihāsa*, III, Pt. I, 51.
[64]Bose, *Hindoos As They Are*, p. 77.

properly serve boiled rice to the Kulīna kinsmen of her husband. This transmutation, by which she became a Kulīna, was effected through a second feast, the *pāka-sparśa* or "touching of cooked food" feast. In order to induce the Kulīna kinsmen of her husband to accept her rice and change her into a Kulīna, the new wife, of course, had to worship the invited Kulīnas with gifts:

> If the newly married wife be the daughter of a Maulika and her husband be a Kulīna the husband's kinsmen and kinswomen are invited to a breakfast to her husband's house and each family receives half the *bidāy* paid to each of the guests who were invited to attend the marriage and a few extra rupees for some petty items before any Kulīna accepts the invitation. Each of the married kinswomen receives a *sāri* for eating with her and those whose feet she can touch get another cloth each. But this does not permit the newly married wife to touch the food of her Kulīna kinsmen. If she wishes to do so then she must again pay another half *bidāy* to the head of every family among her kinsmen and give the kinsmen a feast or she can amalgamate the two feasts together. This last ceremony is called *pāka-sparśa* or touching cooked food. On this occasion, when all the guests are seated for breakfast she enters the room and puts a handful of rice or pilau upon each plate beginning with her husband and retires. Then the servers come and serve other dishes as usual and the breakfast commences. Every family which partakes of this breakfast is bound to take food cooked or touched by her, but if she does not perform this *pāka-sparśa* ceremony then no kinsman is bound to take any cooked food touched by her. But female kinswomen will simply eat with her in the same room, if she performs the first ceremony called *bou-bhāt* or a wife's rice taking. This only raises her to a level with her other kinswomen, Kulīna or Maulika but if she performs the ceremony of *pāka-sparśa* then she raises herself on an equality with kinswomen who are daughters of Kulīna. Nevertheless, no outsider Kulīna is bound to eat any food cooked or touched by her unless some money is paid to him.[65]

Since the Kulīna never returned the gifts of wealth and food he received from the Śrotriya or Maulika, the Kulīna was characterized as the economic and political dependent of the Siddha or "actualized" Śrotriya or Maulika. Among the Brāhmaṇs or Kāyasthas he was the par excellence royal feeder of Kulīnas, the middle period replacement of the old Hindu king. Rāmānanda speaks eloquently of this relationship between the Vaṅgaja Kāyastha Kulīna and the highest, actualized Maulika or Madhyalya in that subcaste:

[65]Bose, *Hindu Customs in Bengal*, pp. 60–61.

> That Madhyalya family (*kula*) is best which, in order to protect the high rank (*kula*) of the Kulīnas, resolves their disputes and shelters their virtues. The Madhyalya is intermediate in rank. The Kulīna, however, is dependent on the Madhyalya. A Kulīna without a Madhyalya is known to have no rank. Like the sky when the moon has set, like the ocean when the wind has died down, like the gods when their power has waned; so is the Kulīna without the Madhyalya. The Madhyalya is an ornament of rank and the Madhyalya born with high rank is, as it were, the king in the kingdom and the crest-jewel on the royal parasol.[66]

Thus, the relationship of the Kulīna and non-Kulīna was a complementary one. The relatively wealthy non-Kulīna, inferior in embodied Vedic rank, and the relatively poor Kulīna, superior in embodied Vedic rank, were properly attracted to each other because of their mutual needs. Yet this complementary interdependence did not imply equality of rank. Nor did it imply that, like apples and pears, the two were incapable of being ranked with respect to each other. The superior goal of a man was to transmute the gross, inferior substances of wealth into their subtle, superior essence, embodied rank. By making nonreciprocal gifts of wealth and food to the Kulīnas, by acting as their "royal" feeders, the Śrotriyas and Maulikas believed that they attained the goal of converting wealth into rank, for they believed that by properly marrying with the Kulīnas, they purified and preserved their inherited ranks as actualized (*siddha*) Śrotriyas and Maulikas and transmuted these embodied ranks into the even subtler essences of fame, respect, reputation, and so forth. These transactions were, therefore, statements of high and low rank, for they asserted that the Kulīna, superior in substance and code, was the suitable source of the subtle and superior embodied rank of the non-Kulīna whereas the non-Kulīna, inferior in substance and code, was the suitable source of the gross and inferior substances of wealth and food for the Kulīna.

From Sādhya to Siddha: Transmutations of Caste Rank

Though the Dakṣiṇa-rāḍhī Kāyastha *jāti* contained only the two contrasting worship *jātis* or grades of Kāyasthas, Siddha and Sādhya, "actualized" and "latent," some of the other territorial *jātis* of Brāhmaṇs and Kāyasthas contained more than two and labeled

[66] Śarmā, "Kula-dīpikā," fol. 17a.

them somewhat differently. Yet in these *jātis*, as in the Dakṣiṇa-rāḍhī Kāyastha, a basic distinction was made between the higher Śrotriya and Maulika grades and the lowest. The Vaṅgaja Kāyastha subcaste, for example, contained three ranked grades of Maulika clans—Madhyalya, Mahāpātra, and Acala or Sādhāraṇa. The Madhyalya, who was born in a clan lower than Kulīna, was thought to be the highest of the three because he was higher in birth and, accordingly, worshiped only the Kulīnas with wealth: "Worship of high rank (*kulārccanā*) uninterrupted for ten generations through marriages in succession when one is born in a successful clan lower than Kulīna is the nature of Madhyalya rank.[67]

The Mahāpātra, lower in birth than the Madhyalya, worshiped and fed both the Kulīna and Madhyalya: "When one is born in a clan lower than Madhyalya, his code for conduct is that of the Mahāpātra. . . . And so, he who makes gifts and acceptances with higher clans and never with those broken in rank, and whose food is pure, is declared a Mahāpātra."[68] Though the Madhyalya and Mahāpātra were lower in rank than the Kulīna, both were similar in their coded bodily substance or rank. Hence, the Kulīna of the middle period could accept their worship and marry with them without ruining his rank. By contrast, the lowest Kāyastha, an ordinary (*sādhāraṇa*) Śūdra of inferior birth and lower caste rank, was characterized as devoid of the good qualities which made up the embodied Kulīna code for conduct. Because of this Śūdra's contrastive inferiority, the Kulīna of the middle period could not accept his worship and marry with him without destroying his Kulīna rank:

> When one makes a marriage with an ordinary (*sādhāraṇa*) person, he abandons his rank and remains shamed.[69]
>
> When a Kulīna and Acala Kāyastha make marriages with each other, there is nothing left; through that inferiorizing fault, he ruins his rank. So say the genealogists, giving the essence.[70]

The Rāḍhī Brāhmaṇ subcaste, which contained four ranked grades of Śrotriya clans—Susiddha, Siddha, Sādhya, and Ari or Kaṣṭa—exhibited a similar contrast. Susiddhas gave daughters to and worshiped the Kulīnas but refused to give daughters to or

[67] *Ibid.*
[68] *Ibid.*, fol. 17b.
[69] Bṛhaspati, "Ḍhākur," in Vasu, *Vaṅger Jātīya Itihāsa*, VI, Pt. I, 96.
[70] *Ibid.*, VI, Pt. I, 98.

worship the Siddhas, and so on.[71] As in the other subcastes, the Kulīnas, who could accept worship from the Susiddha, Siddha, and Sādhya Śrotriyas without ruining their ranks, could not accept worship from the lowest grade of Śrotriya clans. These "enemy" (*ari*) or "troublesome" (*kaṣṭa*) Brāhmaṇs, characterized as "destroyers of rank" (*kula-nāśaka*) and identified with the non-Vedic, fallen (*patita*) Brāhmaṇs of the lower Śūdras, were, according to one text, "to be avoided by the Kulīnas in marriage (*sambandha*), at feasts (*bhojana*), in gifts (*dāna*) and Vedic acts of worship (*yajña*), and at the time of the funeral ceremony (*śrāddha*)."[72] Thus, whatever the Brāhmaṇ or Kāyastha *jāti*, families of their lowest worship *jātis*, possessed of their inferior ranks and unable to make marriages with the Kulīnas without ruining the Kulīnas' ranks, were not in present time Vedic Brāhmaṇs or Kāyasthas. They were in the present only "latent" or "troublesome" Brāhmaṇs or Kāyasthas.

According to the dual classification scheme of Vallāla Sena, the families which belonged to these lowest of worship *jātis* within the Vedic Brāhmaṇ or Kāyastha Śūdra *jātis* could also have been classed as families of the fallen Brāhmaṇ *jātis*, or, in the Śūdra *varṇa*, as families of the occupational *jātis* ranked below the Kāyastha. Those families classed as latent or troublesome Brāhmaṇs or Kāyasthas were those which manifested the capacity to make unselfish worshipful gifts to the Kulīnas and wanted to be proclaimed "actualized" Śrotriya Brāhmaṇs or Maulika Kāyasthas. Having shed their *jāti* occupations and become well-to-do, these families now wished to convert some of their wealth into higher caste rank. Let us see how this was done among the Kāyasthas, about whom we have the most detailed data.

Marriage was, of course, the means by which changes in caste rank were effected in middle period Bengal. Families of inferior Śūdra origin which manifested the conduct and wealth appropriate to a Kāyastha could actualize their latent ranks as Kāyasthas by enacting those marriages with the Kulīnas by which the Siddha Maulikas had originally acquired and now preserved their Kāyastha rank. By making these same marriages, they, too, could become Siddha Maulikas and even masters of the council. Thus, among the Dakṣiṇa-rāḍhī Kāyasthas, "Those among the seventy-two [clans of Sadhya Maulikas] who make the *ādyarasa* and *pratisāri* marriages

[71] Vasu, *Vaṅger Jātīya Itihāsa*, I, Pt. I, 268–71.
[72] Vācaspati, "Kularamā," in Vasu, *Vaṅger Jātīya Itihāsa*, I, Pt. I, 157.

[with the Kulīnas] become kings among the Maulikas, and those who protect the nine seniority grades (*kula*) become masters of the council (*goṣṭhī-pati*)."[73] A passage from another Dakṣiṇa-rāḍhī text makes it quite clear that rank as a Maulika Kāyastha depended not on birth or origin but on marriage with the Kulīnas: "Whether he be Sādhya (latent), Siddha (actualized), Grāmya (rustic) or Kaṣṭa (troublesome) in origin, that Maulika is preeminent and superior whose gifts and acceptance are in the Kulīna clans."[74]

The making of these marriages by an upwardly mobile Śūdra of lower caste was not easy, for they were thought to constitute a "cutting" (*kāṭī*) by him and his family (wife and children) of his "union" (*mela*) with other persons of his caste, an act which was seen to annoy his clansmen:

> Hear carefully the marriage code (*ḍhākuri*) of the Siddha Maulika: the *ādyarasa* gift and the *pratisāraṇa* acceptance are the wealth of life (*prāṇa-dhana*) for his caste (*jāti*). He has two other actions to complete, listen to their ordering. By accepting the son's daughter [of a Kulīna] the rank of his family gains brilliance; while by the second [acceptance] he cuts the union (*meli-kāṭī*) [he had with other Maulikas]. Listen carefully to the essence of this latter. When his clansmen (*jñāti*) see it, then they will not go to his house. That person who, having heard about this, does not perform this action of rank, gives his clansmen virtue and himself obtains shame.[75]

Once the upwardly mobile Śūdra made the decision to pursue a strategy of marrying with Kulīnas, he was to continue marrying with the Kulīnas. His gift of a daughter to a Kulīna made him indebted to the Kulīnas for raising his rank. A subsequent gift of a daughter to a Maulika was called an "after-defect" (*paścād-doṣa*). It was thought to lower his rank by making him indebted to the Maulikas for his rank:

> Hear how the after-defect of a Maulika comes into being. Having exercised judgment (*vicāra*) in this matter, I speak; you should certainly know it. The rule for a Maulika who first makes the *ādyarasa* gift to a Kulīna groom is to do so afterwards. Through the after-defect, a Maulika becomes the debtor (*khātaka*) of another Maulika and it has been correctly judged that becoming such a debtor is very blameworthy.[76]

[73] Kāśīrāma Basu, Kulajī, Dacca University Library MSS (uncataloged), n.d., fol. 2.
[74] Nandarāma Mitra, "Maulika Ḍhākuri," fol. 2a.
[75] Vācaspati, "Kula-sarvvasva," in Vasu, *Vaṅger Jātīya Itihāsa*, VI, Pt. I, 114.
[76] *Ibid.*, 115.

Completing the purification and raising of a family's rank apparently took about three generations, as this typical passage from a genealogy of a Dakṣiṇa-rāḍhī Sinha family indicates:

> Listen, Kulīnas, genealogists, and learned ones, to this account of the preeminent Maulika Sinha family. The very fortunate Santosh Sinha was greatly respected; his prosperity was made manifest in the thirteenth generation. His son, Chandraketu Sinha, whose intelligence was great, settled in Ānuliyā and became known in the world. His son, the intelligent Śrīnakula Sinha made the *ādyarasa* marriage with the young Satyavān Mitra. The honorable Mitra was of the fifteenth generation and all of his own marriages were made in his own generation.[77]

In order to induce a Kulīna to make the appropriate transforming marriages, an upwardly mobile Śūdra had to worship him with wealth, as a Vārendra Kāyastha text states so succinctly: "Look, so many from other castes (*poṭhi*) outside the seven clans have become erect by means of wealth. Recording much of their distribution would not be good. Through marriages with the chief ones, they gained fame and respect."[78] Though there is little middle period evidence on the amounts of wealth given as inducements to the Kulīnas, it is likely that the amounts required were not fixed but negotiated with needy (or greedy) Kulīnas. After all, a Kulīna who made such marriages stood to ruin his Kulīna rank and become a Vaṃśaja. In the nineteenth century, cash offerings (*paṇa*) ranging from 2,000 to 3,000 rupees for a Kulīna bride to 60,000 rupees for a Kulīna groom are reported.[79]

Trade, landholding, and administration seem to have been the economic routes to Kāyastha rank in the middle period. Below are three stories illustrating the process of upward mobility through trade, landholding, and administration. The first is from the Dakṣiṇa-rāḍhī Kāyastha subcaste. The story is set in early nineteenth-century Calcutta at the end of the middle period, and its author is highly critical not of the fact of mobility but of the manipulative, personal gain characteristic of the people in this particular case. Here the low caste Śūdra, continuing to act as a petty merchant, has failed to manifest his "true" conduct as a "latent" Kāyastha and "buys" his way in. Clearly, too, there are Kulīnas who go around selling their rank as well:

[77]Sinha Kulajī, Dacca University Library MSS (uncataloged), n.d., fol. 1.
[78]Yadunandana, *Vārendra Ḍhākur* (Calcutta: Viśvakoṣa Press, 1912), p. 55.
[79]Bose, *Hindu Customs in Bengal*, p. 41.

> Listen, everyone, I beseech you, while I tell of a particular person, the abandonment of Lakṣmī (goddess of family fortune), and of wealth in the house of an inferior. What shall I say? It is the whim of God; everyone has become devoted to inferiors. They make marriages with the Kulīnas skillfully; listen, I relate the account. There was a man named Rādhāmohan Ghosh. In his family was born Gaura Ghosh, a disgrace to the family (*kulāṅgāra*). Listen, I tell of his marriages (*kriyā*). The marriage of his daughter was strange; it took place in an inferior house called ordinary son of the king (Sādhya Maulika). Though his house was in Bebhāgdī village from first to last, he had no roots. Among the Kāyasthas, he was a mere nothing. I speak in detail to all of you. He who skillfully married with the Kulīnas established his rank here. That is why, indeed, it was a great event; the wicked rascal didn't know his own nature and had forgotten about his father. Hāṭurām Bisvās—we don't know where he lived or his origin; he had married with the sister of Jagannātha—this was his rank. He settled there [in Bebhāgdī] and became a Kāyastha, listen to the account. [In the past] with loads on his head, he used to sell betelnut and salt in the markets. He used to sell things for women, in that way he earned his living. In this manner, he somehow made ends meet. In this way he passed his days. It was God's wish, so he had sons. There were three sons—Gupe, Rudra, and Kumriye. They gave up their father's profession and at this point made marriages with Kulīnas. A Kulīna whose caste rank has been ruined sells his rank; he gives daughters in marriage [to Sādhya Maulikas] and goes around saying, "If you make marriages with a Kulīna you get *gotra* and clan name."[80]

The second story, from the Vaṅgaja Kāyastha *jāti*, is earlier, probably from the sixteenth century, and is highly approving in tone, heaping praise upon Dāsa, a *zamindār* or landholder, who, though born of low caste, did manifest the characteristic of a Kāyastha, devoted as he was to selfless worship and giving:

> There was a Dāsa in Rāḍha who had no high rank; he was not accepted in the union of the Śūdras of the five clans at that time. There was, however, a Dāsa in the Vaṅga country who was superior and had unlimited glory. He was Kandrapa Dāsa, whom I record as superior in Vaṅga. He gave and took daughters in every Kulīna clan, and thus became firmly established in the union, and his food was acceptable in every clan. His spotless deeds were great, he was devoted to worship (*dharma*) and truth, and was strict in adhering to the code for conduct of his family. He was a powerful but peaceful *zamindār* and had good

[80]Dakṣiṇa-rāḍhīya Kulajī, Dacca University Library MSS (uncataloged), n.d., fols. 1–2.

characteristics, and his dignity was great. He was truthful—just listen—and was always fortunate. For these reasons all of the genealogists say he is a Madhyalya.[81]

Our last story, from the seventeenth century and the Vārendra Kāyastha *jāti*, relates the transformation of the embodied rank of a Deb family whose men worked in the Muslim government:

> I speak of one more matchless Deb, listen. Sukdeb, by name, settled in Chariyā-grāma. The son of Sukdeb was Bāsudeb Talukdar. Listen to the details of his fame. He was wealthy and famous in worldly affairs. His son had a job in the *nawāb's* (Muslim governor's) administration. Balrām Rāy was born in this family. He took up his grandfather's job in Vārendra. He began to make pure marriages, everything. Dāsa, Chākī, and Nandī, everyone, enjoyed his cooked food and his sons all increased in respect. He was the master of fifty-two lakhs [of rupees].[82]

Realization of Rank in the Council

Councils, Genealogists, and Council Masters

Vicāra, or "judgment," the capacity to distinguish good and bad, high and low, right and wrong, was required in order to resolve disputes about rank so that embodied persons and genera could fully realize the proper fruits of their actions and thereby uphold the embodied ranks of persons, clans, and castes in the ever-changing Hindu community. Before the middle period, judgment had been exercised and ranks upheld by the great kings (*mahārājas*) such as Ādiśūra and Vallāla Sena. In the increasingly localized and particularized Hindu communities of the middle period, judgment comes to be exercised by local subcaste councils (*samāja*, *sabhā*) which convene under the leadership of a master of the council (*goṣṭhī-pati*, *samāja-pati*) and the professional genealogists (*ghaṭaka*, *kulācārya*, *kulajña*). On these occasions, genealogies were recited, disputes resolved, and the persons invited feasted according to the order of the ranks they were judged to possess. Though the persons who attended a particular assembly were usually persons settled in a particular *zamindārī* territory within that of the subcaste, it would be wrong to think of the local subcaste community and its council as a smaller territorial "segment" of

[81] Chuḍāmaṇi, Kulajī, Dacca University Library MSS (uncataloged), n.d., fols. 16, 22.
[82] Yadunandana, *Vārendra Ḍhākur*, pp. 51–52.

the subcaste, for relationships among persons belonging to the same community council were defined not by shared territorial substance but by shared food.

In order to exercise proper judgment, knowledge (*jñāna*, *vidyā*) was required. Knowledge of the highly particular and ever-changing ranks held by the Brāhmaṇs and Kāyasthas of the middle period was supplied by experts in the form of professional genealogists. Often the genealogists were members of the subcaste for which they worked (Nandarāma Mitra was a Dakṣiṇa-rāḍhī Kāyastha, Devīvara and Vācaspati were Rāḍhī Brāhmaṇs), and the title and occupation of *ghaṭaka* were often hereditary. Yet many of the genealogists worked for other than their own subcastes (Rāmānanda Śarmā, a Rāḍhī Brāhmaṇ, worked for the Vaṅgaja Kāyasthas), and no matter what his caste, the genealogist was to be appointed because of his skill in his occupation not because he had inherited the title of *ghaṭaka:*

> The *ghaṭakas* are remembered in six [respects]: they are [with regard to rank], purifiers (*dhāvaka*) and increasers (*bhāvaka*), contactors (*yojaka*) and uniters (*aṃśaka*), and blamers (*dūṣaka*) and praisers (*stāvaka*). They know our generations (*puruṣa*) and the order of generations, our family livelihoods (*varttana*) and which of us maintains his rank (*kula*) on earth. The *ghaṭakas*, foremost of matchmakers, also know very subtle distinctions of rank. These great ones know descent (*vaṃśa*) and marriage (*aṃśa*) as well as their faults (*doṣa*). *Ghaṭakas* are to be known from these actions not afterward from the mere taking of the title "*ghaṭaka*."[83]

These skilled persons, who assisted their patrons in arranging marriages and kept corporate records of their patron subcaste's marriages in their memories and on paper, received invitations to the wedding councils of their patron subcaste. The genealogies they kept not only contained the names of all males in the subcaste and their marriages; they also contained the subtle fruits of the marriages made, as judged by the genealogists.

It was in the context of the public wedding assembly that persons, both as individuals and clansmen, fully realized the superior fruits of their marriages—fame, respect, praise, greatness—as well as their inferior fruits—infamy, disrespect, blame and shame. By reciting the genealogies in front of the subcaste assembly, the genealogists caused these superior and inferior fruits to be made "manifest"

[83] Śarmā, "Kula-dīpikā," fol. 15b.

or "public" (*prakāśa*) and therefore fully realized. Below are two typical passages recited from a Dakṣiṇa-rāḍhī Kāyastha text before a wedding council of that subcaste. The first contains the inferior fruits obtained by Ayodhyārāma Basu, a Mukhya Kulīna who had made inferior marriages. The second contains the superior fruits obtained by another Mukhya Kulīna, Rāmasundara Basu, as a result of his superior marriages:

> Ayodhyārāma has conceit (*abhimāna*), he did not give his eldest daughter to a Mukhya by birth, but to Kāśīrāma Mitra, a Mukhya by increase. His second daughter went to Muchirāma Ghosh, but in that no satisfaction arose. So, he comes to rest through gifts in marriage. I know of his first acceptance, it was from the conceited (*abhimānī*) Raghudeb, a Mukhya by increase. Thus, neither through gift nor acceptance did fame (*yaśa*) arise. Keśarī knows why and speaks, listen; this was great infamy (*apayaśa*).[84]

> Sundara made a beautiful (*sundara*) gift to Nārāyaṇa Ghosh and became faultless (*nirdoṣa*) through acceptance from Kamalākānta. Having increased his rank through one marriage, his reputation (*nāma*) arose in the Basu clan. Kāśīrāma thus sings of his gifts and acceptances with equals.[85]

The council and its master exercised their judgment with respect to the invited genealogists. In order to insure the accuracy of the genealogists' knowledge, contests were sometimes held in which a larger reward was given to the genealogists judged by the entire council to have most correctly recited from memory the genealogies and marriages of the Kulīnas.[86] Persons who tried to bribe or threaten the genealogists in order to circumvent the manifestation of their inferior births and marriages were seen to enjoy the inferior fruits of these inferior acts as well:

> There are Kāhestos (Kāyasthas) without roots and many in whose roots there are defects. When the *ghaṭakas* see them, they rebuke them with great anger. My residence in this country entails great danger. All of these people meet and plan to get rid of the *ghaṭakas*. Nonetheless, Ghaṭaka-chandra speaks these truths. These Kāhestos without roots have become my enemies: Sati, Mati, Pupī, and Bhāskara. Sati Ghosh has no rank and neither does Mati Ghosh. Pupī Ghosh is defective and the rank of Bhāskara is not respected. Of these, there are still no proper roots.[87]

[84]"Dakṣiṇa-rāḍhīya Ḍhākur," in Vasu, *Vaṅger Jātīya Itihāsa*, VI, Pt. I, 202.
[85]*Ibid.*
[86]Wise, *Notes on the Races, Castes and Trades*, pp. 276–77.
[87]Chuḍāmaṇi, Kulajī, fol. 18.

The master of the council (*goṣṭhī-pati*, *samāja-pati*), often chosen from among the wealthier, more powerful Śrotriyas or Maulikas, had as his code the ordered unity and well-being of the community through the exercise of judgment (*vicāra*). By the exercise of his superior judgment, the master of the council was to help resolve disputes (*vivāda*) about rank. There were indeed very subtle differences of rank in the middle period, especially among the Kulīnas who were considered, by virtue of their organization into so many ranked grades, quarrelsome in nature. As one Bengali saying puts it, "Wherever there are Kulīnas, there is quarreling day and night."[88] Resolution of these disputes was essential. While disputes over rank remained unresolved, the Kulīnas could not be seated in rank order for the feast and could not, therefore, complete the process of realizing the fruits of their marriages. Clearly, then, superior knowledge and skill in judgment were needed in order to accomplish this feat.

As this Dakṣiṇa-rāḍhī-Kāyastha definition indicates, the person who was best suited to be the master of the council from all points of view was the one who was to be chosen as master:

> The characteristics of a Kāyastha *goṣṭhī-pati* are as follows: he who is learned in politics, stable, respectable, and endowed with acts of worship; a supporter of high rank by observation of good and bad marriages, ready to make gifts, and show respect; he who is a supporter, knowledgeable about high rank, and, among the good Maulikas, clever in rank; whose pure clan is powerful, who is well known in the world, and a giver, he is a *goṣṭhī-pati*.[89]

The person who held the position of council master was usually the person who held the *zamindārī* in which the council met, and, like the *zamindārī* itself, the position appeared to be transmitted hereditarily to his son. This was not, however, in principle the device by which a man acquired the position. The more powerful king of the past had chosen one of his own sons as his successor. Now, in the middle period when the power of the community council was greater than that of the local king, the position of council master was only incidentally hereditary, for the council chose the successor of the council master by worshipping him with an honorific garland (*mālā*) and sandal-paste mark (*candana*). Hence, local kings who lost their

[88] Sushīl Kumār De, *Bāṃlā Pravāda* (Calcutta: A. Mukherji, 1952), p. 254.

[89] *Śabdakalpadruma*, comp. by Rājā Rādhākānta Deva (Calcutta: Śabdakalpadruma Office, 1821–57), 1st ed., I, 831.

capacity to give generously and to exercise judgment could and did lost the honor of acting as *samāja-pati.*

The relative powers of the council and the coucil master were also demonstrated by the need of the *rājā* or *samāja-pati* to obtain the unanimous consent of those assembled. Take, for example, an amusing case of upward social mobility reported in one of the Vaṅgaja Kāyasthas genealogies. Jitāmitra Nāga, an ordinary Śūdra, had, by following his personal code, made the marriages and gifts of wealth thought proper and necessary in order to increase his rank and become a Kāyastha of Madhyalya rank. It was, therefore, proper for him to come to the council in order to take his proper seat and have made manifest the superior fruits of his actions. The master of the council, following his personal code, properly agreed to make Nāga a Madhyalya. Yet this adjustment of ranks within the community could not take place unless the council master obtained the consent of everyone, including one Vidyānanda Datta, a Madhyalya who believed that Nāga's arrival might detract from his rank:

> Jitāmitra Nāga was greatly endowed with acts of worship; he was skilled in all the virtues and very peaceful and restrained. He [made] an unprecedented gift to the Kāyasthas. His [wish was for them to accept it]. Then the *rājā* of Candradvīp accepted it for the purpose of performing an act of worship, and bringing all of the Kāyasthas together, he honored those with high rank. Then Jitāmitra Nāga came quickly. He brought everyone: Kulīnas of the four clans, Madhyalyas, and many *ghaṭakas.* Then the *rājā* said in the place where everyone was assembled, "For these reasons, Jitāmitra Nāga is a Madhyalya." Having heard the words of the *rājā*, the Kāyasthas gave their consent: "With due haste, then, make Nāga a Madhyalya." Because Vidyānanda Datta Rāy had heard of this, he came to the *rājā*'s assembly. When he came, he was wearing the dress of a Kṣatriya, having put the twice-born thread across his shoulder. With both hands together, Datta gave a benediction (*āśīrvāda*) to the *rājā*, went to one side, and sat down. Seeing this strange act, the *rājā* therefore asked, "I see the twice-born thread across your shoulder; speak to the point and let me hear the reason for this." Datta said, "What is there to say,.o *rājā*; you have the power to do the undoable. If Jitāmitra Nāga can become a Madhyalya, then you can make me a Kṣatriya, honored one." The *rājā* was astonished to hear all these words and spoke quickly yet with good breeding to Datta: "Who can make your Madhyalya rank disappear? Give your consent to my wish for Nāga-

Majumdār to obtain the rank of Madhyalya. If I do not have the consent of everyone, what power have I? You are a Kāhet (Kāyastha) of Vallāla; everyone recognizes that. Who else can be a Madhyalya like you?" Thus spoke the *rājā* to Datta Rāy. And he had spoken good advice. Hence, all the Kāyasthas consulted and spoke especially to Datta Rāy. As a result, the *rājā* obtained the consent of everyone to make Nāga a Madhyalya next in rank to Datta. So, all the Kāyasthas stood before the *rājā* and made Nāga a Madhyalya in Candradvīp.[90]

Feasting and Rank

The giving of wealth, the source of food, and food the source of bodily substance, was the act by which inherited rank was transformed during the middle period into its living, visible fruits. In previous, superior ages, the more powerful king had upheld the ranks of castes and clans through the exercise of coercive power (*daṇḍa*). Now, in the declining Kali era of the middle period, the many less powerful local *rājās*, acting as masters of their local subcaste councils held people to their ranks less by the use of coercive power than the giving of food:

> Listen carefully to how that person who makes marriages with the nine seniority grades (*kulas*) becomes a *goṣṭhī-pati*. All the Kulīnas enjoy benefits through his marriages and he becomes famous with fame in the world. Through gifts of food (*anna-dāna*) he compels the *ghaṭakas* and Kulīnas; that is why he is respected in his own clan. That person who always maintains the union of the clans, his name is *goṣṭhī-pati*, and he then exercises judgment. The Kulīna becomes purified (*śuddha*) through nine moral acts. He has good acts of worship and humility and he is learned; he establishes [deities] in his family and goes on pilgrimages; he displays devotion to family acts of worship and to his chosen deity and he is engaged in the proper occupation of his caste; he should be a giver and he should constantly be purified through austerities. The *goṣṭhī-pati* should know this code for conduct well.[91]

If the *samāja-pati* upheld rank by giving food, the other persons of the council upheld it by receiving food. Cooked food was the daily source of a person's or genus' bodily substance and of the rank embodied therein. During the middle period, the eating of food was an action by which the embodied rank of a being, whether

[90]Chuḍāmaṇi, Kulajī, fols. 14–15.

[91]Vācaspati, "Kula-sarvvasva," in Vasu, *Vaṅger Jātīya Itihāsa*, VI, Pt. I, 115.

a person (*manuṣya*), a clan (*kula*), or a caste *jāti*), was transformed. By sitting in separate rows (*paṅkti*) arranged according to high and low ranks and by accepting the food served in order of rank and eating it, persons publicly realized and expressed the high and low ranks they possessed within the subcaste and at the same time confirmed their unity as persons of the same generic community.

Below are four accounts of the seating and feasting arrangements made in the assemblies of different subcastes. The first relates how persons of the nine ranked clans were seated in the Uttara-rāḍhī Kāyastha subcaste:

> [First to take their seats] are the pair of clans, Vātsya [Sinha] and Saukālina [Ghosh], who are famed in the world and spotless in prestige. After them, Maudgalya [Dāsa], whose gain with regard to high rank is through marriage with the good clans, [takes his seat]. After him, Viśvāmitra [Mitra] and Kāśyapa] Datta, those whose greatness and duty lie in marriage with the three superior clans, [take their seats]. After them, the Śāṇḍilya Ghosh clan sits sixth, and Kāśyapa [Dāsa], harsh-sounding to the ear and a Kaṣṭa, [takes his seat]. The next two places [are taken by] broken clans, which are well known in marriage as the essence of [the subcaste's] limits; these are the places of [Maudgalya] Kara and Bharadvāja [Sinha].[92]

Next is a secondary account of the impressive arrangements made by the rājā of Candradvīp, who was the master of the Candradvīp council of Vaṅgaja Kāyasthas. Of particular interest is the fact that Kāyasthas in this council had to obtain permission from the *rājā* to make their marriages. Here, in a remote area of east Bengal, the distribution of wealth and the transmutation of ranks were apparently more controllable by the local *rājā*.

> When the council of Candradvīp was established, the *samāja-pati* gave the responsibility of performing two duties to several Brāhmaṇs. For performing these two duties they received the title of *ghaṭaka* and *svarṇāmātya*. . . . To the *ghaṭakas* this responsibility was given, that they would record in their books the increasing genealogies of the Kāyasthas, the number of their marriages, and who married into superior clans and who into inferior clans. They would remain in the royal court and submit accounts of the marriages of the Kāyasthas in detail to the *rājā*. To the *svarṇāmātyas* was given the responsibility of assigning places to the Kāyasthas by looking at the books of the *ghaṭakas*, but later, they themselves began to keep a book of the

[92] "Uttara-rāḍhīya Kula-pañjikā," in Vasu, *Vaṅger Jātīya Itihāsa*, III, Pt. I, 44-45.

> marriages of the Kāyasthas similar to the *ghaṭakas*'. These two positions and their duties are still current. So that the Kāyasthas might feast in the royal compound, the *rājā* built a large building called the Cil-chātor of Cil-chatra. The *rājā*'s seat was placed in the middle of it. The Kulīnas used to sit next to him; and after them the Kulaja, Madhyalya, Mahāpātra, and other Kāyasthas used to sit in order on four sides. . . . When a Kāyastha in Candradvīp *samāja* had to give the marriage of his son or daughter, before the marriage he had to take the permission of the *rājā* and the *rāja* had to exercise royal mediation. If some Kulīna made a marriage without the *rājā*'s permission, he had to be punished before the *rājā*. The *rājā* had several people named *khās-khāl*, and they made that faulty person appear before the *rājā*. The *rājā* judged him and fixed his punishment.[93]

The last two are accounts of two of the subcaste-wide councils of Dakṣiṇa-rāḍhī Kāyastha Kulīnas, called *eka-jāi*, which convened only once in every generation. First is a description of the eighteenth-generation assembly convened by Kiṅkara Sena (d. 1708 A.D.). It is followed by a description of the twenty-fourth generation-assembly, convened in 1854 A.D. by Āśutosh Deb:

> In the eighteenth generation, Kiṅkara invited all the Kulīnas together with the genealogists. At the invitation of Kiṅkara, all of them came; and, at great expense, Kiṅkara made an *eka-jāi*. He honored the Kulīnas for their marriages: first, the Prakṛta-rāja received honor; second, the Sahaja Mukhyas, third the Komala Mukhyas, fourth the Kaniṣṭhas, and fifth the Chabhāyās. The Madhyāṃśas and Teojas were honored sixth and seventh; and the Kaniṣṭha Doja-pos, eighth. The Chabhāyā Doja-pos received honor ninth, and the Madhyāṃśa Doja-pos were honored tenth. The Teoja Doja-pos received honor eleventh. In this way, he honored all the Kulīnas for their marriages. The Kulīnas and genealogists accepted these honors and they accepted Kiṅkara as *goṣṭhī-pati*. The Kulīnas and genealogists accepted these honors and, satisfied, they gave him mastery (*adhikāra*) in the form of the garland and sandal-mark.[94]

> The *kulācāryas* (genealogists) received letters of invitation and all all of them, happy in their hearts, went. All of the Kāyastha *ghaṭakas*, several of whose names I mention here—Mādhava, Rāmachandra, Hara Kulārṇava, Mahesh, Kulārṇava, and others, storehouses of virtue among the *ghaṭakas*, came quickly. The Mukhyas, Kaniṣṭhas, Chabhāyās, Madhyāṃśas, and Teojas came, and the other four

[93]Braj Sundar Mitra, *Candradvīper Rāja-vaṃśa o Vaṅgaja Kāyasthagaṇer Vivarana* (Bariśāl: Kumudakanta Basu, 1913), pp. 22–23.

[94]Maheśchandra Mukhopādhyay, *Vāsuki-kula-grantha* (Calcutta: n.p., 1913), p. 10.

seniority grades came too when they found out about it. Some received letters, some did not receive letters; nonetheless, they came running, invited by word of mouth or not invited at all. Then the genealogists caused the judgment (*vicāra*) of ranks—Mukhya, Kaniṣṭha, and all the others—to take place. When they heard from the mouths of the *ghaṭakas* who had what prestige (*māna*), everyone gave him a position in the appropriate place in the assembly. The genealogists who were there were all learned and deliberated over the marriages which had been made. The Kulīnas who agreed with the *ghaṭakas* took their appointed places in the assembly. Āśutosh, whom the people of Aṅga, Vaṅga, and Kaliṅga praise in worldly affairs, became *goṣṭhī-pati*. The Mukhyas and the others gave him the sandal-mark. In this brilliant acts were achieved in the assembly and he became *goṣṭhī-pati* in the twenty-fourth generation.[95]

To sum up, the relative ranks of the high and low grades of clans, maintained by the making of worshipful, nonreciprocal exchanges of daughters, wealth, and food, were established at the outset of the middle period (c. 1450 A.D.) and endured without significant change into the nineteenth century. Yet the ranks of male householders and their family dependents were not seen as necessarily enduring over long periods of time. To the contrary, families were viewed as frequently lowering or raising their embodied ranks as a result of the marriages they made. Kulīnas moved up and down within the ranked Kulīna grades "like waves"; some of the Kulīnas, those who made very improper marriages, "fell like over-ripe fruit from a tree" and became Vaṃśajas—fallen or broken Kulīnas. Others, such as the Mukhya Kulīnas among the Dakṣiṇa-rāḍhī Kāyasthas, became pinnacles of perfection, endowed with "nine-colored" rank. Even more significant than the fluctuation of clan rank (*kula*) was the fluctuation of caste rank (*jāti*). Throughout the middle period, families of the inferior Brāhmaṇ and Śūdra castes were seen to become high caste Brāhmaṇs and Kāyasthas by transforming their embodied ranks.

Two connected points about this mobility are important. First, social mobility was not an activity that took place around the margins of a social order that was conceived of a "static" and given by "tradition." To the contrary, the very organization of the Brāhmaṇs and Kāyasthas was premised on the existence of and the need for social mobility. Yet it would be a mistake to go to the other extreme and conclude that mobility took place within the same context as

[95]"Samīkaraṇa-kārikā," in Vasu, *Vaṅger Jātīya Itihāsa*, VI, Pt. I, 158.

in a "modern" class society. Whence the second point. Mobility was not viewed as simply a matter of personal or familial loss or gain, as a competition for scarce resources. The purpose of mobility was to sustain the solidarity, unity, and integrity of the Kulīnas, those who most embodied the coded substance of the Veda. Hence acts of upward mobility were themselves defined as acts which promoted unity and prosperity, as selfless acts of worship.

CONCLUSION

The medieval Bengali conception of clan rank as an inherited substance maintained or altered by marriage rested on the cultural definition of castes (*jāti*) and clans (*kula*) as units defined by features from a single order at once natural, moral, and divine. A caste or clan was conceived of as a "genus" defined by the possession of inherited bodily substance and an inborn code for conduct. Each genus contained within it the divine power (*śakti*) to transform substances into their superior forms of fruits. Specifically, each genus contained the divine power to transform repeatedly its inherited rank into a wide range of superior fruits—prosperity, protection, maintenance, fame, respect, and so forth. And this was done by following the genus' inborn code.

Though these codes varied considerably in their content from one genus to another, the defining action enjoined by each generic code was the worship of higher, more divine genera. The content of worship varied as widely as the content of the codes themselves. Yet there, too, it is possible to generalize. At the caste level, worship always seems to have involved the service of the higher, more divine genus by the lower, less divine. At the clan level, worship always seems to have involved the exchange of a daughter in marriage. At either level, worship had as its central element the unselfish feeding or nourishing of the higher genus either with gifts of food, considered to be the source of a genus' bodily substance and rank, or with gifts of wealth, considered to be the source of food.

Worship was central to a genus' code for conduct because the divine power to transform bodily substance varied from caste to caste and clan to clan. Higher castes and clans were thought to be higher because of their greater power to generate and transform coded substances as demonstrated in acts of worship. Thus, at the caste level, the Brāhmaṇ was more powerful and higher than the Śūdra because he possessed the Veda, the corpus of sounds considered to be the source of the divine power (*brahman*) by which the Hindu community itself was generated. Similarly, at the clan level, the Kulīna was more powerful and higher than the non-Kulīna because, generated himself by the gods and endowed by them with Vedic power, he had the divine power to generate Vedic Brāhmaṇs (Śrotriyas) out of fallen non-Vedic Brāhmaṇs and to generate Kāyasthas (Maulikas) out of ordinary, inferior Śūdras. It was through worship of the higher, generating genus that the lower, generated genus obtained the superior fruits of his inherited rank. Thus, it was by worshiping the Brāhmaṇ that the Śūdra obtained maintenance, protection, and prosperity as the fruits of his rank, and it was by worshipping the Kulīnas that the non-Kulīnas continued to obtain the superior fruits of fame, prestige, and respect inherent in their Vedic Brāhmaṇ or Kāyastha Śūdra ranks.

The ranked grades of Brāhmaṇ and Kāyastha clans, which I have characterized as worship *jātis*, did not, then, resemble an aristocratic system of ranks in the European sense. Clan ranks were not based on the holding of ranked political offices or on the holding of lands given by a king. Many Brāhmaṇs and Kāyasthas did in fact hold political offices and lands in middle period Bengal, but patterns of office and land holding did not correlate with clan rank. Indeed, Maulikas and Śrotriyas in their respective Kāyastha and Brāhmaṇ subcastes were often, like the Kṣatriya in relation to the Brāhmaṇ, considered to be the great possessors of wealth.

On the other hand, it would be equally incorrect to see the system of ranks as a purely spiritual or religious one, based on the possession of higher and lower spiritual qualities. The high and low Vedic qualities and codes of the ranked worship *jātis* were not transcendant "spiritual" or "ritual" elements with respect to the "material" flesh, wealth, and power of the humans who possessed them. On the contrary, these elements were imbedded in the bodily substances of the Kulīnas and non-Kulīnas and fed by the wealth and food offered in worship. Thus, the relationship between the two was a transformational one. Selfless gifts of wealth and food caused the worshiper's embodied Vedic rank to be transformed into fame, respect, and prestige or even into higher clan or caste rank, and the acceptance of wealth and food caused the bodily substance of the worshiped to be nourished.

The act of worship was, then, at both the caste and clan level the act of *dharma* par excellence, a concise statement or symbol of the ordered unity of the total community. By worshiping a higher more divine genus, by honoring a divine superior with gifts of wealth and food in accord with its capacity to give, a genus subordinated its own gain (*artha*) and enjoyment (*kāma*) to the higher goal of nourishing and upholding the embodied Veda, the primary source of community well-being and prosperity, and transformed its own embodied rank into the share of well-being, fame, and respect it rightly deserved.

One remarkable aspect of the system of clan ranking in middle period Bengal was the importance attached to social mobility on the part of male householders (*kartā*) and their family dependents (*parivāra*). Only the genera of Kulīna clans, defined as those Brāhmaṇs or Kāyasthas who had sustained their embodied Vedic ranks since the time of their generation by the gods, were closed to upward mobility on the part of male householders of lower grades or castes. The genera of Śrotriya Brāhmaṇs contained families which had, through misconduct, broken their embodied Vedic ranks and become fallen Brāhmaṇs. The genera of Maulika Kāyasthas contained families of Śūdras which had ruined their ranks as superior Śūdras and been born in inferior occupational *jātis*.

The higher grades of Śrotriyas and Maulikas, were considered to be the descendants of fallen Brāhmaṇs or ordinary Śūdras who had "actualized" (*siddha*) their potential as Vedic Brāhmaṇs and Kāyastha Śūdras by worshiping the Kulīnas with gifts of daughters, wealth, and food. The Kulīnas, by accepting their worship, had transformed them into genera of Vedic Brāhmaṇs or Kāyastha Śūdras. The lowest grades of Śrotriyas and Maulikas contained families of the lower castes of fallen Brāhmaṇs or ordinary Śūdras, which appeared to possess the "potential" (*sādhya*) to become Vedic Brāhmaṇs or Kāyastha Śūdras but had not yet realized it. By worshiping the Kulīnas with gifts of daughters and exceptional gifts of wealth and food, a fortunate family of a fallen Brāhmaṇ or inferior Śūdra caste was able to "actualize" its "potential" and transform its lower caste rank into higher caste rank.

Thus, the Śrotriya and Maulika grades were, in a sense, "open" genera. Now, the idea of an "open" caste seems to be a contradiction in terms, but only if we adhere to a Euro-American definition of caste as a group whose membership is defined by blood as natural substance which is beyond the power of men to change. Bengalis did not view caste in this way. For them, "natural" substance and "moral" code were inseparable, homologous elements transformable by acts of worship. Hence, caste blood as well as caste code could be and were changed in middle period Bengal.

Why, according to the Brāhmaṇs and Kāyasthas, did their middle period systems of clan ranking develop? Order, prosperity, and well-being emanated, in their view, from the sounds of the Veda and the acts of worship enjoined in them. Among the *jātis* making up the Hindu community of Bengal, the Vedic Brāhmaṇ and Kāyastha were the highest and most important. The Vedic Brāhmaṇ fully embodied the Veda and its worship code; and the Kāyasthas, the foremost of the Śūdras, had, by virtue of their devoted service of the Brāhmaṇs, become partially imbued with the Veda and came to stand as the par excellence generic worshipers or feeders of the Brāhmaṇs. Hence, upon the conduct of these *jātis*, upon their handling of the coded substances of Vedic worship, rested the prosperity of the entire Hindu community. The conduct of the Brāhmaṇs and Kāyasthas also affected immediately their own embodied ranks. Those whose conduct was in accord with their inborn codes transmuted their inherited ranks into fame, respect, and glory and gained prosperity in the form of wealth, food, and sons. The Brāhmaṇs and Kāyasthas who did not ruin their inherited ranks and went hungry.

The part played by the Hindu king in sustaining the ranks of the Brāhmaṇs and Kāyasthas before the Muslim conquest had been critical, for he had periodically summoned the Brāhmaṇs and Kāyasthas to his court, judged their past conduct, resolved disputes, made their ranks manifest to those assembled, and rewarded those who adhered to their worship codes with appropriate gifts of wealth. Even before the Muslim conquest, the Hindu community, and especially the Brāhmaṇs and the king, oscillated between good conduct and bad, producing important changes. Improper conduct caused the coded bodily substances that defined *jātis* and *kulas* to become mixed and confused, creating problems for successive Hindu king. Improper marriages among different *jātis* were most threatening, for they directly mixed and inferiorized all of the coded substances which defined a *jāti*. The Brāhmaṇs and Kāyasthas of middle period Bengal traced their origin to just such events. The ancestors of the Kulīna Brāhmaṇs and Kāyasthas of middle period Bengal, possessed of superior Vedic ranks, had come and regenerated the Hindu community of Bengal at the request of King Ādiśūra.

Subsequently, these superior Brāhmaṇs and Kāyasthas began to intermarry with the indigenous and inferior Brāhmaṇs and Śūdras, once again threatening the worshipful order of castes and clans. The king Vallāla Sena solved the recurring problem created by the confusion of coded bodily substances by inaugurating his "dual" organization scheme of ranked worship *jātis* or grades for classifying and ranking the Brāhmaṇs and Śūdras of Bengal. The descendants of the Ādiśūra Brāhmaṇs and Kāyasthas who had acted in accord with their ninefold Kulīna code were made into a worship *jāti* dubbed Kulīna. The Brāhmaṇs of Bengal who were fallen and inferior were made into a worship *jāti* called Śrotriya, and the fallen and inferior Śūdras into a worship *jāti* of Kāyasthas called Maulika. Those who had improved their Vedic codes and worshipfully married with the Kulīnas were proclaimed Siddha or "actualized," but those who had not were declared to be Sādhya, "latent," or Kaṣṭa, "troublesome."

The event which moved marriage onto the center of the cultural stage was the Muslim conquest of Bengal. By destroying the Hindu king of Bengal, the Muslims ushered in a new period of misconduct and disorder among the Brāhmaṇs and Kāyasthas. Now there was no Hindu king to judge conduct and make manifest the ranks of the Brāhmaṇs and Kāyasthas and honor them with gifts. The Brāhmaṇs and Kāyasthas met this problem by narrowing the standard of good conduct to marriage alone and by collectively taking up the functions of the single Hindu king. Proper marriage had always been necessary to the maintenance of embodied rank, but it had not been the definitive act by which inherited ranks were sustained and transformed into fame and respect. Now, marriage with a Kulīna becomes an act of worship which requires the gift of wealth—*paṇa*—to the Kulīna and bring in return the transmutation of inherited rank into fame, glory, and respect. And newly formed subcaste councils which convene on the occasion of a marriage judge marriage conduct and make public the ranks of the Brāhmaṇs. By stressing marriage in this way, the Brāhmaṇs and Kāyasthas were thus able to do what the Hindu king had done before—nourish and sustain their embodied Vedic ranks and maintain order among themselves.

This explanation for the highly particularistic and localized systems of rank in terms of a decentralization of distinctively Hindu political functions in relation to the Hindu community is worth further exploration. It is especially interesting in light of the developments of the last seventy-five years of Bengal's history. This period has seen the development of a centralized political administration concerned with changing Hindu codes, first under the British, now under independent rule. And in conjunction with this increasing centralization, the particularity of the middle period society has gradually been disappearing. Marriages no longer sustain the ranked genera of Kulīnas, nor do they at present maintain any distinction of rank between Kulīna and non-Kulīna; and subcaste boundaries themselves seem to have all but disappeared among the Brāhmaṇs and Kāyasthas as a result of recent migrations and intermarriages. At the same time, marriage for at least some Brāhmaṇs and Kāyasthas has begun to lose its centrality as the act by which ranks are generated and transformed and has begun to be replaced by new educational and occupational activities. But an account of these changes is, naturally and properly, the subject of another study.

BIBLIOGRAPHY

KULAJĪS

Rāḍhī Brāhmaṇ

Bandya, Śrīnāth. "Saptaśati-kārikā," in Nagendranāth Vasu, *Vaṅger Jātīya Itihāsa*. Calcutta: Viśvakoṣa Press, 1911–33. I, Pt. I. 98–99.

Devīvara. "Kula-kārikā," in Vasu, *Vaṅger Jātīya Itihāsa*. I, Pt. I, 172–73; VI, Pt. I, 51–52.

"Kula-mañjarī," in Vasu, *Vaṅger Jātīya Itihāsa*. I, Pt. I. 143–46.

Nula Pañchānana. "Goṣṭhī-kathā," in Lālmohan Vidyānidhi, *Sambandha-nirnaya*. Calcutta: M. C. Bhaṭṭāchārya, 1949. I, 201–6, 272–76, 297–304.

Vācaspati. "Kularamā," in Chandrakānta Ghaṭaka-vidyānidhi, *Kulakalpadruma*. Calcutta: Bhavānīpur Press, 1912.

Dakṣiṇa-rāḍhī Kāyastha

Basu, Baradākānta Ghaṭaka. Kulajī. Dacca University Library MSS (uncataloged), n.d.

Basu, Kāśīrāma. Kulajī. Dacca University Library MSS (uncataloged), n.d.

Dīnabandhu Kulabhūṣaṇa Ghaṭaka. *Kāyastha-kārikā*. Calcutta: n.p., 1886.

Ghaṭakāchārya. "Kārikā," in Vasu, *Vaṅger Jātīya Itihāsa*. VI, Pt. I. 107–8.

"Kula-pradīpa." Dacca University Library MSS (uncataloged), n.d.

Mitra, Nandarāma. Kulajī. Dacca University Library MSS (uncataloged), n.d.

———. "Maulika Ḍhākurī." Dacca University Library MSS (uncataloged), n.d.

———. "Vaṃśaja Ḍhākurī." Dacca University Library MSS (uncataloged), n.d.

Rajanikara Ghaṭaka. "Dakṣiṇa-rāḍhīya Kula-kārikā," in Vasu, *Vaṅger Jātīya Itihāsa*. VI, Pt. I, 108–12.

Sarvabhauma Ghaṭaka. "Ḍhākurī," in Vasu, *Vaṅger Jātīya Itihāsa*. VI, Pt. I, 104–5.

Vācaspati. "Kula-sarvvasva," in Vasu, *Vaṅger Jātīya Itihāsa*. VI. Pt. I. 112–15.

Vaṅgaja Kāyastha

Bṛhaspati. "Ḍhākur," in Vasu, *Vaṅger Jātīya Itihāsa*. VI, Pt. I, 95–99.

Chuḍāmani. Kulajī. Dacca University Library MSS (uncataloged), n.d.

Śarmā, Rāmānanda. "Kula-dīpikā." Dacca University Library MSS (uncataloged), n.d.

Uttara-rāḍhī Kāyastha

Ghaṭaka-keśarī. "Kula-kārikā," in Vasu, *Vaṅger Jātīya Itihāsa*, III, Pt. I, 51.

Sinha, Śukadeva. "Uttara-rāḍhīya Kula-kārikā," in Vasu, *Vaṅger Jātīya Itihāsa*. III. Pt. I, 68–69.

Uttara-rāḍhī Kāyastha Kulajī. Dacca University Library MSS (uncataloged), n.d.

"Uttara-rāḍhīya Kula-pañjikā," in Vasu, *Vaṅger Jātīya Itihāsa*. III, Pt. I, 54–55.

Vārendra Kāyastha

Yadunandana. *Mūla Ḍhākur o Samālocanā; arthāt, Kāyastha Samājer Vivaraṇa*. Calcutta: Bhārat Mihir Press, 1891.

Yadunandana. *Vārendra Ḍhākur*. Calcutta: Viśvakoṣa Press, 1912.

Ethnographies

Bhaṭṭāchārya, Jogendra Nāth. *Hindu Castes and Sects*. Calcutta: Editions Indian, 1968. 1st ed., 1896.

Bose, B. C. *Hindu Matrimony*. Calcutta: J. N. Ghose & Co., 1880.

Bose, Basanta Coomar. *Hindu Customs in Bengal*. Calcutta: Book Company, 1928.

Bose, Shib Chunder. *The Hindoos As They Are*. Calcutta: W. Newman & Co., 1881.

Ghaṭaka-vidyānidhi, Chandrakānta. *Kulakalpadruma*. Calcutta: Bhavānīpur Press, 1912.

Ghosh, Rājendrakumār. *Kāyastha-samāja-tattva*. Calcutta: By the Author, 1931.

Majumdār, Mahimāchandra. *Gaude Brāhmaṇ*. Calcutta: B. L. Chakravarti, New School-Book Press, 1886.

Mitra, Braj Sundar. *Candradvīper Rāja-vaṃśa o Vaṅgaja Kāyasthagaṇer Vivaraṇa*. Bariśāl: Kumudakanta Basu, 1913.

Mitra Mustauphi, Srijanāth. *Ulār Mustauphi Vaṃśa*. Ulā: By the Author, 1930.

Putatuṇḍa, Brindāban Chandra. *The Manners and Customs in Bengal in the Seventeenth and Eighteenth Centuries*. Bariśāl: Bariśāl Śākhā-Pariṣad, 1916.

Ray Choudhury, Dīnabandhu. *Paricaya: Vaṅgaja Kāyastha-gaṇer Sāmājika Itihāsa saha Dakṣiṇa Farīdpurer Bil-pradeśer Vivaraṇa*. Calcutta: Amūlya Chandra De, 1937.

Risley, Herbert H. *Tribes and Castes of Bengal. Ethnographic Glossary*. Calcutta: Bengal Secretariat Press, 1891.

Vasu, Nagendranāth. *Vaṅger Jātīya Itihāsa*. Calcutta: Viśvakoṣa Press, 1911–33.

Vidyānidhi, Lālmohan. *Sambandhanirnaya*. Calcutta: M. C. Bhattacharya, 1949. 4th ed. 1st ed., 1865.

Wise, James. *Notes on the Races, Castes, and Trades of Eastern Bengal*. London: Harrison & Sons, 1883.

Other Sources

Brahma-vaivartta Purāṇa. Translated into Bengali by Pañchānana Tarkaratna. Calcutta: Natavara Chakravartti, 1925.

Mahānirvāṇa-tantra. Ed. Jībānanda Vidyāsāgara. Calcutta: New Valmiki Press, 1884.

Raghunandana Bhaṭṭāchārya. *Institutes of the Hindoo Religion* ["Smṛti-tattva"]. Śrīrāmpur: Śrīrāmpur Press, 1834–35.

Śabdakalpadruma. Comp. by Rājā Rādhākānta Deva. Calcutta: Śabdakalpadruma Office. 1st ed., 1821–57; 2nd ed., 1874–75.

Theoretical Works

Dumont, Louis. *Homo Hierarchicus*. Chicago: University of Chicago Press, 1970.

Marriott, McKim. "Caste Ranking and Food Transactions: A Matrix Analysis," in *Structure and Change in Indian Society*. Ed. Milton Singer and Bernard S. Cohn. Chicago: Aldine, 1968.

Schneider, David M. *American Kinship: A Cultural Account*. Englewood Cliffs, N. J.: Prentice-Hall, 1968.

Histories

History of Bengal, vol. I, ed. R. C. Majumdār. Dacca: University of Dacca, 1943.

Kane, Pandurang Vaman. *History of Dharmaśāstra*. Poona: Bhandarkar Oriental Research Institute, 1930–62.

Paul, Pramode Lāl. *The Early History of Bengal*. Calcutta: Indian Research Institute, 1939–40.

Rahim, M. A. *Social and Cultural History of Bengal*. Karachi: Pakistan Historical Society, 1963.

INDEX